Mastering Spring Application Development

Gain expertise in developing and caching your applications running on the JVM with Spring

Anjana Mankale

BIRMINGHAM - MUMBAI

Mastering Spring Application Development

First published: May 2015

Production reference: 1270515

Published by Packt Publishing Ltd.
Livery Place
35 Livery Street
Birmingham B3 2PB, UK.

ISBN 978-1-78398-732-0

www.packtpub.com

Credits

Author
Anjana Mankale

Reviewers
Nanda Nachimuthu
Chandan Sharma

Commissioning Editor
Julian Ursell

Acquisition Editor
Sonali Vernekar

Content Development Editor
Athira Laji

Technical Editor
Chinmay S. Puranik

Copy Editors
Sonia Michelle Cheema
Brandt D'Mello
Ulka Manjrekar

Project Coordinator
Harshal Ved

Proofreaders
Stephen Copestake
Safis Editing

Indexer
Monica Ajmera Mehta

Graphics
Disha Haria
Abhinash Sahu

Production Coordinator
Nilesh R. Mohite

Cover Work
Nilesh R. Mohite

About the Author

Anjana Mankale is a tech lead and has 8 years of experience in developing web applications. She has developed applications for healthcare, e-commerce portals, media portals, and content management systems using Spring and Struts2. She is extensively involved in application design and implementation. She has worked on Amazon Cloud and Spring Web Services and has recently been involved in deploying and designing cloud-based multitenant applications. Anjana has also authored a cookbook, *Spring Security 3.x Cookbook, Packt Publishing*.

Anjana is passionate about blogging (`http://jtechspace.blogspot.in/`), where she shares her write-ups and technical code that she has worked on.

I would like to thank my husband, Raghavendra S., for providing complete support and encouragement by intimating me about the timelines. This book is dedicated to my father, M. G. Prasad. Lastly, I would like to thank my parents and in-laws for their encouragement in completing this book.

About the Reviewers

Nanda Nachimuthu studied at IIT Kharaghpur and specializes in advanced Internet programming. He has 18 years of IT experience, which includes 10 years as an architect in various technologies, such as J2EE, SOA, ESB, Cloud, big data, and mobility.

He has designed, architected, and delivered many national projects and large-scale commercial projects. He is also involved in product design and development of various products in the insurance, finance, logistics, and life sciences domains.

Chandan Sharma is currently a software program analyst at Mroads, located in the US. It focuses on building the next generation workforce and leverages technology and awareness.. At Mroads, his primary responsibility is designing and implementing solutions that use Liferay, Spring Framework, and Hibernate for Portals, as well as for RESTful/SOAP Web services. Previously, he has worked as a senior consultant for Cignex Datamatics and TransIT mPower Labs. He also likes to coach people in the technology. Due to the experience he's gained throughout his career, he has developed hands-on experience in Liferay with Spring Framework, Hibernate and Liferay Integration with other applications, cloud technology, and so on. He also has his own technical blog at `http://codingloading.com`.

I would like to thank Packt Publishing for the opportunity given to me to review this book. I would like to thank Gaurav Vaish (author of *Getting started with NoSQL, Packt Publishing*) who inspired me to review this book. I would like to express my gratitude to my "rakhi" sister, Meenu Gupta, for her support and encouragement while reviewing this book. I am also grateful to my "cracked" group of friends (Monalisa Sahu, Manoj Patro, and Debasis Padhi) for encouraging me to do new things in my life. I would like to especially thank my best friend who helped me review this book.

www.PacktPub.com

Support files, eBooks, discount offers, and more

For support files and downloads related to your book, please visit www.PacktPub.com.

Did you know that Packt offers eBook versions of every book published, with PDF and ePub files available? You can upgrade to the eBook version at www.PacktPub.com and as a print book customer, you are entitled to a discount on the eBook copy. Get in touch with us at service@packtpub.com for more details.

At www.PacktPub.com, you can also read a collection of free technical articles, sign up for a range of free newsletters and receive exclusive discounts and offers on Packt books and eBooks.

https://www2.packtpub.com/books/subscription/packtlib

Do you need instant solutions to your IT questions? PacktLib is Packt's online digital book library. Here, you can search, access, and read Packt's entire library of books.

Why subscribe?

- Fully searchable across every book published by Packt
- Copy and paste, print, and bookmark content
- On demand and accessible via a web browser

Free access for Packt account holders

If you have an account with Packt at www.PacktPub.com, you can use this to access PacktLib today and view 9 entirely free books. Simply use your login credentials for immediate access.

Table of Contents

Preface

Spring is an open source Java application development framework that is used to build and deploy systems and applications that run on a JVM. It makes efficiently built modular and testable web applications, by using a Model-View-Controller paradigm and dependency injection. It seamlessly integrates with numerous frameworks (such as Hibernate, MyBatis, Jersey, and so on), and reduces boilerplate code when using standard technologies, such as JDBC, JPA, and JMS.

The purpose of this book is to teach intermediate-level Spring developers to master Java application development with Spring, applying advanced concepts and using additional modules to extend the core framework. This is done to develop more advanced, strongly integrated applications.

What this book covers

Chapter 1, *Spring Mongo Integration*, demonstrates the integration of a Spring MVC with MongoDB along with installing MongoDB, to create database and collections.

Chapter 2, *Messaging with Spring JMS*, teaches you to install Apache ActiveMQ and different types of messaging. This chapter also demonstrates the creation of multiple queues and communicating with these queue using Spring templates with the help of screenshots.

Chapter 3, *Mailing with Spring Mail*, creates a mailing service and configures it using the Spring API, and demonstrates how to send mails with attachments using MIME messages.

Chapter 4, *Jobs with Spring Batch*, illustrates how Spring Batch can be used to read an XML file, and also how to create Spring-based batch applications to read a CSV file. This chapter also demonstrates how to write simple test cases using Spring Batch.

Chapter 5, Spring Integration with FTP, gives you an overview of different types of adapters, such as inbound and outbound adapters, with an outbound gateway and its configurations . This chapter also looks into two important classes, FTPSessionFactory and FTPsSessionFactory, by using getter and setter.

Chapter 6, Spring Integration with HTTP, takes you through the use of a multivalue map to populate a request and put the map in the HTTP header. Also, it will provide you with information about HTTP and Spring integration support, which can be used to access HTTP methods and requests.

Chapter 7, Spring with Hadoop, shows how Spring integrates with Apache Hadoop and provides Map and Reduce processes to search and count data. The chapter also discussed installing a Hadoop instance on Unix machines and configuring Hadoop jobs in a Spring framework.

Chapter 8, Spring with OSGI, develops a simple OSGI application, and also demonstrates how a Spring dynamic module supports OSGI development and reduces the creation of files, thereby making things easier with configuration.

Chapter 9, Bootstrap your Application with Spring Boot, starts with setting up a simple Spring boot project, along with the process of using a Spring Boot to bootstrap applications. This chapter also gives information about how a Spring Boot supports a cloud foundry server and helps to deploy applications on cloud.

Chapter 10, Spring Cache, implements our own caching algorithm and teaches you to make a generic algorithm. This chapter also discusses the classes and interface that support a caching mechanism in a Spring Framework.

Chapter 11, Spring with Thymeleaf Integration, integrates the Thymeleaf templating engine into a Spring MVC application, and also uses a Spring Boot to start Spring with a Thymeleaf application.

Chapter 12, Spring with Web Service Integration, integrates JAX_WS with Spring Web Service. It demonstrates how to create spring Web services and an endpoint class, accessing the web service by accessing the WSDL URL.

What you need for this book

A computer with Mac OS, Ubuntu, or Windows is needed. To build Spring applications, you will need at least Java and Maven 3.

Who this book is for

If you are a Java developer with experience in developing applications with Spring, then this book is perfect for you. A good working knowledge of Spring programming conventions and applying dependency injection is recommended to make the most of this book.

Conventions

In this book, you will find a number of text styles that distinguish between different kinds of information. Here are some examples of these styles and an explanation of their meaning.

Code words in text, database table names, folder names, filenames, file extensions, pathnames, dummy URLs, user input, and Twitter handles are shown as follows: "We have used the `@Controller` annotation to indicate that the `ProductController.java` class is a controller class."

A block of code is set as follows:

```
@Controller
public class ProductController {
  @Autowired
  private ProductRepository respository;
  private List <Product>productList;
  public ProductController() {
    super();
  }
}
```

When we wish to draw your attention to a particular part of a code block, the relevant lines or items are set in bold:

```
public class MailAdvice {
  public void advice (final ProceedingJoinPoint
    proceedingJoinPoint) {
    new Thread(new Runnable() {
    public void run() {
```

Any command-line input or output is written as follows:

```
cd E:\MONGODB\mongo\bin

mongod -dbpath e:\mongodata\db
```

New terms and **important words** are shown in bold. Words that you see on the screen, for example, in menus or dialog boxes, appear in the text like this: "The next step is to create a rest controller to send a mail; to do so, click on **Submit**."

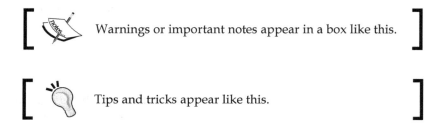

Warnings or important notes appear in a box like this.

Tips and tricks appear like this.

Reader feedback

Feedback from our readers is always welcome. Let us know what you think about this book—what you liked or disliked. Reader feedback is important for us as it helps us develop titles that you will really get the most out of.

To send us general feedback, simply e-mail feedback@packtpub.com, and mention the book's title in the subject of your message.

If there is a topic that you have expertise in and you are interested in either writing or contributing to a book, see our author guide at www.packtpub.com/authors.

Customer support

Now that you are the proud owner of a Packt book, we have a number of things to help you to get the most from your purchase.

Downloading the example code

You can download the example code files from your account at http://www.packtpub.com for all the Packt Publishing books you have purchased. If you purchased this book elsewhere, you can visit http://www.packtpub.com/support and register to have the files e-mailed directly to you.

Errata

Although we have taken every care to ensure the accuracy of our content, mistakes do happen. If you find a mistake in one of our books—maybe a mistake in the text or the code—we would be grateful if you could report this to us. By doing so, you can save other readers from frustration and help us improve subsequent versions of this book. If you find any errata, please report them by visiting http://www.packtpub.com/submit-errata, selecting your book, clicking on the **Errata Submission Form** link, and entering the details of your errata. Once your errata are verified, your submission will be accepted and the errata will be uploaded to our website or added to any list of existing errata under the Errata section of that title.

To view the previously submitted errata, go to https://www.packtpub.com/books/content/support and enter the name of the book in the search field. The required information will appear under the **Errata** section.

Piracy

Piracy of copyrighted material on the Internet is an ongoing problem across all media. At Packt, we take the protection of our copyright and licenses very seriously. If you come across any illegal copies of our works in any form on the Internet, please provide us with the location address or website name immediately so that we can pursue a remedy.

Please contact us at copyright@packtpub.com with a link to the suspected pirated material.

We appreciate your help in protecting our authors and our ability to bring you valuable content.

Questions

If you have a problem with any aspect of this book, you can contact us at questions@packtpub.com, and we will do our best to address the problem.

1
Spring Mongo Integration

MongoDB is a popular NoSQL database and is a document-based one too. It is written using the popular and powerful C++ language, which makes it a document-oriented database. Queries are also document-based, and it also provides indexing using JSON style to store and retrieve data. MongoDB works on the concept of **collection** and **documentation**.

Let's look at few terminology differences between MySQL and MongoDB:

MySQL	MongoDB
Table	Collection
Row	Document
Column	Field
Joins	Embedded documents linking

In MongoDB, a collection is a set or a group of documents. It is the same as RDBMS tables.

In this chapter, we shall start by setting up a MongoDB NoSQL database and will integrate a spring application with MongoDB to perform CRUD operations. The first example demonstrates updating single document values. The second example considers an order use case where it requires two document references to be stored in the collection. It demonstrates the flexibility in referencing different documents of MongoDB using objectId references.

We need to go for a NoSQL database only if the applications have heavy write operations. MongoDB also suits the cloud environment very well, where we can take copies of databases easily.

In the next section, we shall see how we can get started with MongoDB, beginning with installing it, using the Spring Framework, and integrating MongoDB. To get started, we shall show basic **Create, Retrieve, Update, and Delete (CRUD)** operations with various use cases.

Installing MongoDB and creating a database

In this section we shall install MongoDB and create a database:

1. Download the MongoDB database at `http://www.mongodb.org/downloads`.

2. Configure the data folder by executing the following command in the `bin` folder:

   ```
   >mongod.exe -dbpath e:\mongodata\db
   ```

3. Start `mongod.exe` in another Command Prompt.

4. Execute the following command:

   ```
   >show databaseExecute
   ```

   The `>show dbs` command also works fine with MongoDB.

5. Execute the following command to create a new database, namely `eshopdb`.

   ```
   >use new-eshopdb
   ```

6. Executing `> show dbs` will still show that `eshopdb` hasn't been created yet; this is because it doesn't contain any collections. Let's add some collections in the next step, once a collection is added.

7. Execute the following snippet in the Command Prompt. The following snippets will insert sample documents into the collection:

   ```
   db.eshopdb.insert({cust_id:1,name:"kishore",address:"jayangar"
   })

   db.eshopdb.insert({cust_id:2,name:"bapi",address:"HAL
   Layout"})

   db.eshopdb.insert({cust_id:3,name:"srini",address:"abbigere
   street"})

   db.eshopdb.insert({cust_id:4,name:"sangamesha",address:
   "Kattarigupee layout"})
   ```

Setting up a batch file for MongoDB

It's always easy to create a batch file to start MongoDB, and it's best to create a script file to start Mongo. This way, we won't have an error with the configuration. This would also save us a lot of time.

1. Create a `mongodbstart.bat` file.

2. Edit the file and type in the following command and save it:

   cd E:\MONGODB\mongo\bin

   mongod -dbpath e:\mongodata\db

The next time you want to start MongoDB, just click on the batch file.

Order use case with Spring and MongoDB

Let us look at the Order use case to implement a simple CRUD operation using Spring and MongoDB. We are performing CRUD operations on Product, Customer, and Order documents. The scenario is this: a customer selects a product and places an order.

Following is the Order use case. The actor is the application user and will have the following options:

- CRUD operation on Product Document
- CRUD operation on Customer Document
- CRUD operation on Order by selecting Product and Customer
- Saving the Product Document Object ID and Customer Document Object ID in Order Document

Mapping a Mongo document to Spring Bean

Spring provides a simple way to map Mongo documents. The following table depicts the mapping of Bean with MongoDB collections:

Bean	Mongo Collections
Customer.java	db.customer.find()
Order.java	db.order.find()
Product.java	db.product.find()

Setting up a Spring-MongoDB project

We need to create a simple web application project using Maven.

1. Execute the following command in your Maven command prompt:

   ```
   mvn archetype:generate -DgroupId=com.packtpub.spring -
   DartifactId=spring-mongo -DarchetypeArtifactId=maven-
   archetype-webapp
   ```

2. Create a simple Maven project with a web application archetype. Add the latest 4.0.2.RELEASE spring dependency.

3. The following is an extract from the pom.xml file. These are the mandatory dependencies to be added to the pom.xml file.

   ```xml
   <!-- Spring dependencies -->
   <dependency>
   <groupId>org.mongodb</groupId>
   <artifactId>mongo-java-driver</artifactId>
   <version>2.9.1</version>
   </dependency>
   <dependency>
   <groupId>org.springframework.data</groupId>
   <artifactId>spring-data-mongodb</artifactId>
   <version>1.2.0.RELEASE</version>
   </dependency>
   <dependency>
   <groupId>org.springframework.data</groupId>
   <artifactId>spring-data-mongodb</artifactId>
   <version>1.2.0.RELEASE</version>
   </dependency>
   <dependency>
   <groupId>org.springframework</groupId>
   <artifactId>spring-core</artifactId>
   <version>${spring.version}<//}</version>
   <scope>runtime</scope>
   </dependency>
   <dependency>
   <groupId>org.springframework</groupId>
   <artifactId>spring-context</artifactId>
   <version>4.0.2.RELEASE </version>
   <scope>runtime</scope>
   </dependency>
   <dependency>
   <groupId>org.springframework</groupId>
   <artifactId>spring-context-support</artifactId>
   ```

```
<version>4.0.2.RELEASE </version>
<scope>runtime</scope>
</dependency>
<dependency>
<groupId>org.springframework</groupId>
<artifactId>spring-beans</artifactId>
<version>4.0.2.RELEASE </version>
<scope>runtime</scope>
</dependency>
<dependency>
<groupId>org.springframework</groupId>
<artifactId>spring-web</artifactId>
<version>4.0.2.RELEASE </version>
<scope>runtime</scope>
</dependency>
<dependency>
<groupId>org.springframework</groupId>
<artifactId>spring-webmvc</artifactId>
<version>4.0.2.RELEASE </version>
<scope>runtime</scope>
</dependency>
```

Application design

The following table contains the classes used to develop a simple CRUD application. The request flows from controller to model and back. The Repository classes are marked with the @Repository annotation and connect to MongoDB using the mongoTemplate class.

Controller	Model	JSP	Bean
Customer Controller.java	Customer Repository.java	customer.jsp editcutomer.jsp allcustomers.jsp	Customer.java
Order Controller.java	Order Repository.java	order.jsp editorder.jsp allorders.jsp	Order.java
Product Controller.java	Product Repository.java	product.jsp editproduct.jsp allproducts.jsp	Product.java

Application implementation of Spring with MongoDB

The following are the steps are for the implementation of the `Spring4MongoDB_Chapter1` application:

1. Create a web-based Maven project with the name `Spring4MongoDB_Chapter1`.

2. Import the project into Eclipse for the implementation. I have used Eclipse Juno.

We need to create the controller to map the requests.

The controller request is mapped to the `GET` and `POST` methods, as shown in the following table:

Request	Request Method	Model Attributes
`/product`	`GET`	`productList`
`/product/save`	`POST`	`productList`
`/product/update`	`POST`	`productList`
`/product/geteditproduct`	`GET`	`productAttribute`
`/product/deleteproduct`	`GET`	`productAttribute`
`/product/getallproducts`	`GET`	`productList`

Following is the implementation of `ProductController.java`. We have used the `@Controller` annotation to indicate that the `ProductController.java` class is a controller class. The `@Autowired` annotation ties the `ProductRepository` class with the `ProductController.java` file.

The property `productList` is a list of type `Product` that holds the products that are to be displayed on screen. The `@PostConstruct` annotation will call the method decorated by it. Once the constructor of the class is called and all properties are set, and before any business methods are called, it's worthy to note as it's only called once.

```
@Controller
public class ProductController {
  @Autowired
  private ProductRepository respository;
  private List <Product>productList;
  public ProductController() {
    super();
  }
  @PostConstruct
```

```java
public void init(){
  this.productList=respository.getAllObjects();
}
//to get the list of products
@RequestMapping(value="/product", method = RequestMethod.GET)
public String getaddproduct(Model model) {
  model.addAttribute("productList", productList);
  model.addAttribute("productAttribute", new Product());
  return "product";
}
//to save the product
@RequestMapping(value="/product/save", method =
  RequestMethod.POST)
public String addproduct(@ModelAttribute Product prod,Model
  model) {
  if(StringUtils.hasText(prod.getProdid())) {
    respository.updateObject(prod);
  } else {
    respository.saveObject(prod);
  }
  this.productList=respository.getAllObjects();
  model.addAttribute("productList", productList);
  return "product";
}
//to update the edited product
@RequestMapping(value="/product/update", method =
  RequestMethod.POST)
public String updatecustomer(@ModelAttribute Product prod,Model
  model) {
  respository.updateObject(prod);
  this.productList=respository.getAllObjects();
  model.addAttribute("productList", productList);
  return "product";
}
//to edit a product based on ID
@RequestMapping(value = "/product/geteditproduct", method =
  RequestMethod.GET)
public String geteditproduct(
@RequestParam(value = "prodid", required = true) String prodid,
Model model) {
  model.addAttribute("productList", productList);
  model.addAttribute("productAttribute",
    respository.getObject(prodid));
  return "editproduct";
}
```

```
//to delete a product based on ID
@RequestMapping(value="/product/deleteproduct", method =
  RequestMethod.GET)
public String deleteproduct(
@RequestParam(value = "prodid", required = true) String prodid,
  Model model) {
  respository.deleteObject(prodid);
  this.productList=respository.getAllObjects();
  model.addAttribute("productList", this.productList);
  return "product";
}
//to get all the products
@RequestMapping(value = "/product/getallproducts", method =
  RequestMethod.GET)
public String getallproducts(Model model) {
  this.productList=respository.getAllObjects();
  model.addAttribute("productList", this.productList);
  return "allproducts";
}
}
```

The `Product.java` file has an `@Document` annotation and an `@ID` annotation, which is identified as a MongoDB collection that maps the `Product` entity to product collection in MongoDB.

```
@Document
public class Product {
  /*Bean class product with getter and setters*/
  @Id
  private String prodid;
  private Double price;
  private String name;
  public Product() {
    super();
  }
  public String getProdid() {
    return prodid;
  }
  public void setProdid(String prod_id) {
    this.prodid = prod_id;
  }
  public Double getPrice() {
    return price;
  }
  public void setPrice(Double price) {
```

```
      this.price = price;
    }
    public String getName() {
      return name;
    }
    public void setName(String name) {
      this.name = name;
    }
  }
```

The `ProducRepository.java` file has `@Repository` annotation. This is the persistence layer, and tells spring that this class performs operations on the database. The connection to Mongo is set up in Mongo template.

ProductRepository.java

```
@Repository
public class ProductRepository {
  @Autowired
  MongoTemplate mongoTemplate;
  public void setMongoTemplate(MongoTemplate mongoTemplate) {
    this.mongoTemplate = mongoTemplate;
  }

  public List<Product> getAllObjects() {
    return mongoTemplate.findAll(Product.class);
  }

  /**
   * Saves a {@link Product}.
   */
  public void saveObject(Product Product) {
    Product.setProdid(UUID.randomUUID().toString());
    mongoTemplate.insert(Product);
  }

  /**
   * Gets a {@link Product} for a particular id.
   */
  public Product getObject(String id) {
    return mongoTemplate.findOne(new Query(Criteria.where("_id").
is(id)),
    Product.class);
  }
```

```
/**
 * Updates a {@link Product} name for a particular id.
 */
public void updateObject(Product object) {
  Query query = new Query();
  query.addCriteria(Criteria.where("_id")
    .is(object.getProdid()));
  Product prod_tempObj = mongoTemplate.findOne(query,
    Product.class);
  System.out.println("cust_tempObj - " + prod_tempObj);
  //modify and update with save()
  prod_tempObj.setName(object.getName());
  prod_tempObj.setPrice(object.getPrice());
  mongoTemplate.save(prod_tempObj);
}

/**
 * Delete a {@link Product} for a particular id.
 */
public void deleteObject(String id) {
  mongoTemplate.remove(new
    Query(Criteria.where("_id").is(id)),Product.class);
}

/**
 * Create a {@link Product} collection if the collection does not
     already
 * exists
 */
public void createCollection() {
  if (!mongoTemplate.collectionExists(Product.class)) {
    mongoTemplate.createCollection(Product.class);
  }
}

/**
 * Drops the {@link Product} collection if the collection does
     already exists
 */
public void dropCollection() {
  if (mongoTemplate.collectionExists(Product.class)) {
    mongoTemplate.dropCollection(Product.class);
  }
}
}
```

The `.jsp` file displays the products available and allows the user to perform CRUD operations on the `Product` bean. The following screenshot is the output of editing product information using the product `ObjectId` stored in MongoDB.

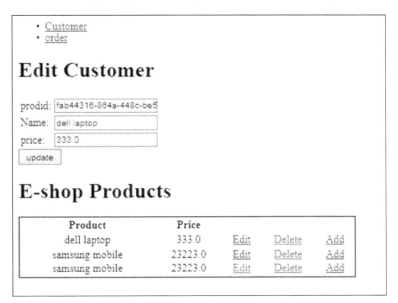

Product.jsp file

This file serves as a view layer to the user. This has the product creation form and includes a file that lists all the products stored in MongoDB.

```
<%@ taglib uri="http://java.sun.com/jsp/jstl/core" prefix="c" %>
<%@ taglib uri="http://www.springframework.org/tags/form"
prefix="form" %>
<%@ page language="java" contentType="text/html; charset=UTF-8"
    pageEncoding="UTF-8"%>
<!DOCTYPE html PUBLIC "-//W3C//DTD HTML 4.01 Transitional//EN"
  "http://www.w3.org/TR/html4/loose.dtd">
<html>
<head>
<meta http-equiv="Content-Type" content="text/html; charset=UTF-
  8">
<title>Register Product</title>
</head>
<body>

<h1>Register Product</h1>
<ul>
```

```
<li><a href="/Spring4MongoDB_Chapter1/customer">Customer</a>
</li>
<li>r<a href="/Spring4MongoDB_Chapter1/order">Product</a>
</li></ul>
<form  method="post"
  action="/Spring4MongoDB_Chapter1/product/save">
  <table>
    <tr>
      <td> Name:</td>
      <td><input type=text name="name"/></td>
    </tr>
    <tr>
      <td>Price</td>
      <td><input type=text name="price"/></td>
    </tr>
      </table>
  <input type="hidden" name="prod_id"  >
  <input type="submit" value="Save" />
</form>
<%@ include file="allproducts.jsp" %>
</body>
</html>
```

If all goes well, you should see the following screen, where you can play around with products. The following screenshot is the output of the **Register Product** and list Product functionality using Spring and MongoDB.

The following `dispatcher-servlet.xml` file shows the configuration for component scan and MongoDB template. It also shows the MongoDB database name configuration.

dispatcher-servlet.xml

```xml
<?xml version="1.0" encoding="UTF-8"?>
<beans xmlns="http://www.springframework.org/schema/beans"
  xmlns:xsi="http://www.w3.org/2001/XMLSchema-instance"
  xmlns:context="http://www.springframework.org/schema/context"
  xmlns:mongo="http://www.springframework.org/schema/data/mongo"
  xmlns:p="http://www.springframework.org/schema/p"
  xsi:schemaLocation="http://www.springframework.org/schema/beans
  http://www.springframework.org/schema/beans/spring-beans-4.0.xsd
  http://www.springframework.org/schema/data/mongo
  http://www.springframework.org/schema/data/mongo/
    spring-mongo-1.0.xsd

  http://www.springframework.org/schema/context
  http://www.springframework.org/schema/context/
    spring-context-4.0.xsd">

  <context:component-scan base-package="com.packt" />

  <!-- Factory bean that creates the Mongo instance -->
    <bean id="mongo"
      class="org.springframework.data.mongodb.
      core.MongoFactoryBean">
      <property name="host" value="localhost" />
    </bean>
    <mongo:mongo host="127.0.0.1" port="27017" />
    <mongo:db-factory dbname="eshopdb" />

  <bean id="mongoTemplate"
    class="org.springframework.data.mongodb.
    core.MongoTemplate">
    <constructor-arg name="mongoDbFactory" ref="mongoDbFactory" />
  </bean>

  <!-- Use this post processor to translate any MongoExceptions
    thrown in @Repository annotated classes -->
    <bean class="org.springframework.dao.annotation.
      PersistenceExceptionTranslationPostProcessor" />
    <bean id="jspViewResolver"
      class="org.springframework.web.servlet.view.
      InternalResourceViewResolver"
```

```
       p:prefix="/WEB-INF/myviews/"
       p:suffix=".jsp" />

</beans>
```

You can see that the `mongoDbFactory` bean has been configured with MongoDB database details. You will also observe that `mongoTemplate` has also been configured. The property of the `mongoTemplate` bean is `mongoDbFactory` bean, and so when the template is called the connection gets established.

Just run the following commands in the MongoDB database in order to test the Order use case:

- `db.order.find()`
- `db.order.remove()`

 RoboMongo is a free tool like `Toad` to access the MongoDB database.

Order management use case

Let's consider a complex scenario for this section. In the use case that we have considered, the Order use case has customer and product objects in the class. When a user places an order, the user will select a product and customer.

Our aim here is to store the `customer` and `product` classes directly in the `Order` collection in MongoDB. Let's first implement the `OrderBean` class with getter and setters.

Order.java

```
package com.packt.bean;
import org.springframework.data.annotation.Id;
import org.springframework.data.mongodb.core.mapping.Document;

@Document
public class Order {
  private String order_id;
  private Customer customer;
  private Product product;
  private String date;
  private String order_status;
  private int quantity;
```

```java
public Order() {
  super();
  // TODO Auto-generated constructor stub
}

@Id
public String getOrder_id() {
  return order_id;
}
public void setOrder_id(String order_id) {
  this.order_id = order_id;
}

public String getDate() {
  return date;
}
public void setDate(String date) {
  this.date = date;
}
public int getQuantity() {
  return quantity;
}
public void setQuantity(int quantity) {
  this.quantity = quantity;
}
public String getOrder_status() {
  return order_status;
}
public void setOrder_status(String order_status) {
  this.order_status = order_status;
}

public Customer getCustomer() {
  return customer;
}
public void setCustomer(Customer customer) {
  this.customer = customer;
}
public Product getProduct() {
  return product;
}
public void setProduct(Product product) {
  this.product = product;
}
}
```

The next step would be to define the methods in the `OrderRepository.java` file.

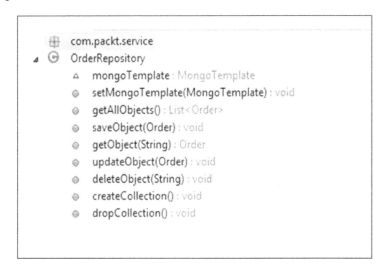

Below are the code snippets of the `update` and `save` methods in the `repository` class.

Creating and inserting Order

We see that the update `Order` method accepts the `Order` object. We used the `addCriteria()` method to get a particular order based on the object ID. The `Order` object retrieved is stored in the `temp` object. The values are then set to the `temp` object based on the object that is passed to the method. Then, the `mongoTemplate.save(Object)` method is called to update the saved object.

```
public void updateObject(Order order) {
  Query query = new Query();
  query.addCriteria(Criteria.where("_id").
    is(order.getOrder_id()));
  Order order_tempObj = mongoTemplate.findOne(query, Order.class);
    order_tempObj.setCustomer(order.getCustomer());
    order_tempObj.setProduct(order.getProduct());
    order_tempObj.setQuantity(order.getQuantity());
    mongoTemplate.save(order_tempObj);
}
```

The `saveObject` method only accepts the `Order` object and sets the ID to the `Order` object before saving it.

We have seen how to perform an update and an insert. The following method is invoked to save the Order details. This shows that `mongoTemplate` has the methods `insert()` and `save()`.

```
public void saveObject(Order Order) {
  Order.setOrder_id(UUID.randomUUID().toString());
  mongoTemplate.insert(Order);
}
```

Controller to handle requests

The `controller` class has the customer repository and product repository references as per the use case. The application user needs to select the customer and product to place an order.

The initial Skelton of `OrderController` is shown here:

```
@Controller
public class OrderController {
  @Autowired
  private OrderRepository respository;
  @Autowired
  private CustomerRepository customerRespository;
  @Autowired
  private ProductRepository productRespository;
  private List<Order> orderList;
  private List<Customer> customerList;
  private List<Product> productList;

  public OrderController() {
    super();
  }
}
```

Adding the @Modelattribute annotation at the Method level

The `controller` class is to handle the `Order` requests. The `@ModelAttribute` annotation is added to the method. The product list and customer list is always available as a model attribute to the controller. The following is the code snippet of the `OrderController` class:

```
@ModelAttribute("orderList")
  public List<Order> populateOrderList() {
```

```
    this.orderList = respository.getAllObjects();
    return this.orderList;
}
@ModelAttribute("productList")
public List<Product> populateProductList() {
  this.productList = productRespository.getAllObjects();
  return this.productList;
}
@ModelAttribute("customerList")
public List<Customer> populateCstomerList() {
  this.customerList = customerRespository.getAllObjects();
  return this.customerList;
}
```

CRUD operations of the OrderController class

The methods are mapped to a particular request, `@ModelAttribute("Order")`, to make the order object easily accessible at the JSP level. You can observe that using `@ModelAttribute` at the method level; this will minimize adding `@ModelAttribute` to the method.

```
@RequestMapping(value = "/order", method = RequestMethod.GET)
// request show add order page
public String addOrder(@ModelAttribute("Order") Order order,
  Map<String, Object> model) {
  model.put("customerList", customerList);
  model.put("productList", productList);
  return "order";
}
@RequestMapping(value = "/order/save", method =
RequestMethod.POST)
// request to insert the record
public String addorder(@ModelAttribute("Order") Order order,
  Map<String, Object> model) {
  order.setCustomer(customerRespository.getObject
    (order.getCustomer().getCust_id()));
  order.setProduct(product_respository.getObject
    (order.getProduct().getProdid()));
  respository.saveObject(order);
  model.put("customerList", customerList);
  model.put("productList", productList);
  return "order";
}
```

```
@RequestMapping(value = "/orde`r/update", method =
  RequestMethod.POST)
public String updatecustomer(@ModelAttribute("Order") Order
  order,
  Map<String, Object> model) {
  order.setCustomer(customerRespository.getObject
    (order.getCustomer().getCust_id()));
  order.setProduct(product_respository.getObject
    (order.getProduct().getProdid()));
  respository.updateObject(order);
  model.put("customerList", customerList);
  model.put("productList", productList);
  return "order";
}
@RequestMapping(value = "/order/geteditorder", method =
  RequestMethod.GET)
public String editOrder(
  @RequestParam(value = "order_id", required = true)
  String order_id, @ModelAttribute("Order") Order order,
  Map<String, Object> model) {
  model.put("customerList", customerList);
  model.put("productList", productList);
  model.put("Order",respository.getObject(order_id));
  return "editorder";
}
@RequestMapping(value = "/order/deleteorder", method =
  RequestMethod.GET)
public String deleteorder(
  @RequestParam(value = "order_id", required = true)
  String order_id, @ModelAttribute("Order") Order order,
  Map<String, Object> model) {
  respository.deleteObject(order_id);
  model.put("customerList", customerList);
  model.put("productList", productList);
  return "order";
}
}
```

JSP files

The Order.jsp file demonstrates the use of @ModelAttribute, which gets mapped to the Model Order defined in the controller class. The setter methods set the values to the objects, which minimizes the coding. This showcases a feature in spring, which simplifies the coding process.

Orders.jsp

```
<h1>Orders </h1>
<ul>
<li><a href="/Spring4MongoDB_Chapter1/customer">Customer</a>
</li>
<li>r<a href="/Spring4MongoDB_Chapter1/product">Product</a>
</li></ul>

<form:form action="/Spring4MongoDB_Chapter1/order/save"
modelAttribute="Order">
  <table>
    <tr>
      <td>Add your Order:</td>
      <td><form:input path="quantity" size="3"/></td>
    </tr>
    <tr>
      <td>Select Product:</td>
      <td>
        <form:select path="product.prodid">
        <form:option value="" label="--Please Select"/>
        <form:options items="${productList}" itemValue="prodid"
          itemLabel="name"/>
        </form:select>
      </td>
    </tr>
    <tr>
      <td>Select Customer:</td>
      <td>
        <form:select path="customer.cust_id">
        <form:option value="" label="--Please Select"/>
        <form:options items="${customerList}" itemValue="cust_id"
          itemLabel="name"/>
        </form:select>
      </td>
    </tr>
    <tr>
      <td colspan="2" align="center">
        <input type="submit" value="Submit" />
      </td>
    </tr>
  </table>
</form:form>

<%@ include file="allorders.jsp" %>
</body>
</html>
```

The `allorders.jsp` file displays the list of orders with an option to edit. Use of MongoDB has made displaying the `orderList` simpler.

Allorders.jsp

```
<h1> E-shop Orders</h1>
<table style="border: 1px solid; width: 500px; text-align:center">
  <thead style="background:#fffcc">
    <tr>
      <th>Order Id</th>
      <th>Customer Name</th>
      <th>Customer Address</th>
      <th>Product Address</th>
      <th>Product Price</th>
      <th>Product Quantity</th>
      <th colspan="2"></th>
    </tr>
  </thead>
  <tbody>

  <c:forEach items="${orderList}" var="order">
    <c:url var="editUrl"
      value="/order/geteditorder?order_id=${order.order_id}" />
    <c:url var="deleteUrl"
      value="/order/deleteorder?order_id=${order.order_id}" />
    <c:url var="addUrl" value="/order/" />
    <tr>
    <td><c:out value="${order.order_id}" /></td>
      <td><c:out value="${order.customer.name}" /></td>
      <td><c:out value="${order.customer.address}" /></td>
        <td><c:out value="${order.product.name}" /></td>
        <td><c:out value="${order.product.price}" /></td>
        <td><c:out value="${order.quantity}" /></td>
      <td><a href="${editUrl}">Edit</a></td>
      <td><a href="${deleteUrl}">Delete</a></td>
      <td><a href="${addUrl}">Add</a></td>
    </tr>
  </c:forEach>
  </tbody>
```

The following is a screenshot of the page to add your order:

Orders

- Customer
- rProduct

Add your Order: 8
Select Product: samsung mobile ∨
Select Customer: Ravindrav ∨

Submit

E-shop Orders

Order Id	Customer Name	Customer Address	Product Address	Product Price	Product Quantity			
7a616788-bb47-4166-bb73-da1f125d6f53	Ravindrav	MILKCOLONY	samsung mobile	23223.0	8	Edit	Delete	Add
b6c40f70-653b-41a7-a25e-65fbb43cfc2a	anju	hnagar	samsung mobile	23223.0	8	Edit	Delete	Add
c68b5bc6-cb5e-4a61-8b9e-ec8230523bad	Ravindrav	MILKCOLONY	samsung mobile	23223.0	34	Edit	Delete	Add

The following is a screenshot of the page to edit your order:

Orders

- Customer
- rProduct

Order id: `7a616788-bb47-4166-bb`

Quantity: `8`

Select Product: `samsung mobile ∨`

Select Customer: `Ravindrav ∨`

`Submit`

E-shop Orders

Order Id	Customer Name	Customer Address	Product Address	Product Price	Product Quantity			
7a616788-bb47-4166-bb73-da1f125d6f53	Ravindrav	MILKCOLONY	samsung mobile	23223.0	8	Edit	Delete	Add
b6c40f70-653b-41a7-a25e-65fbb43cfc2a	anju	hnagar	samsung mobile	23223.0	8	Edit	Delete	Add
c68b5bc6-cb5e-4a61-8b9e-ec8230523bad	Ravindrav	MILKCOLONY	samsung mobile	23223.0	34	Edit	Delete	Add
c9b9ab9c-f06f-43d3-8555-d17339596d23	Ravindrav	MILKCOLONY	samsung mobile	23223.0	8	Edit	Delete	Add

Summary

In this chapter, we learned how to install MongoDB and create a database and collections. In MongoDB, we have used the latest version of spring that was available during the writing of this chapter. We also learned how to integrate Spring MVC with MongoDB. We have built a CRUD operation. We have also seen the usage of annotations such as @Repository, @Document, and @Controller. In the next chapter, let us see how we can integrate spring message brokers using jms templates.

2
Messaging with Spring JMS

Java Messaging Services (JMS) is an API used to communicate between the components in an application or between applications. The messages can be sent and received between applications and components. The messaging agents behave like middlemen to create, receive, read, and send messages. The message consumer does not need to be available at all times to receive the message. The messaging agents store the messages and they can be read whenever required.

An architect would choose JMS to achieve a loosely coupled design. The messages are asynchronous, they are delivered as soon as they arrive, and there is no request sent for the messages. It also prevents redundancy and ensures that a particular message is delivered only once.

Types of messaging

There are two types of messaging domains to be chosen from, as per the requirement:

- Point-to-point messaging:
    - Each message has only one consumer
    - There is no timing dependency

- Publish-Subscribe messaging:
    - Each message has many consumers
    - Messages have a timing dependency - when an application sends a message to the messaging agent, the consumer needs to subscribe and be active to receive the messages

Message consumers

These are the ways of consuming messages provided by JMS API:

- Message listeners
  - ° They provide an asynchronous messaging model
  - ° Listeners are like event watchers/listeners; whenever a message is available, the listener ensures that it reaches its destination
  - ° Listeners will call the onMessage() method

- The receive() method
  - ° It provides a synchronous messaging model()
  - ° Messages are consumed by explicitly calling the receive() method from the connection factory

Message structure

A message consists of three parts:

- **Header**: This contains information about the destination and timestamp, and has messageID, which is set by the send() or publish() methods.
- **Properties**: Some properties can be set for the message.
- **Body**: The message body can be of any of the following five types:
  - ° TextMessage: This is used to send string objects as messages
  - ° ObjectMessage: This is used to send serializable objects as messages
  - ° MapMessage: This is used to send maps with key-value pairs
  - ° BytesMessage: This is used to send bytes in messages
  - ° StreamMessage: This is used to send I/O streams in messages

Message-driven POJOs and listeners

As we all know, **Enterprise JavaBeans** (**EJB**) offers a message-driven bean to communicate with the EJB container. Similar to this, Spring also offers Message Driven Pojos, which communicate with the messaging middleware using the Message Listener container.

The Message Listener container communicates between the message-driven Pojo and the message provider. It registers the messages and helps with transaction and exception handling by acquiring and releasing the messaging resources.

The following is a list of message listener containers offered by the Spring JMS package:

- **Simple Message Listener Container**: Provides a fixed number of JMS sessions and doesn't participate in externally managed transactions.

- **Default Message Listener Container**: Participates in externally managed transactions and gives a good performance. This listener container is widely used.

- **Server Message Listener Container**: Offers provider-driven runtime tuning and provides a pool of message sessions and participates in transactions.

Open source messaging tools

The following are some open source messaging middleware available under open source licenses:

- Glassfish OpenMQ

- Apache ActiveMQ

- JORAM

- Presumo

Apache ActiveMQ

Apache ActiveMQ has many features that have made it a choice for messaging. The latest release is 5.10. The advantages of using ActiveMQ are as follows:

- It supports REST API

- It supports CXF Web services

- It supports AJAX implementations

- It provides complete support to the Spring framework

- It works with all the major application servers, such as JBoss, Tomcat, Weblogic and Glassfish servers

Setting up ApacheMQ for point-to-point messaging

The following are the steps for setting up ApacheMQ:

1. Download the latest `Apache ActiveMQ.zip` from `http://activemq.apache.org/download.html`.

2. Unzip the ZIP file to `E:\apachemq\`.

3. In the Command Prompt, go to the location `E:\apachemq\apache-activemq-5.10-SNAPSHOT\bin\win32` and then click on `apachemq.bat` to start Apache ActiveMQ.

4. Apache ActiveMQ will run on Jetty Server and is hence accessible through a URL.

5. Click on the link `http://localhost:8161/admin/index.jsp`.

6. The first time you do this, you will be asked for credentials; enter `admin/admin`.

7. In the console, you will see a **Welcome** section and a **Broker** section.

8. The **Broker** section gives the following information about Apache message broker:
   - Name: `localhost` or the name of the server
   - Version 5.10 Snapshot
   - ID: `ID:BLRLANJANA-55074-1397199950394-0:1`
   - Uptime: 1 hour 24 minutes
   - Store percent used: 0
   - Memory percent used: 0
   - Temp percent used: 0

9. Click on **Queues**.

10. Enter `orderQueue` in the **Queue name** field and click on **Create**.

Use case for ApacheMq with Spring JmsTemplate

In the previous chapter, we demonstrated order management using MongoDB. Let us consider that the order placed from one application needs to be read into different applications and stored in a different database.

The design for **Order Management Message Broker** is as follows:

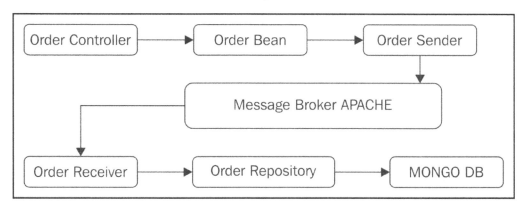

Let's use the same use case with **Message Broker**. The request flows from the controller, and when the user enters order details and clicks on **Save**, the order bean is set in the controller, which sends the request to the JMS sender, that is, the Order Sender.

The order sender sends the message to the queue in the form of a map. The receiver reads the message and saves the message into the MongoDB database. The receiver can be a different application as well; all the application needs to know is the queue name, in case there are many queues configured in the application.

Spring dependency

Use the same source code from *Chapter 1, Spring Mongo Integration*, and the pom.xml file. Update the pom.xml file with Spring JMS dependencies. For this chapter, we have the Spring 4.0.3 release available, which is the latest one to date. The following is the code for the Pom.xml file:

```
<project xmlns="http://maven.apache.org/POM/4.0.0"
  xmlns:xsi="http://www.w3.org/2001/XMLSchema-instance"
  xsi:schemaLocation="http://maven.apache.org/POM/4.0.0
    http://maven.apache.org/maven-v4_0_0.xsd">
  <modelVersion>4.0.0</modelVersion>
  <groupId>com.packt.web</groupId>
  <artifactId>Spring4JMS_Chapter2</artifactId>
  <packaging>war</packaging>
  <version>0.0.1-SNAPSHOT</version>
  <name>Spring4JMS_Chapter2</name>
```

```
<url>http://maven.apache.org</url>
<properties>
<spring.version>4.0.3.RELEASE</spring.version>
</properties>

<dependencies>

<!-- Spring JMS dependencies -->
  <dependency>
  <groupId>org.springframework</groupId>
  <artifactId>spring-jms</artifactId>
  <version>${spring.version}</version>
  <scope>runtime</scope>
  </dependency>

  <dependency>
  <groupId>org.apache.activemq</groupId>
  <artifactId>activemq-core</artifactId>
  <version>5.3.1</version>
  <scope>runtime</scope>
  </dependency>
  <dependency>
  <groupId>org.apache.xbean</groupId>
  <artifactId>xbean-spring</artifactId>
  <version>3.5</version>
  <scope>runtime</scope>
  </dependency>
  <dependency>
  <groupId>org.apache.geronimo.specs</groupId>
  <artifactId>geronimo-jms_1.1_spec</artifactId>
  <version>1.1.1</version>
  <scope>runtime</scope>
  </dependency>
</dependencies>
<build>
  <finalName>Spring4JMS_Chapter2</finalName>
</build>
</project>
```

Implementing the Order Management Messaging System with SpringJMS and ActiveMQ

In the preceding section about Apache ActiveMQ, we discussed the steps required to create a message queue and created an order queue. Now, let's send messages to the queue from the application.

The following table depicts the components of the application with JMS integrated with it.

The request flows from JSP to a Spring controller, which sets the order bean object and sends it orderSender (which is a JMS message sender class). The class puts the order object in the queue.

The JMS Receiver is the class which reads from the queue. The read object is sent to the OrderRepository class, which is a Mongo Repository class, and posts the messages to the MongoDB database.

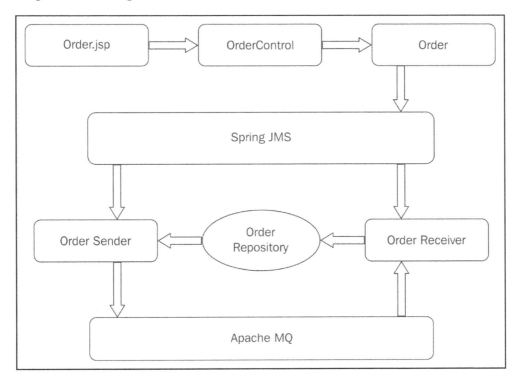

The following table gives us an overview about the classes used to communicate with JMS with a Spring MVC application:

JSP	Controller	Bean	JMS sender	JMS receiver	MongoRepository
order.jsp allorders. jsp	Order Controller. java	Order. java	OrderSender	OrderReceiver	OrderRepository

Configuring dispatcherservlet.xml to use JMS

You can see that we have configured the following in the XML file:

- connectionFactory: It creates a jmsconnection object. This jmsconnection object connects to **Message Orientated Middleware** (**MOM**), that is, Apache ActiveMQ. The jmsconnection object provides a JMS session object, and using that, the application interacts with Apache ActiveMQ. The broker URL gives information about the host and the port the message broker interface is listening at.

- destination: It's the name of the queue with which the application needs to communicate.

```
<bean id="destination"
  class="org.apache.activemq.command.ActiveMQQueue">
  <constructor-arg value="orderQueue"/>
</bean>
```

- jmstemplate: This takes the destination and connectionFactory bean as the argument.

```
<bean id="jmsTemplate"
  class="org.springframework.jms.core.JmsTemplate">
  <property name="connectionFactory"
    ref="connectionFactory" />
  <property name="defaultDestination"
    ref="destination" />
</bean>
```

- orderSender: This is the class that uses the jms template to send a message to the queue.

```
<bean id="orderSender" class="com.packt.jms.OrderSender" />
```

- `orderReceiver`: This class reads the messages from the queue. It has the `connectionFactory` so that it can connect to the JMS provider to read the message.

```
<bean id="orderReceiver"
  class="com.packt.jms.OrderReceiver" />

<jms:listener-container
  connection-factory="connectionFactory">
<jms:listener destination="orderQueue"
  ref="orderReceiver" method="orderReceived" />
</jms:listener-container>
```

The following is the complete configuration of `dispacherservlet.xml`. We will observe that the configuration file has been updated with `activemq` configurations.

dispatcherservlet.xml

```
<?xml version="1.0" encoding="UTF-8"?>
<beans xmlns="http://www.springframework.org/schema/beans"
  xmlns:xsi="http://www.w3.org/2001/XMLSchema-instance"
  xmlns:context="http://www.springframework.org/schema/context"
  xmlns:mongo="http://www.springframework.org/schema/data/mongo"
  xmlns:p="http://www.springframework.org/schema/p"
  xmlns:jms="http://www.springframework.org/schema/jms"
  xsi:schemaLocation="http://www.springframework.org/schema/beans
  http://www.springframework.org/schema/beans/spring-beans-3.2.xsd
  http://www.springframework.org/schema/data/mongo
  http://www.springframework.org/schema/data/mongo/
    spring-mongo-1.0.xsd

  http://www.springframework.org/schema/context
  http://www.springframework.org/schema/context/
    spring-context-3.2.xsd
  http://www.springframework.org/schema/jms
  http://www.springframework.org/schema/jms/spring-jms.xsd
  http://activemq.apache.org/schema/core
  http://activemq.apache.org/schema/core/activemq-core.xsd">
<context:component-scan base-package="com.packt" />
  <!-- JMS Active MQQueue configuration -->
  <bean id="connectionFactory"
    class="org.apache.activemq.ActiveMQConnectionFactory">
  <property name="brokerURL">
    <value>tcp://localhost:61616</value>
  </property>
  </bean>
```

```xml
<bean id="destination"
  class="org.apache.activemq.command.ActiveMQQueue">
<constructor-arg value="orderQueue"/>
</bean>

<bean id="jmsTemplate"
  class="org.springframework.jms.core.JmsTemplate">
<property name="connectionFactory" ref="connectionFactory" />
<property name="defaultDestination" ref="destination" />
</bean>
<bean id="orderSender" class="com.packt.jms.OrderSender" />
<bean id="orderReceiver" class="com.packt.jms.OrderReceiver" />
<jms:listener-container  connection-factory="connectionFactory">
<jms:listener destination="orderQueue" ref="orderReceiver"
  method="orderReceived" />
</jms:listener-container>

<!-- Factory bean that creates the Mongo instance -->
<bean id="mongo"
  class="org.springframework.data.mongodb.
  core.MongoFactoryBean">
  <property name="host" value="localhost" />
</bean>
<mongo:mongo host="127.0.0.1" port="27017" />
<mongo:db-factory dbname="eshopdb" />

<bean id="mongoTemplate"
  class="org.springframework.data.mongodb.core.MongoTemplate">
  <constructor-arg name="mongoDbFactory" ref="mongoDbFactory" />
</bean>
<!-- Use this post processor to translate any MongoExceptions
  thrown in @Repository annotated classes -->
<bean class="org.springframework.dao.annotation.
  PersistenceExceptionTranslationPostProcessor" />

  <bean id="jspViewResolver" class="org.springframework.web.
    servlet.view.InternalResourceViewResolver"
    p:prefix="/WEB-INF/myviews/"
    p:suffix=".jsp" />
</beans>
```

Order.java

```
package com.packt.bean;
import org.springframework.data.annotation.Id;
import org.springframework.data.mongodb.core.mapping.Document;

@Document
public class Order {
  private String order_id;
  private Customer customer;
  private Product product;
  private String date;
  private String order_status;
  private int quantity;

  public Order() {
    super();
    // TODO Auto-generated constructor stub
  }

  @Id
  public String getOrder_id() {
    return order_id;
  }
  public void setOrder_id(String order_id) {
    this.order_id = order_id;
  }

  public String getDate() {
    return date;
  }
  public void setDate(String date) {
    this.date = date;
  }
  public int getQuantity() {
    return quantity;
  }
  public void setQuantity(int quantity) {
    this.quantity = quantity;
  }
  public String getOrder_status() {
    return order_status;
  }
  public void setOrder_status(String order_status) {
```

```
      this.order_status = order_status;
    }

    public Customer getCustomer() {
      return customer;
    }
    public void setCustomer(Customer customer) {
      this.customer = customer;
    }
    public Product getProduct() {
      return product;
    }
    public void setProduct(Product product) {
      this.product = product;
    }
  }
```

The `OrderController` class calls the sender to send the order to the message broker queue. The controller does some basic CRUD operations using MongoDB. The following code demonstrates the `Create` operation only.

When `/order/save` is invoked, the controller sends the order object to `orderSender`, which keeps the order details in the queue.

OrderCOntroller.java

```
Order details is saved with JMS.The Order Object is passed to
orderSender, which will store the order details in the queue.
@RequestMapping(value = "/order/save", method = RequestMethod.POST)
  // request insert order recordhrecord
  public String addorder(@ModelAttribute("Order") Order order,
    Map<String, Object> model) {
    orderSender.sendOrder(order);
    model.put("customerList", customerList);
    model.put("productList", productList);
    return "order";
  }
```

Let's look at the JMS sender and receiver classes. Both classes use the Spring JMS template to receive and send messages. The `org.springframework.jms.core.` `MessageCreator` class creates the message to be placed in the queue.

The following is the code for `orderSender`, which gets an object that needs to be passed to the queue. The `JMSTemplate` prepares the message format so that it is acceptable for the queue.

OrderSender

```
package com.packt.jms;

import javax.jms.JMSException;
import javax.jms.MapMessage;
import javax.jms.Message;
import javax.jms.Session;
import org.springframework.beans.factory.annotation.Autowired;
import org.springframework.jms.core.JmsTemplate;
import org.springframework.jms.core.MessageCreator;
import com.packt.bean.Order;

public class OrderSender {

  @Autowired
  private JmsTemplate jmsTemplate;
  public void sendOrder(final Order order){
    jmsTemplate.send(
    new MessageCreator() {
      public Message createMessage(Session session)
        throws JMSException {
        MapMessage mapMessage = session.createMapMessage();
        mapMessage.setInt("quantity", order.getQuantity());
        mapMessage.setString("customerId",
          order.getCustomer().getCust_id());
        mapMessage.setString("productId",
          order.getProduct().getProdid());
        return mapMessage;

      }
    }
    );
    System.out.println("Order: "+ order);
  }
}
```

The following is a screenshot at the time of adding the order case:

Orders

- Customer
- rProduct

Add your Order: [8]
Select Product: [samsung mobile ∨]
Select Customer: [Ravindrav ∨]
[Submit]

E-shop Orders

Order Id	Customer Name	Customer Address	Product Address	Product Price	Product Quantity			
7a616788-bb47-4166-bb73-da1f125d6f53	Ravindrav	MILKCOLONY	samsung mobile	23223.0	8	Edit	Delete	Add
b6c40f70-653b-41a7-a25e-65fbb43cfc2a	anju	hnagar	samsung mobile	23223.0	8	Edit	Delete	Add
c68b5bc6-cb5e-4a61-8b9e-ec8230523bad	Ravindrav	MILKCOLONY	samsung mobile	23223.0	34	Edit	Delete	Add

Working with multiple queues in ApacheMQ

In the preceding section, we demonstrated sending messages using Map Message to Order Queue. Now, we can have a look at how to work with multiple queues in ApacheMQ:

1. Start the Apache ActiveMQ server, and in the console, click on **Queues** and create two queues.

2. Let us create two queues and name the queues as follows:
   - `PacktTestQueue1`
   - `PacktTestQueue2`

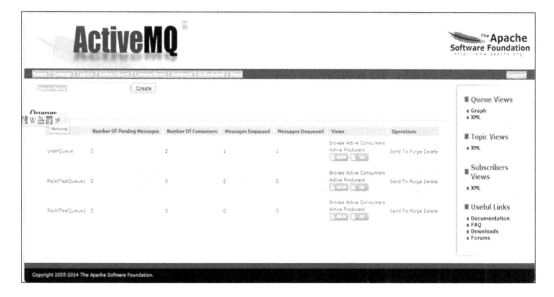

3. Create a new Spring project with the same dependency as the first example in the chapter.

4. Create a `PacktMessageListener` class that implements the `MessageListener` interface. The class overrides the `onMessage(Message message)` method.

5. Spring's `DefaultMessageListener` consumes the messages from the queue and calls the `onMessage(Message message)` method.

```
PacktMessageListener:
package com.packt.jms;

import javax.jms.JMSException;
import javax.jms.Message;
import javax.jms.MessageListener;
import javax.jms.TextMessage;

public class  PacktMessageListener implements
  MessageListener{
  private PacktMessageSender packtmessagesender;
  public void onMessage(Message message){
    if (message instanceof TextMessage){
      try{
        String msgText = ((TextMessage) message).getText();
        packtmessagesender.sendMessage(msgText);
      }
      catch (JMSException jmsexception){
        System.out.println(jmsexception.getMessage());
      }
    }
    else{
      throw new RuntimeException("exception runtime");
    }
  }

  public void setTestMessageSender(PacktMessageSender
    packtmessagesender){
    this.packtmessagesender = packtmessagesender;
  }
}
```

6. Let's now look at the message sender class, which sends the text message to the queue using `JmsTemplate`.

Here, we have provided setters for `JmsTemplate` object and `queue` object and we defined a method to send messages. The class has been configured in the XML file with the application.

PacktMessageSender

```
package com.packt.jms;
import javax.jms.MessageListener;
import javax.jms.Queue;
```

```
import org.springframework.jms.core.JmsTemplate;

public class PacktMessageSender {
  private JmsTemplate jmsTemplate;
  private Queue queue;
  public void setJmsTemplate(JmsTemplate jmsTemplate){
    this.jmsTemplate = jmsTemplate;
  }
  public void setQueue(Queue queue) {
    this.queue = queue;
  }
  public void sendMessage(String msgText) {
  jmsTemplate.convertAndSend(queue, msgText);
  }
}
```

7. Let us first create resource references in the `context.xml` file under the `meta-inf` folder. This is where we will configure **Java Naming and Directory Interface (JNDI)** for JMS.

```
<?xml version="1.0" encoding="UTF-8"?>
<Context>
<!—connection factory details-->
<Resource name="jms/mqConnectionFactory" auth="Container"
  type="org.apache.activemq.ActiveMQConnectionFactory"
  description="JMS Connection Factory"
  factory="org.apache.activemq.jndi.JNDIReferenceFactory"
  brokerURL="tcp://localhost:61616" />

<!—queue details-->

<Resource name="jms/PacktTestQueue1" auth="Container"
  type="org.apache.activemq.command.ActiveMQQueue"
  factory="org.apache.activemq.jndi.JNDIReferenceFactory"
  physicalName="PacktTestQueue1"/>

<!—queue details-->

<Resource name="jms/PacktTestQueue2" auth="Container"
  type="org.apache.activemq.command.ActiveMQQueue"
  factory="org.apache.activemq.jndi.JNDIReferenceFactory"
  physicalName="PacktTestQueue2"/>
</Context>
```

8.   The following are the configuration changes that need to be made in the `spring-configuration.xml` file to configure multiple queues:

     ○   Use Spring JNDI to look up for `queueNames` and JMS `connectionFactory`

     ○   Pass the `ConnectionFactory` reference to `JmsTemplate`

     ○   Configure the `MessageSender` and `MessageListener` classes

     ○   The `MessageSender` class will have `JmsTemplate` and `queue` object as the property

     ○   `MessageListener` will have `MessageSender` as the property

     ○   Configure the `DefaultMessageListenerContainer` class, this class consumes the message from the queue

9.   The following is the code for the configuration file:

Spring-configuration.xml

```xml
<?xml version="1.0" encoding="UTF-8"?>
<beans xmlns="http://www.springframework.org/schema/beans"
  xmlns:xsi="http://www.w3.org/2001/XMLSchema-instance"
  xmlns:context="http://www.springframework.org/schema/context"
  xmlns:jee="http://www.springframework.org/schema/jee"
  xsi:schemaLocation="http://www.springframework.org/schema/beans
  http://www.springframework.org/schema/beans/spring-beans-4.0.xsd
  http://www.springframework.org/schema/context
  http://www.springframework.org/schema/context/
    spring-context-4.0.xsd
  http://www.springframework.org/schema/beans
  http://www.springframework.org/schema/beans/spring-beans-4.0.xsd
  http://www.springframework.org/schema/jee
  http://www.springframework.org/schema/jee/spring-jee-4.0.xsd">

  <jee:jndi-lookup id="apachemqConnectionFactory"
    jndi-name="java:comp/env/jms/mqConnectionFactory" />
  <jee:jndi-lookup id="PacktTestQueue1"
    jndi-name="java:comp/env/jms/PacktTestQueue1" />
  <jee:jndi-lookup id="PacktTestQueue2"
    jndi-name="java:comp/env/jms/PacktTestQueue2" />

  <bean id="packtMessageListener"
    class="com.packt.jms.PacktMessageListener">
    <property name="packtMessageSender"
      ref ="packtMessageSender" />
  </bean>

  <bean id="defaultMessageListenerContainer"
```

```
class="org.springframework.jms.listener.
DefaultMessageListenerContainer">
  <property name="connectionFactory"
    ref ="apachemqConnectionFactory" />
  <property name="destination" ref ="PacktTestQueue1"/>
  <property name="messageListener" ref ="packtMessageListener"/>
  <property name="concurrentConsumers" value="2" />
</bean>

<bean id="packtMessageSender"
  class="com.packt.jms.PacktMessageSender">
  <property name="jmsTemplate" ref="jmsTemplate"/>
  <property name="queue" ref="PacktTestQueue2"/>
</bean>

<bean id="jmsTemplate"
  class="org.springframework.jms.core.JmsTemplate">
  <property name="connectionFactory"
  ref="apachemqConnectionFactory" />
</bean>

</beans>
```

10. The following code will be configuring the web.xml file. In web.xml, we are actually providing the information about the spring-configuration.xml file location so that the web container can load it.

```
<?xml version="1.0" encoding="UTF-8"?>
<web-app xmlns:xsi="http://www.w3.org/2001/XMLSchema-instance"
  xmlns="http://java.sun.com/xml/ns/javaee"
  xmlns:web="http://java.sun.com/xml/ns/javaee/
    web-app_2_5.xsd"
  xsi:schemaLocation="http://java.sun.com/xml/ns/javaee
  http://java.sun.com/xml/ns/javaee/web-app_2_5.xsd"
  id="WebApp_ID"
  version="2.5">
  <context-param>
    <param-name>contextConfigLocation</param-name>
    <param-value>
      /WEB-INF/configuration/spring-configuration.xml
    </param-value>
  </context-param>
  <listener>
    <listener-class>org.springframework.web.context.
      ContextLoaderListener</listener-class>
  </listener>
</web-app>
```

11. If you are using Maven as the build tool, ensure that you compile the source code and run the application on Tomcat or any other server of your choice. Also keep the Apache ActiveMQ server console up and running.

12. In the ActiveMQ console, click on **Queues**.

13. Click on the **Send** button to link in the `PacktTestQueue1` row.

14. Enter some message text and click on the **Send** button.

15. In the console, you will see that a message was sent from queue 1 to queue 2. Our application consumes messages from `PacktTestQueue1` and push it to `PacktTestQueue2`.

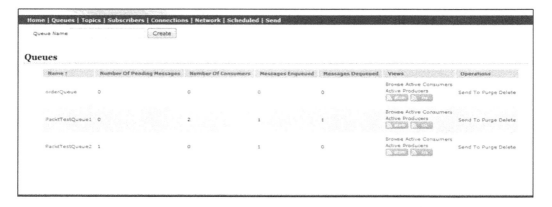

16. Now, let's increase the number of messages to send and see how it behaves.

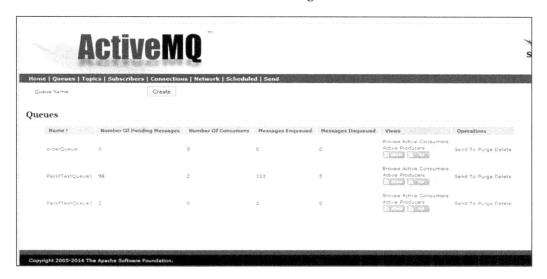

17. Click on **PacktTestQueue2** and you will see all the messages getting pushed to `PacktTestQueue2`.

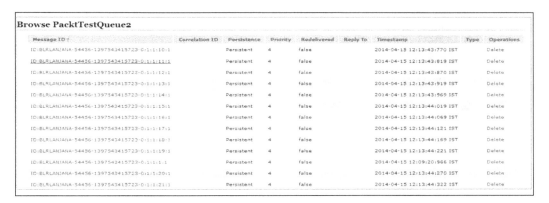

Configuring JMS transactions

When we use transactions, we can handle the preceding scenario better. The messages will be processed within the transactions, and in case of exceptions in the listener, will be rolled back for the complete source code. Refer to the source code present in `repository-Spring4JMS_TransactionChapter2`.

Here are the steps required for including transactions in messaging:

1. Add the following property to the ActiveMQ connection factory bean configuration:

```
<property name="redeliveryPolicy">
  <bean class="org.apache.activemq.RedeliveryPolicy">
<property name="maximumRedeliveries" value="3"/>
  </bean>
</property>
```

2. Update the listener definition as follows:

```
<jms:listener-container
  connection-factory="connectionFactory"
  acknowledge="transacted">
  <jms:listener destination="orderQueue"
    ref="orderReceiver" method="orderReceived" />
</jms:listener-container>
```

Let us revisit the scenarios to learn what happened after adding transactions to the jmsTemplate:

- **Scenario 1**: Success Scenario

- **Scenario 2**: The message producer sends information to the queues, the consumer reads it and processes it into the database; then, an error occurs.

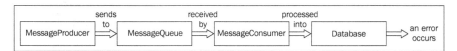

After adding the transaction, the message will be sent by the broker three times. On the fourth attempt, it will be sent to a new queue so that the message is not lost.

- **Scenario 3**: The message producer sends information to the queues, the consumer reads it and processes it into the database; then, an error occurs.

After adding the transaction, if the execution fails with the listener before completing the process, the message broker resends the information.

Configuring multiple JMS listeners and adapters

We may come across an instance where we need to have more JMS listeners and adapters. We can configure multiple listeners when we have to process multiple queues easily with Spring Template. To process multiple listeners, we also need adapters, which will delegate to different listeners.

```xml
<bean id="jmsMessageAdapter"
  class="org.springframework.jms.listener.adapter.
  MessageListenerAdapter">
<property name="delegate" ref="jmsMessageReceiverDelegate" />
<property name="defaultListenerMethod" value="processMessage" />
</bean>

<jms:listener-container container-type="default"
  connection-factory="connectionFactory" acknowledge="auto">
<jms:listener destination="queue1"
  ref="jmsMessageReceiverDelegate" method="processMessage" />
<jms:listener destination="queue2"
  ref="jmsMessageReceiverDelegate" method="processMessage" />
</jms:listener-container>
```

JMS transactions

In this section, let's see how we can include transactions in messaging. We shall first demonstrate messaging without transactions using a few scenarios. We shall first describe the scenarios and write a test case. Then, we shall develop an application around it. We shall demonstrate sending messages using the `convertandsendmessage()` method.

- **Scenario 1**: This is a positive use case, which we have seen in previous sections as well.

```java
@Test
public void testCorrectMessage() throws InterruptedException {
    Order order = new Order(0, "notification to deliver correctly");
    ordersender.convertAndSendMessage(QUEUE_INCOMING, order);

    Thread.sleep(6000);
```

```
  printResults();

  assertEquals(1, getSavedOrders());
  assertEquals(0, getMessagesInQueue(QUEUE_INCOMING));
  assertEquals(0, getMessagesInQueue(QUEUE_DLQ));
}
```

- **Scenario 2**: Here, let's use a negative scenario. The message producer sends information to the queues and the consumer reads it, but an exception occurs before reaching the database.

```
@Test
public void testFailedAfterReceiveMessage()
  throws InterruptedException {
  Order order = new Order(1, "ordernotification to fail
    after receiving");
  ordersender.convertAndSendMessage(QUEUE_INCOMING, order);
  Thread.sleep(6000);
  printResults();
  assertEquals(0, getSavedOrders());
  assertEquals(0, getMessagesInQueue(QUEUE_INCOMING));
  assertEquals(1, getMessagesInQueue(QUEUE_DLQ));
  //Empty the dead letter queue
  jmsTemplate.receive(QUEUE_DLQ);
}
```

In this scenario we have lost the message.

- **Scenario 3**: Here, let's use another negative scenario. The message producer sends information to the queues and the consumer reads it and processes it into the database; then, an error occurs

```
@Test
public void testFailedAfterProcessingMessage()
  throws InterruptedException {
  Order order = new Order(2, "ordernotification to fail
    after processing");
  ordersender.convertAndSendMessage(QUEUE_INCOMING, order);
```

```
    Thread.sleep(6000);
    printResults();
    assertEquals(2, getSavedOrders());
    assertEquals(0, getMessagesInQueue(QUEUE_INCOMING));
    assertEquals(0, getMessagesInQueue(QUEUE_DLQ));
}
```

The message gets delivered and gets stored in the database before the message fails.

Summary

In this chapter, we learned the steps required to install Apache ActiveMQ and different types of messaging. We demonstrated integrating Spring `jms` templates with the application. We also demonstrated, with screenshots, how to create multiple queues and how to communicate with a queue using Spring templates. In the next chapter, we will look at Spring JAVA mail APIs.

Mailing with Spring Mail

3

A mailing API is a part of all modern web applications. End users prefer to be intimated by mail on details of the transactions performed with the application.

Spring has made it easier to provide mailing abilities to any Java application. In this chapter, we shall see how we can use the Spring mail template to e-mail recipients. In the previous chapter, we used messaging as the middleware to store messages in the queue, and now in this chapter, we shall demonstrate using Spring mailing template configurations using different scenarios.

Spring mail message handling process

The following diagram depicts the flow of a Spring mail message process. With this, we can clearly understand the process of sending mail using a Spring mailing template.

A message is created and sent to the transport protocol, which interacts with internet protocols. Then, the message is received by the recipients.

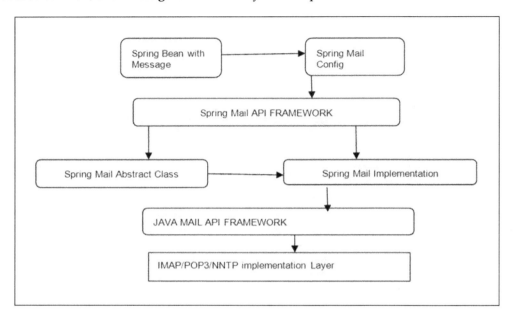

The Spring mail framework requires a mail configuration, or SMTP configuration, as the input and message that needs to be sent. The mail API interacts with internet protocols to send messages. In the next section, we shall look at the classes and interfaces in the Spring mail framework.

Interfaces and classes used for sending mails with Spring

The package `org.springframework.mail` is used for mail configuration in the spring application.

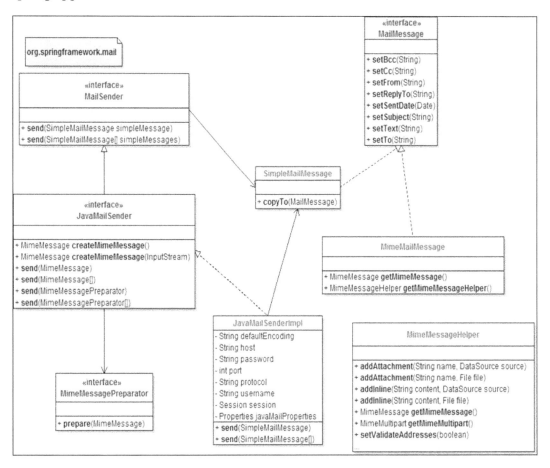

The following are the three main interfaces that are used for sending mail:

- `MailSender`: This interface is used to send simple mail messages.

- `JavaMailSender`: This interface is a subinterface of the `MailSender` interface and supports sending mail messages.

- `MimeMessagePreparator`: This interface is a callback interface that supports the `JavaMailSender` interface in the preparation of mail messages.

The following classes are used for sending mails using Spring:

- `SimpleMailMessage`: This is a class which has properties such as `to`, `from`, `cc`, `bcc`, `sentDate`, and many others. The `SimpleMailMessage` interface sends mail with `MailSenderImp` classes.

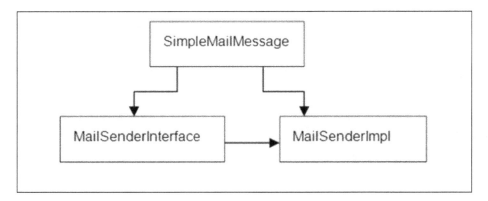

- `JavaMailSenderImpl`: This class is an implementation class of the `JavaMailSender` interface.

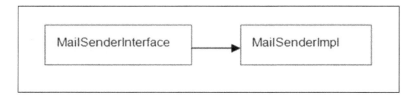

- `MimeMessageHelper`: This class helps with preparing MIME messages.

Sending mail using the @Configuration annotation

We shall demonstrate here how we can send mail using the Spring mail API.

1. First, we provide all the SMTP details in the `.properties` file and read it to the class file with the `@Configuration` annotation. The name of the class is `MailConfiguration`.

   `mail.properties` file contents are shown below:

   ```
   mail.protocol=smtp
   mail.host=localhost
   mail.port=25
   ```

```
mail.smtp.auth=false
mail.smtp.starttls.enable=false
mail.from=me@localhost
mail.username=
mail.password=

@Configuration
@PropertySource("classpath:mail.properties")
public class MailConfiguration {
  @Value("${mail.protocol}")
  private String protocol;
  @Value("${mail.host}")
  private String host;
  @Value("${mail.port}")
  private int port;
  @Value("${mail.smtp.auth}")
  private boolean auth;
  @Value("${mail.smtp.starttls.enable}")
  private boolean starttls;
  @Value("${mail.from}")
  private String from;
  @Value("${mail.username}")
  private String username;
  @Value("${mail.password}")
  private String password;

  @Bean
  public JavaMailSender javaMailSender() {
    JavaMailSenderImpl mailSender = new JavaMailSenderImpl();
    Properties mailProperties = new Properties();
    mailProperties.put("mail.smtp.auth", auth);
    mailProperties.put("mail.smtp.starttls.enable", starttls);
    mailSender.setJavaMailProperties(mailProperties);
    mailSender.setHost(host);
    mailSender.setPort(port);
    mailSender.setProtocol(protocol);
    mailSender.setUsername(username);
    mailSender.setPassword(password);
    return mailSender;
  }
}
```

2. The next step is to create a rest controller to send mail; to do so, click on **Submit**. We shall use the `SimpleMailMessage` interface since we don't have any attachment.

```
@RestController
class MailSendingController {
  private final JavaMailSender javaMailSender;
  @Autowired
  MailSubmissionController(JavaMailSender javaMailSender) {
    this.javaMailSender = javaMailSender;
  }
  @RequestMapping("/mail")
  @ResponseStatus(HttpStatus.CREATED)
  SimpleMailMessage send() {
    SimpleMailMessage mailMessage = new SimpleMailMessage();
    mailMessage.setTo("packt@localhost");
    mailMessage.setReplyTo("anjana@localhost");
    mailMessage.setFrom("Sonali@localhost");
    mailMessage.setSubject("Vani veena Pani");
    mailMessage.setText("MuthuLakshmi how are you?Call
      Me Please [...]");
    javaMailSender.send(mailMessage);
    return mailMessage;
  }
}
```

Sending mail using MailSender and SimpleMailMessage with the XML configuration

"Simple mail message" means the e-mail sent will only be text-based with no HTML formatting, no images, and no attachments. In this section, consider a scenario where we are sending a welcome mail to the user as soon as the user gets their order placed in the application. In this scenario, the mail will be sent after the database insertion operation is successful.

Create a separate folder, called `com.packt.mailService`, for the mail service. The following are the steps for sending mail using the `MailSender` interface and `SimpleMailMessage` class.

1. Create a new Maven web project with the name `Spring4MongoDB_MailChapter3`.

2. The example used the MongoDB database created in *Chapter 1, Spring Mongo Integration*. We have also used the same Eshop db database with MongoDB for CRUD operations on `Customer`, `Order`, and `Product`. We have also used the same `mvc` configurations and source files.

3. Use the same dependencies as used in *Chapter 2, Messaging with Spring JMS*.

4. We need to add dependencies to the `pom.xml` file:

```
<dependency>
    <groupId>org.springframework.integration</groupId>
    <artifactId>spring-integration-mail</artifactId>
    <version>3.0.2.RELEASE</version>
    <scope>runtime</scope>
</dependency>
<dependency>
    <groupId>javax.activation</groupId>
    <artifactId>activation</artifactId>
    <version>1.1-rev-1</version>
    <scope>runtime</scope>
</dependency>
<dependency>
    <groupId>javax.mail</groupId>
    <artifactId>mail</artifactId>
    <version>1.4.3</version>
</dependency>
```

5. Compile the Maven project. Create a separate folder called `com.packt.mailService` for the mail service.

6. Create a simple class named `MailSenderService` and autowire the `MailSender` and `SimpleMailMessage` classes. The basic skeleton is shown here:

```
public class MailSenderService {
  @Autowired
  private MailSender mailSender;
  @AutoWired
  private SimpleMailMessage simplemailmessage;
  public void sendmail(String from, String to, String
    subject, String body){
    /*Code */
  }

}
```

7. Next, create an object of `SimpleMailMessage` and set mail properties, such as `from`, `to`, and `subject` to it.

```
public void sendmail(String from, String to, String
  subject, String body){
  SimpleMailMessage message=new SimpleMailMessage();
  message.setFrom(from);
  message.setSubject(subject);
  message.setText(body);
  mailSender.send(message);
}
```

8. We need to configure the SMTP details. Spring Mail Support provides this flexibility of configuring SMTP details in the XML file.

```
<bean id="mailSender"
  class="org.springframework.mail.javamail.
  JavaMailSenderImpl">
  <property name="host" value="smtp.gmail.com" />
  <property name="port" value="587" />
  <property name="username" value="username" />
  <property name="password" value="password" />

  <property name="javaMailProperties">
  <props>
    <prop key="mail.smtp.auth">true</prop>
    <prop key="mail.smtp.starttls.enable">true</prop>
  </props>
</property>
</bean>

<bean id="mailSenderService" class="
  com.packt.mailserviceMailSenderService ">
  <property name="mailSender" ref="mailSender" />
</bean>

</beans>
```

We need to send mail to the customer after the order has been placed successfully in the MongoDB database. Update the `addorder()` method as follows:

```
@RequestMapping(value = "/order/save", method =
  RequestMethod.POST)
  // request insert order recordh
  public String addorder(@ModelAttribute("Order")
    Order order,Map<String, Object> model) {
    Customer cust=new Customer();
```

```
cust=customer_respository.getObject
    (order.getCustomer().getCust_id());

order.setCustomer(cust);
order.setProduct(product_respository.getObject
    (order.getProduct().getProdid()));
respository.saveObject(order);
mailSenderService.sendmail
    ("anjana.mprasad@gmail.com",cust.getEmail(),
    "Dear"+cust.getName()+"Your order
    details",order.getProduct().getName()+"-price-"+order
    .getProduct().getPrice());
model.put("customerList", customerList);
model.put("productList", productList);
return "order";
}
```

Sending mails to multiple recipients

If you want to intimate the user regarding the latest products or promotions in the application, you can create a mail sending group and send mail to multiple recipients using Spring mail sending support.

We have created an overloaded method in the same class, MailSenderService, which will accept string arrays. The code snippet in the class will look like this:

```
public class MailSenderService {
  @Autowired
  private MailSender mailSender;
  @AutoWired
  private SimpleMailMessage simplemailmessage;
  public void sendmail(String from, String to, String subject,
    String body){
    /*Code */
  }

  public void sendmail(String from, String []to, String subject,
    String body){
    /*Code */
  }

}
```

The following is the code snippet for listing the set of users from MongoDB who have subscribed to promotional e-mails:

```
public List<Customer> getAllObjectsby_emailsubscription(String
  status) {
  return mongoTemplate.find(query(
    where("email_subscribe").is("yes")), Customer.class);
}
```

Sending MIME messages

Multipurpose Internet Mail Extension (MIME) allows attachments to be sent over the Internet. This class just demonstrates how we can send mail with MIME messages. Using a MIME message sender type class is not advisable if you are not sending any attachments with the mail message. In the next section, we will look at the details of how we can send mail with attachments.

Update the MailSenderService class with another method. We have used the MIME message preparator and have overridden the prepare method() to set properties for the mail.

```
public class MailSenderService {
  @Autowired
  private MailSender mailSender;
  @AutoWired
  private SimpleMailMessage simplemailmessage;

  public void sendmail(String from, String to, String subject,
    String body){
    /*Code */
  }
  public void sendmail(String from, String []to, String subject,
    String body){
    /*Code */
  }
  public void sendmime_mail(final String from, final String to,
    final String subject, final String body) throws MailException{
    MimeMessagePreparator message = new MimeMessagePreparator() {
      public void prepare(MimeMessage mimeMessage)
        throws Exception {
        mimeMessage.setRecipient(Message.RecipientType.TO,new
          InternetAddress(to));
        mimeMessage.setFrom(new InternetAddress(from));
        mimeMessage.setSubject(subject);
        mimeMessage.setText(msg);
```

```
        }
    };
    mailSender.send(message);
}
```

Sending attachments with mails

We can also attach various kinds of files to the mail. This functionality is supported by the `MimeMessageHelper` class. If you just want to send a MIME message without an attachment, you can opt for `MimeMesagePreparator`. If the requirement is to have an attachment to be sent with the mail, we can go for the `MimeMessageHelper` class with file APIs.

Spring provides a file class named `org.springframework.core.io.FileSystemResource`, which has a parameterized constructor that accepts file objects.

```java
public class SendMailwithAttachment {
    public static void main(String[] args)
        throws MessagingException {
        AnnotationConfigApplicationContext ctx =
            new AnnotationConfigApplicationContext();
        ctx.register(AppConfig.class);
        ctx.refresh();
        JavaMailSenderImpl mailSender =
            ctx.getBean(JavaMailSenderImpl.class);
        MimeMessage mimeMessage = mailSender.createMimeMessage();
        //Pass true flag for multipart message
        MimeMessageHelper mailMsg = new MimeMessageHelper(mimeMessage,
            true);
        mailMsg.setFrom("ANJUANJU02@gmail.com");
        mailMsg.setTo("RAGHY03@gmail.com");
        mailMsg.setSubject("Test mail with Attachment");
        mailMsg.setText("Please find Attachment.");
        //FileSystemResource object for Attachment
        FileSystemResource file = new FileSystemResource(new
            File("D:/cp/ GODGOD. jpg"));
        mailMsg.addAttachment("GODGOD.jpg", file);
        mailSender.send(mimeMessage);
        System.out.println("---Done---");
    }

}
```

Sending preconfigured mails

In this example, we shall provide a message that is to be sent in the mail, and we will configure it in an XML file. Sometimes when it comes to web applications, you may have to send messages on maintenance. Think of a scenario where the content of the mail changes, but the sender and receiver are preconfigured. In such a case, you can add another overloaded method to the `MailSender` class.

We have fixed the subject of the mail, and the content can be sent by the user. Think of it as "an application which sends mails to users whenever the build fails".

```xml
<?xml version="1.0" encoding="UTF-8"?>
<beans xmlns="http://www.springframework.org/schema/
beans" xmlns:xsi="http://www.w3.org/2001/XMLSchema-instance"
xmlns:context="http://www.springframework.org/schema/context"
xsi:schemaLocation="http://www.springframework.org/schema/beans
http://www.springframework.org/schema/beans/spring-beans-3.0.xsd
http://www.springframework.org/schema/context
http://www.springframework.org/schema/
  context/spring-context-3.0.xsd">
<context:component-scan base-package="com.packt" />
<!-- SET default mail properties -->
<bean id="mailSender" class=
  "org.springframework.mail.javamail.JavaMailSenderImpl">
  <property name="host" value="smtp.gmail.com"/>
  <property name="port" value="25"/>
  <property name="username" value="anju@gmail.com"/>
  <property name="password" value="password"/>
  <property name="javaMailProperties">
  <props>
    <prop key="mail.transport.protocol">smtp</prop>
    <prop key="mail.smtp.auth">true</prop>
    <prop key="mail.smtp.starttls.enable">true</prop>
    <prop key="mail.debug">true</prop>
  </props>
  </property>
</bean>

<!-- You can have some pre-configured messagess also which are
  ready to send -->
<bean id="preConfiguredMessage" class=
  "org.springframework.mail.SimpleMailMessage">
  <property name="to" value="packt@gmail.com"></property>
  <property name="from" value="anju@gmail.com"></property>
  <property name="subject" value="FATAL ERROR- APPLICATION AUTO
    MAINTENANCE STARTED-BUILD FAILED!!"/>
```

```
    </bean>
  </beans>
```

Now we shall sent two different bodies for the subjects.

```
public class MyMailer {
  public static void main(String[] args){
    try{
      //Create the application context
      ApplicationContext context = new
        FileSystemXmlApplicationContext(
        "application-context.xml");
      //Get the mailer instance
      ApplicationMailer mailer = (ApplicationMailer)
        context.getBean("mailService");
      //Send a composed mail
      mailer.sendMail("nikhil@gmail.com", "Test Subject",
        "Testing body");
    }catch(Exception e){
      //Send a pre-configured mail
      mailer.sendPreConfiguredMail("build failed exception occured
        check console or logs"+e.getMessage());
    }
  }
}
```

Using Spring templates with Velocity to send HTML mails

Velocity is the templating language provided by Apache. It can be integrated into the Spring view layer easily. The latest Velocity version used during this book is 1.7. In the previous section, we demonstrated using Velocity to send e-mails using the `@Bean` and `@Configuration` annotations. In this section, we shall see how we can configure Velocity to send mails using XML configuration.

All that needs to be done is to add the following bean definition to the `.xml` file. In the case of `mvc`, you can add it to the `dispatcher-servlet.xml` file.

```
<bean id="velocityEngine" class=
  "org.springframework.ui.velocity.VelocityEngineFactoryBean">
  <property name="velocityProperties">
  <value>
    resource.loader=class
    class.resource.loader.class=org.apache.velocity
```

```
    .runtime.resource.loader.ClasspathResourceLoader
  </value>
  </property>
</bean>
```

1. Create a new Maven web project with the name `Spring4MongoDB_Mail_VelocityChapter3`.

2. Create a package and name it `com.packt.velocity.templates`.

3. Create a file with the name `orderconfirmation.vm`.

```
<html>
<body>
<h3> Dear Customer,<h3>
<p>${customer.firstName} ${customer.lastName}</p>
<p>We have dispatched your order at address.</p>
${Customer.address}
</body>
</html>
```

4. Use all the dependencies that we have added in the previous sections.

5. To the existing Maven project, add this dependency:

```
<dependency>
  <groupId>org.apache.velocity</groupId>
  <artifactId>velocity</artifactId>
  <version>1.7</version>
</dependency>
```

6. To ensure that Velocity gets loaded on application startup, we shall create a class. Let's name the class `VelocityConfiguration.java`. We have used the annotations `@Configuration` and `@Bean` with the class.

```
import java.io.IOException;
import java.util.Properties;

import org.apache.velocity.app.VelocityEngine;
import org.apache.velocity.exception.VelocityException;
import org.springframework.context.annotation.Bean;
import
  org.springframework.context.annotation.Configuration;
import
  org.springframework.ui.velocity.VelocityEngineFactory;
@Configuration
public class VelocityConfiguration {
  @Bean
  public VelocityEngine getVelocityEngine()
```

```
  throws VelocityException, IOException{
    VelocityEngineFactory velocityEngineFactory = new
      VelocityEngineFactory();
    Properties props = new Properties();
    props.put("resource.loader", "class");
    props.put("class.resource.loader.class",
      "org.apache.velocity.runtime.resource.loader." +
      "ClasspathResourceLoader");
    velocityEngineFactory.setVelocityProperties(props);
    return factory.createVelocityEngine();
  }
}
```

7. Use the same `MailSenderService` class and add another overloaded `sendMail()` method in the class.

```
public void sendmail(final Customer customer){
  MimeMessagePreparator preparator = new
    MimeMessagePreparator() {
    public void prepare(MimeMessage mimeMessage)
    throws Exception {
      MimeMessageHelper message =
        new MimeMessageHelper(mimeMessage);
      message.setTo(user.getEmailAddress());
      message.setFrom("webmaster@packt.com"); // could be
        parameterized
      Map model = new HashMap();
      model.put("customer", customer);
      String text =
        VelocityEngineUtils.mergeTemplateIntoString(
        velocityEngine, "com/packt/velocity/templates/
        orderconfirmation.vm", model);
      message.setText(text, true);
    }
  };
  this.mailSender.send(preparator);
}
```

8. Update the controller class to send mail using the Velocity template.

```
@RequestMapping(value = "/order/save", method =
  RequestMethod.POST)
// request insert order recordh
public String addorder(@ModelAttribute("Order") Order
  order,Map<String, Object> model) {
  Customer cust=new Customer();
  cust=customer_respository.getObject(order.getCustomer()
```

```
        .getCust_id());

    order.setCustomer(cust);
    order.setProduct(product_respository.getObject
        (order.getProduct().getProdid()));
    respository.saveObject(order);
    // to send mail using velocity template.
    mailSenderService.sendmail(cust);

    return "order";
    }
```

Sending Spring mails over a different thread

There are other options for sending Spring mail asynchronously. One way is to have a separate thread to the mail sending job. Spring comes with the `taskExecutor` package, which offers us a thread pooling functionality.

1. Create a class called `MailSenderAsyncService` that implements the `MailSender` interface.

2. Import the `org.springframework.core.task.TaskExecutor` package.

3. Create a private class called `MailRunnable`. Here is the complete code for `MailSenderAsyncService`:

```
public class MailSenderAsyncService implements MailSender{
    @Resource(name = "mailSender")
    private MailSender mailSender;

    private TaskExecutor taskExecutor;

    @Autowired
    public MailSenderAsyncService(TaskExecutor taskExecutor){
        this.taskExecutor = taskExecutor;
    }
    public void send(SimpleMailMessage simpleMessage) throws
        MailException {
        taskExecutor.execute(new MailRunnable(simpleMessage));
    }

    public void send(SimpleMailMessage[] simpleMessages)
        throws MailException {
        for (SimpleMailMessage message : simpleMessages) {
```

```
          send(message);
      }
  }

  private class SimpleMailMessageRunnable implements
    Runnable {
    private SimpleMailMessage simpleMailMessage;
    private SimpleMailMessageRunnable(SimpleMailMessage
      simpleMailMessage) {
      this.simpleMailMessage = simpleMailMessage;
    }

    public void run() {
    mailSender.send(simpleMailMessage);
    }
  }
  private class SimpleMailMessagesRunnable implements
    Runnable {
    private SimpleMailMessage[] simpleMessages;
    private SimpleMailMessagesRunnable(SimpleMailMessage[]
      simpleMessages) {
      this.simpleMessages = simpleMessages;
    }

    public void run() {
      mailSender.send(simpleMessages);
    }
  }
}
```

4. Configure the `ThreadPool` executor in the `.xml` file.

```xml
<bean id="taskExecutor" class="org.springframework.
  scheduling.concurrent.ThreadPoolTaskExecutor"
  p:corePoolSize="5"
  p:maxPoolSize="10" p:queueCapacity="100"
    p:waitForTasksToCompleteOnShutdown="true"/>
```

5. Test the source code.

```java
import javax.annotation.Resource;

import org.springframework.mail.MailSender;
import org.springframework.mail.SimpleMailMessage;
import org.springframework.test.context.ContextConfiguration;

@ContextConfiguration
```

```java
public class MailSenderAsyncService {
  @Resource(name = " mailSender ")
  private MailSender mailSender;
  public void testSendMails() throws Exception {
    SimpleMailMessage[] mailMessages = new
      SimpleMailMessage[5];

    for (int i = 0; i < mailMessages.length; i++) {
      SimpleMailMessage message = new SimpleMailMessage();
      message.setSubject(String.valueOf(i));
      mailMessages[i] = message;
    }
    mailSender.send(mailMessages);
  }
  public static void main (String args[]){
    MailSenderAsyncService asyncservice=new
      MailSenderAsyncService();
    Asyncservice. testSendMails();
  }
}
```

Sending Spring mails with AOP

We can also send mails by integrating the mailing functionality with **Aspect Oriented Programming (AOP)**. This can be used to send mails after the user registers with an application. Think of a scenario where the user receives an activation mail after registration. This can also be used to send information about an order placed on an application. Use the following steps to create a `MailAdvice` class using AOP:

1. Create a package called `com.packt.aop`.

2. Create a class called `MailAdvice`.

```java
public class MailAdvice {
  public void advice (final ProceedingJoinPoint
    proceedingJoinPoint) {
    new Thread(new Runnable() {
    public void run() {
      System.out.println("proceedingJoinPoint:"+
        proceedingJoinPoint);
      try {
        proceedingJoinPoint.proceed();
      } catch (Throwable t) {
        // All we can do is log the error.
        System.out.println(t);
```

```
        }
      }
   }).start();
   }
}
```

This class creates a new thread and starts it. In the `run` method, the `proceedingJoinPoint.proceed()` method is called. `ProceddingJoinPoint` is a class available in `AspectJ.jar`.

3. Update the `dispatcher-servlet.xml` file with `aop` configurations. Update the `xlmns` namespace using the following code:

```
xmlns:aop=http://www.springframework.org/schema/aop
```

4. Also update the `xsi:schemalocation`, as shown in the following code:

```
xsi:schemaLocation="http://www.springframework.org/
   schema/aop http://www.springframework.org/
   schema/aop/spring-aop-2.5.xsd
```

5. Update the bean configuration in the `.xml` file:

```
<aop:config>
   <aop:aspect ref="advice">
   <aop:around method="fork"
     pointcut="execution(* org.springframework.mail
     .javamail.JavaMailSenderImpl.send(..))"/>
   </aop:aspect>
</aop:config>
```

Summary

In this chapter, we demonstrated how to create a mailing service and configure it using Spring API. We also demonstrated how to send mails with attachments using MIME messages. We also demonstrated how to create a dedicated thread for sending mails using `ExecutorService`. We saw an example in which mail can be sent to multiple recipients, and saw an implementation of using the Velocity engine to create templates and send mails to recipients. In the last section, we demonstrated how the Spring framework supported mails can be sent using Spring AOP and threads.

In the next chapter, we will look at Spring Batch framework.

4

Jobs with Spring Batch

Enterprise applications often have requirements for processing bulk information by applying complex business rules. Some applications require automated jobs to run and provide large chunks of data as input for further processing. Such functions are always time-based jobs, which don't require any user intervention. Batch processing is widely used in banking and insurance domains where large sets of data are processed at scheduled times. A **job** is a process while a **batch job** implies a set of processes that run to perform a task at a scheduled time.

Introduction to Spring Batch

Spring Batch is itself a batch framework that is used to develop applications to do batch jobs. It supports batch optimization and job partitioning and is highly scalable, which provokes us to consider it in the development of batch applications.

Use cases for using Spring Batch

Let us list a few use cases where we can use Spring batch in the application:

- To send bulk mails to the user at a scheduled time
- To read messages from the queue
- To update transactions at a given time
- To process all the received files from the user at a given time

Goals of batch processing

The batch processing key goal is to fulfill the following set of steps in order to complete the batch job:

1. Locating a job.
2. Identifying the input.
3. Scheduling the job.
4. Starting the job.
5. Processing the job.
6. Go to step 2 (for fresh input).

Architecture of a batch job

Let's depict the basic architecture of a batch processor; we can also see the components involved in the batch processing. From the following diagram you can figure out the main components of Spring Batch:

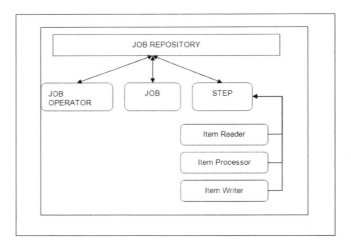

Let's now have a look at the components individually.

- JobRepository: This container is where we need to register our jobs or processes.

- JobOperator: This is the one that triggers the registered job. It also provides APIs for accessing the register. It is an interface.

- Job: It is a process or task in the jobRepository. This consists of one more step.

- `Step`: This actually contains the logic that needs to be executed. Each step consists of an `ItemReader`, `ItemProcessor`, and `ItemWriter` interface. First, the `ItemReader` interface reads one step at a time in a job and gives it to `ItemProcessor` which processes the job. For example, it might collect some data required. Then, the `ItemWriter` interface writes the data to the database or it might execute a transaction or log a message. There are two kinds of steps:

  - `ChunkStyle`: A `ChunkStyle` step has exactly one `ItemReader`, one `ItemProcessor`, and one `ItemWriter`.

  - `BatchLet`: In Spring, `BatchLet` is called `TaskLetStep`. `BatchLet` is a custom-made step that can be used for sending bulk mails or text messages.

Now that we know the basics of a batch, in the next section we shall see how to implement or use a batch.

Using an enterprise batch

We have the following two options for implementing a batch:

- Using JVM and starting JVM for each job run
- Deploying a batch job management application in a J2EE container

JSR-352 is the standard specification available for implementing batch processing. The Spring framework supports this specification to a great extent. Most JEE containers, such as **Glassfish**, **Jboss- JMX**, and Web Sphere are bound to support the JSR-352 specifications. As a developer, we can choose the Spring framework and deploy the batch on a J2EE container.

You can also use restful APIs to pool the data into and out of the batch application. In the next section, let's use the Spring Batch framework to create a job. We shall first look at the dependency.

Dependency for Spring Batch

To get started with Spring Batch, we need to look at the dependencies. Assuming that the user is familiar with the Maven application, we can look at the following dependencies that need to be added to the `pom.xml` file to use Spring Batch:

```
<dependency>
    <groupId>org.springframework.batch</groupId>
    <artifactId>spring-batch-core</artifactId>
    <version>3.0.0.RELEASE</version>
```

```
    </dependency>
    <dependency>
      <groupId>org.springframework</groupId>
      <artifactId>spring-core</artifactId>
      <version>${spring.version}</version>
    </dependency>

    <dependency>
      <groupId>org.springframework</groupId>
      <artifactId>spring-context</artifactId>
      <version>${spring.version}</version>
    </dependency>
```

Key components of Spring Batch

You can see that the key components of Spring Batch are very similar to the JSR specification for batch processing in Java.

- `JobRepository`: This is again a repository for jobs. But, in the Spring Batch framework, the core API has `JobRepository`. It provides the `create`, `update`, `read`, and `delete` methods for `JobLauncher`, `JobReader`, `ItemProcessor`, and `ItemWriter`. The class responsible for `JobRepository` in the Spring framework is `SimpleJobRepository`. There are two ways of storing the jobs: one in the database and another in memory (which will have to make use of `HashMaps`).

  `SimpleJobRepositoryConstructor` looks like this:

  ```
  public SimpleJobRepository(JobInstanceDao jobInstanceDao,
      JobExecutionDao jobExecutionDao,
      StepExecutionDao stepExecutionDao,
      ExecutionContextDao ecDao)
  ```

- `JobLauncher`: `JobLauncher` is just a simple interface used for launching jobs. Jobs are registered at the `jobRepository`.

  ```
  public interface JobLauncher {
      public JobExecution run(Job job, JobParameters
        jobParameters)
      throws JobExecutionAlreadyRunningException,
        JobRestartException;
  }
  ```

  A `SimpleJobLauncher` class implements the `JobLauncher` interface. This class has a `setJobRepository` method.

  ```
  public void setJobRepository(JobRepository jobRepository)
  ```

- `ItemReader`: It is an interface in `org.springframework.batch.item` package. ItemReader is used for providing data. The data can be from a database, XML, or from a flat file.

  Implementation classes are expected to be stateful and will be called multiple times for each batch, with each call to `read()` returning a different value and finally returning null when all input data is exhausted. Implementation classes need not be thread-safe, and clients of an `ItemReader` interface need to be aware that this is the case.

```
public interface ItemReader<T> {
  T read() throws Exception, UnexpectedInputException,
    ParseException;
}
```

- `ItemProcessor`: This is an interface that can be used for processing data and does the intermediate processing of data. Before it is given to `ItemWriter`, `ItemProcessor` can be used for implementing certain business logic.

```
public interface ItemProcessor<I, O> {
  O process(I item) throws Exception;
}
public class ProductBean {}

public class RelatedProductsBean {
  public RelatedProductsBean(ProductBean productBean) {}
}
public class ProductBeanProcessor implements
  ItemProcessor<ProductBean, RelatedProductsBean >{
  public RelatedProductsBean process(ProductBean
    productBean) throws Exception {
    //Perform simple transformation, convert a ProductBean
    to a RelatedProductsBean
    return new RelatedProductsBean(productBean);
  }
}
public class ProductBeanWriter implements
  ItemWriter<ProductBean>{
  public void write(List<? extends ProductBean>
    productBeans) throws Exception {
    //write productBeans
  }
}
```

Assume that an `ItemReader` interface provides a class of type `ProductBean` and this class needs to be converted to type `RelatedProductsBean` before being written out. An `ItemProcessor` can be written to perform the conversion. In this very simple example, there is a class `ProductBean`, a class `RelatedProductsBean`, and a class `ProductBeanProcessor` that adhere to the `ItemProcessor` interface. The transformation is simple, but any type of transformation could be done here. The `RelatedProductsBean` writer will be used to write out `RelatedProductsBean` objects, throwing an exception if any other type is provided. Similarly, `ProductBeanProcessor` will throw an exception if anything but `ProductBean` is provided.

`ProductBeanProcessor` can then be injected into a step:

```
<job id="ioSampleJob">
  <step name="step1">
  <tasklet>
  <chunk reader="ProductReader" processor="ProductProcessor"
    writer="RelatedProductsWriter"
    commit-interval="2"/>
  </tasklet>
  </step>
</job>
```

- `Item Writer`: This is an interface and here are its frequently used implementation classes.

  The `write` method defines the most essential contract of the ItemWriter interface. It will attempt to write out the list of items passed in as long as it is open. As it is expected that items will be batched together into a chunk and then the output given, the interface accepts a list of items rather than an item by itself. Once the items are written out, any flushing that may be necessary can be performed before returning from the `write` method. For example, if writing to a Hibernate DAO, multiple calls to `write` can be made, one for each item.

  The writer can then call close on the hibernate session before returning.

  Here is a frequently used implementation of `ItemWriter`:

- `FlatFileItemWriter`: This writes data to a file or stream. It uses a buffered writer to improve performance.

  ```
  StaxEventItemWriter: This is an implementation of
     ItemWriter that uses StAX and Marshaller for serializing
     objects to XML.
  ```

Developing a sample batch application

Now that we have covered the basics of batch processing and the components of Spring Batch, let's develop a simple example in which names starting with $$ are recognized as nonvegetarian food items and names starting with ## are vegetarian. Names that do not start with either of these characters need to be ignored. Our job must generate an HTML string with the font color red for nonvegetarian recipes and a green font color for vegetarian recipes.

You need to create a Maven project named `recipeMarker` with the previously mentioned dependency. Also add all the Spring Framework core dependencies. We shall work on the `context.xml` file. We need to configure the job repository and job launcher.

Look at the `applicationContext.xml` file:

```
<?xml version="1.0" encoding="UTF-8"?>
<beans xmlns="http://www.springframework.org/schema/beans"
  xmlns:xsi="http://www.w3.org/2001/XMLSchema-instance"
  xmlns:context="http://www.springframework.org/schema/context"
  xsi:schemaLocation="http://www.springframework.org/schema/beans
    http://www.springframework.org/schema/beans/
    spring-beans-2.5.xsd
  http://www.springframework.org/schema/context
  http://www.springframework.org/schema/context/
    spring-context-2.5.xsd">
  <bean id="transactionManager"
    class="org.springframework.batch.support.transaction
    .ResourcelessTransactionManager"/>
  <bean id="jobLauncher"
    class="org.springframework.batch.core.launch.support
    .SimpleJobLauncher">
    <property name="jobRepository" ref="jobRepository"/>
  </bean>
  <bean id="jobRepository"
    class="org.springframework.batch.core.repository
    .support.MapJobRepositoryFactoryBean">
    <property name="transactionManager" ref="transactionManager"/>
  </bean>
  <bean id="simpleJob"
    class="org.springframework.batch.core.job.SimpleJob"
    abstract="true">
    <property name="jobRepository" ref="jobRepository" />
  </bean>
</beans>
```

You can see that we have used `MapJobRepositoryFactoryBean` to create a job repository. It's a `FactoryBean` that automates the creation of `SimpleJobRepository` using nonpersistent, in-memory **data access object (DAO)** implementations. This repository is only really intended for use in testing and rapid prototyping. In such settings, you might find that `ResourcelessTransactionManager` is useful (as long as your business logic does not use a relational database). It is not suited for use in multi-threaded jobs with splits, although it should be safe to use in a multi-threaded step.

Next, we shall create implementation classes using the `ItemReader` and `ItemWriter` interfaces.

1. The following is the `ItemReader` implementation class. It reads the data in the overridden `read()` method which returns an object.

```
package com.packt.batchjob;
import java.util.List;
import org.springframework.batch.item.ItemReader;
import org.springframework.batch.item.ParseException;
import
   org.springframework.batch.item.UnexpectedInputException;
public class CustomItemReader implements ItemReader {
  private int index = 0;
  private List<String> itemList;
  public Object read() throws Exception,
    UnexpectedInputException,
    ParseException {
    if (index < itemList.size()) {
      String str = itemList.get(index++);
      System.out.println("Read[ " + index + " ] = " + str);
      return str;
    } else {return null;}
  }
  public List<String> getItemList() {
    return itemList;
  }
  public void setItemList(List<String> itemList) {
    this.itemList = itemList;
  }
}
```

2. Here we have `ItemProcessor`. It applies the logic of marking the recipe list with red and green colors.

```
package com.packt.batchjob;
import org.springframework.batch.item.ItemProcessor;
public class CustomItemProcessor implements ItemProcessor {
```

```
public Object process(Object arg0) throws Exception {
  String input = (String) arg0;
  if (input.contains("$$")) {
    input = input.substring(3, input.length());
    input = "<font colour="red">(.Non-Veg)</font> " +
      input;
  } else if (input.contains("##")) {
  input = input.substring(3, input.length());
  input = "<font colour="green">(.Veg)</font> " + input;
  } else
  return null;
  System.out.println("Process : " + input);
  return input;
  }
}
```

3. Lastly, let's write the implementation class for reading the modified data from the `ItemProcessor` and write it.

```
import java.util.List;
import org.springframework.batch.item.ItemWriter;
public class CustomItemWriter implements ItemWriter {
  public void write(List arg0) throws Exception {
    System.out.println("Write   : " + arg0 + "\n");
  }
}
```

In the next step, we shall combine `ItemReader`, `ItemProcessor`, and `ItemWriter` into a job.

Let us create an `itemreaderprocessorwriter.xml` file. We shall pass the list of recipes in the XML file. We have included the `applicationContext.xml` file. A commit interval has been defined to say that the writer should commit after it writes two elements at a time. You can also observe that the step consists of `reader`, `writer`, and `jobRepository`.

```
<?xml version="1.0" encoding="UTF-8"?>
<beans xmlns="http://www.springframework.org/schema/beans"
  xmlns:xsi="http://www.w3.org/2001/XMLSchema-instance"
  xmlns:context="http://www.springframework.org/schema/context"
  xsi:schemaLocation="http://www.springframework.org/schema/beans
  http://www.springframework.org/schema/beans/spring-beans-2.5.xsd
  http://www.springframework.org/schema/context
  http://www.springframework.org/schema/context/
    spring-context-2.5.xsd">
  <import resource="applicationContext.xml"/>
```

```
<bean id="customReader"
  class="com.packt.batchjob.CustomItemReader" >
  <property name="itemList" >
  <list>
  <value>$$Chicken65</value>
  <value>$$ChickenTikkaMasala</value>
  <value>$$GingerChicken</value>
  <value>$$GarlicChicken</value>
  <value>##Dal Makani</value>
  <value>##Stuffed Capsicum</value>
  <value>##Bendi Fry</value>
  <value>##Alo Bartha</value>
  </list>
  </property>
</bean>
<bean id="customProcessor"
  class="com.packt.batchjob.CustomItemProcessor" />
<bean id="customWriter"
  class="com.packt.batchjob.CustomItemWriter" />
<bean id="simpleStep"
  class="org.springframework.batch.core.step
  .item.SimpleStepFactoryBean">
  <property name="transactionManager"
    ref="transactionManager" />
  <property name="jobRepository" ref="jobRepository" />
  <property name="itemReader" ref="customReader"/>
  <property name="itemProcessor" ref="customProcessor"/>
  <property name="itemWriter" ref="customWriter"/>
  <property name="commitInterval" value="2" />
</bean>
<bean id="readerWriterJob" parent="simpleJob">
  <property name="steps">
  <list>
  <ref bean="simpleStep"/>
  </list>
  </property>
</bean>
</beans>
```

The next step is to launch the job using a command-line interface provided by the Spring Batch framework.

```
D:\SpringBatch\receipeMarker>java -classpath "lib\*;src"
org.springframework.batch.core.launch.support
  .CommandLineJobRunner
  itemReaderWriter.xml readerWriterJob
```

Let us create a file named `itemreaderprocessorwriter.xml`. We shall pass the list of recipes in the XML file. We have included the `applicationContext.xml` file. A commit interval has been defined to say that the writer should commit after it writes two elements at a time. You can also observe that the step consists of `reader`, `writer`, and `jobRepository`.

```
OUTPUT:
Read[ 1 ] = $$Chicken65
Read[ 2 ] = $$ChickenTikkaMasala
Process : "<font colour="red">(.Non-Veg)</font> $$Chicken65
Process : "<font colour="red">(.Non-
  Veg)</font>$$ChickenTikkaMasala
Write   : [<font colour="red">(.Non-Veg)</font>$$Chicken65 , <font
  colour="red">(.Non-Veg)</font> $$ChickenTikkaMasala
Read[ 3 ] = $$GingerChicken
Read[ 4 ] = $$GarlicChicken
Process : "<font colour="red">(.Non-Veg)</font> $$GingerChicken
Process : "<font colour="red">(.Non-Veg)</font>$$GarlicChicken
Write   : [<font colour="red">(.Non-Veg)</font>$$GingerChicken ,
  <font colour="red">(.Non-Veg)</font> $$GarlicChicken
Read[ 5 ] = ##Dal Makani
Read[ 6 ] = ##Stuffed Capsicum
Process : "<font colour="green">(. Veg)</font> ##Dal Makani
Process : "<font colour=" green ">(.Non-Veg)</font>##Stuffed
  Capsicum
Write   : [<font colour=" green ">(.Veg)</font>##Dal Makani ,
  <font colour=" green ">(. Veg)</font> ##Stuffed Capsicum
Read[ 7 ] = ##Bendi Fry
Read[ 8 ] = ##Alo Bartha
Process : "<font colour=" green ">(. Veg)</font> ##Bendi Fry
Process : "<font colour=" green ">(. Veg)</font>##Alo Bartha
Write   : [<font colour=" green ">(. Veg)</font>##Bendi Fry ,
  <font colour="red">(.Non-Veg)</font> ##Alo Bartha
```

Creating a sample batch application using the Tasklet interface

Let's create another batch application that runs on the command line. This batch application prints the message. We have already spoken about Tasklet in the beginning of the chapter. A job compromises of steps and a step can be one of two types: chunk style step and Tasklet.

We are using the `Tasklet` interface in this example. In Spring Batch, `Tasklet` is an interface called to perform a single task, like to clean or set up resources before or after a step execution. This interface comes with a method called `executeStatus`, which should be overridden by the class that implements it.

```
RepeatStatus execute(StepContribution contribution,
                     ChunkContext chunkContext)
           throws java.lang.Exception
RepeatStatus: CONTINUABLE and FINISHED
```

In the following example, `TaskLetImpl` implements the `Tasklet` interface. We have also used the `TaskLetStep` class for configuring the `JobRepository` in the configuration file. The public class `TaskletStep` extends `AbstractStep`.

`TaskletStep` is a simple implementation of executing the step as a call to `Tasklet`, possibly repeated, and each call is surrounded by a transaction. The structure is therefore that of a loop with a transaction boundary inside the loop. The loop is controlled by the step operations (`setStepOperations(RepeatOperations)`).

Clients can use interceptors in the step operations to intercept or listen to the iteration on a step-wide basis—for instance, to get a callback when the step is complete. Those that want callbacks at the level of an individual task can specify interceptors for the chunk operations.

Let's understand the flow through the following diagram:

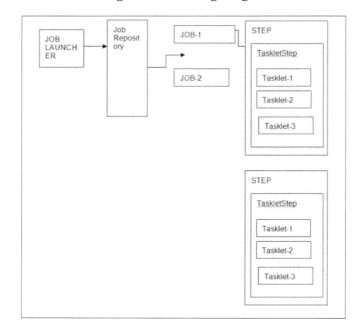

Let's create a simple Java batch application project named
Chapter4-SpringBatchCommandLine

1. Create a Maven folder structure for Chapter4-SpringBatchCommandLine,
    as follows:
    ○   src/main/java
    ○   src/main/resources
    ○   src/pom.xml

2. Create a package called com.packt.example.

3. Create a class called TaskletImpl. This class implements the Tasklet
    interface and overrides the execute() method.

    ```
    import org.springframework.batch.core.step.tasklet.Tasklet;
    import org.springframework.batch.repeat.ExitStatus;
    public class TaskletImpl implements Tasklet{
      private String message;
      public void setMessage(String message) {
        this.message = message;
      }
      public ExitStatus execute() throws Exception {
        System.out.print(message);
        return ExitStatus.FINISHED;
      }
    }
    ```

4. Configure the simpleJob.xml file.

5. Place this file in the resources folder.

6. You can see that we have created three instances of the TaskletImpl class:
    object1, object2, and object3.

7. In each instance, we are setting the message property. We are passing the
    object instance to TaskletStep.

    ```
    <?xml version="1.0" encoding="UTF-8"?>
    <beans xmlns="http://www.springframework.org/schema/beans"
      xmlns:xsi="http://www.w3.org/2001/XMLSchema-instance"
      xsi:schemaLocation="http://www.springframework.org/
        schema/beans
      http://www.springframework.org/schema/beans/
        spring-beans-4.0.xsd">
    <import resource="applicationContext.xml"/>

    <bean id="object1" class="com.packt.example.TaskletImpl">
      <property name="message" value="Dad not well"/>
    ```

```xml
      </bean>

      <bean id="object2" class="com.packt.example.TaskletImpl">
        <property name="message" value="Call the doctor"/>
      </bean>

      <bean id="object3" class="com.packt.example.TaskletImpl">
        <property name="message" value="He is sweating"/>
      </bean>

      <bean id="taskletStep" abstract="true"
        class="org.springframework.batch.core
        .step.tasklet.TaskletStep">
        <property name="jobRepository" ref="jobRepository"/>
      </bean>

      <bean id="simpleJob"
        class="org.springframework.batch.core.job.SimpleJob">
        <property name="name" value="simpleJob" />
        <property name="steps">
        <list>
        <bean parent="taskletStep">
        <property name="tasklet" ref="object1"/>
        </bean>
        <bean parent="taskletStep">
        <property name="tasklet" ref="object2"/>
        </bean>
        <bean parent="taskletStep">
        <property name="tasklet" ref="object3"/>
        </bean>
        </list>
        </property>
        <property name="jobRepository" ref="jobRepository"/>
      </bean>
    </beans>
```

8. Configure jobLauncher and JobRepository.

```xml
    <bean id="jobLauncher"
      class="org.springframework.batch.core
      .launch.support.SimpleJobLauncher">
      <property name="jobRepository" ref="jobRepository"/>
    </bean>
    <bean id="jobRepository"
      class="org.springframework.batch.core
      .repository.support.SimpleJobRepository">
```

```
  <constructor-arg>
    <bean
      class="org.springframework.batch.core.repository
      .dao.MapJobInstanceDao"/>
  </constructor-arg>
  <constructor-arg>
    <bean class="org.springframework.batch.core.repository.
      dao.MapJobExecutionDao" />
  </constructor-arg>
  <constructor-arg>
    <bean class="org.springframework.batch.core
      .repository.dao.MapStepExecutionDao"/>
  </constructor-arg>
</bean>
```

9. You can run the project with MVN Compile, as follows:

   mvn clean compile exec:java -Dexec.mainClass=org.springframework. batch.core.launch.support.CommandLineJobRunner -Dexec. args="simpleJob.xml simpleJob"

   OUTPUT:

   Dad not well

   Call the Doctor

   He is sweating

Using Spring Batch to read a CSV file

Let us create another batch application that reads a CSV file from a directory and uses commandlinerunner to run the job. The output is again a CSV file that will be available in the output folder.

This example is about showing the various options of the ItemWriter and ItemReader implementations available in the Spring Batch framework. We have used flatFileItemReader and flatFileItemWriter implementations available in the Spring Framework here.

We shall begin with application development and check out how these ItemReader implementation classes are used.

1. Create a Spring Java application using Maven and name it SpringBatchCommandLine-Chapter4Example2.

2. Create a domain class Employee with two instance variables, empId and name, with getters and setters:

   ```
   package com.packt;
   public class Employee {
   ```

```
      int empId;
      String name;
      public int getEmpId() {
        return empId;
      }
      public void setEmpId(int empId) {
        this.empId = empId;
      }
      public String getName() {
        return name;
      }
      public void setName(String name) {
        this.name = name;
      }
    }
```

3. Use the `ItemWriter` interface and implement a `CustomeItemWriter` class. This class overrides the `write` method, which is defined in the `ItemWriter` interface.

4. You will observe that the `write` method accepts `List` as input. In the `write` method, we are just parsing the list and typecasting the list index value to the `Employee` object and printing it.

```
package com.packt;
import java.util.List;
import org.springframework.batch.item.ItemWriter;
public class CustomItemWriter<T> implements ItemWriter<T> {
  @Override
  public void write(List<? extends T> items) throws
    Exception {
    for (int i = 0; items.size() > i; i++) {
      Employee obj = (Employee) items.get(i);
      System.out.println(obj.getEmpId() + ":" +
        obj.getName());
    }

  }

}
```

5. Create a `Main` class with `public static void main()` with a `jobrun()` method:

```
public class Main {
  public static void main(String[] args) {
    Main obj = new Main();
    obj.run();
```

```
    }

    private void run() {
      /*config files are present in the resource folder*/
      String[] springConfig = {
        "spring/batch/config/context.xml",
        "spring/batch/jobs/job-read-files.xml" };

      ApplicationContext context = new
        ClassPathXmlApplicationContext(springConfig);

      JobLauncher jobLauncher = (JobLauncher)
        context.getBean("jobLauncher");
      Job job = (Job) context.getBean("readMultiFileJob");
      try {
        JobExecution execution = jobLauncher.run(job, new
          JobParameters());
        System.out.println("Exit Status : " +
          execution.getStatus());
        System.out.println("Exit Status : " +
          execution.getAllFailureExceptions());

      } catch (Exception e) {
        e.printStackTrace();

      }

      System.out.println("COMPLETED");

    }
  }
  /*config files are present in the resource folder*/
```

6. Let us set the bean id to JobRepository in the context.xml file:

```
<bean id="jobRepository"
  class="org.springframework.batch.core.repository
  .support.MapJobRepositoryFactoryBean">
  <property name="transactionManager"
    ref="transactionManager" />
</bean>

<bean id="transactionManager"
  class="org.springframework.batch.support.transaction
  .ResourcelessTransactionManager" />
```

```
<bean id="jobLauncher"
  class="org.springframework.batch.core.launch
  .support.SimpleJobLauncher">
<property name="jobRepository" ref="jobRepository" />
</bean>

/*
```

The `Job Read files.xml` file is present in the resource folder `*`/`Job Read files.xml`.

We have used `flatfileItemReader` and `FlatFileItemWriter`. These classes read the input and recreate the files in the `output` folder.

Let's look at a prototype of `FlatFileItemReader` and learn what it does in the application:

```
public class FlatFileItemReader<T> extends
  AbstractItemCountingItemStreamItemReader<T>
implements ResourceAwareItemReaderItemStream<T>,
  org.springframework.beans.factory.InitializingBean
```

Restartable `ItemReader` reads lines from input `setResource(Resource)`. A line is defined by `setRecordSeparatorPolicy(RecordSeparatorPolicy)` and mapped to an item using `setLineMapper(LineMapper)`.

If an exception is thrown during line mapping, it is rethrown as `FlatFileParseException`, adding information about the problematic line and its line number.

```
public class FlatFileItemWriter<T>
extends AbstractItemStreamItemWriter<T>
implements ResourceAwareItemWriterItemStream<T>,
  org.springframework.beans.factory.InitializingBean
```

This class is an item writer that writes data to a file or stream. The writer also provides a restart. The location of the output file is defined by a resource and must represent a writable file and use buffered writer to improve performance. The implementation is not thread-safe.

In the file we have done the following:

- We have configured the job with the name `readMultiFileJob`
- We must observe that `tasklet` has a step which is configured with the `ItemReader` and `ItemWriter` classes
- We have again used `tasklet`, but we have used step as a chunk reader that accepts `MultiResourceReader`

To understand `MultiResourceReader`, we shall look at the prototype:

```
public class MultiResourceItemReader<T>extends
  AbstractItemStreamItemReader<T>
```

`MultiResourceReader` reads items from multiple resources sequentially. The resource list is given by `setResources(Resource[])`, and the actual reading is delegated to `setDelegate(ResourceAwareItemReaderItemStream)`. Input resources are ordered using `setComparator(Comparator)` to make sure that resource ordering is preserved between job runs in a restart scenario.

Now, let's see what step of the type chunk is about. In a chunk, a reader and a writer are mandatory! However, the `ItemProcessor` is optional.

```xml
<import resource="../config/context.xml"/>
  <bean id="employee" class="com.packt.Employee" />
  <job id="readMultiFileJob"
    xmlns="http://www.springframework.org/schema/batch">

    <step id="step1">
    <tasklet>
    <chunk reader="multiResourceReader"
      writer="flatFileItemWriter"
      commit-interval="1" />
    </tasklet>
    </step>

  </job>
  <! --create folder structure in the project root csv/inputs
    and add the csv files-->
  <bean id="multiResourceReader"
    class=" org.springframework.batch.item.file
    .MultiResourceItemReader">
    <property name="resources" value="file:csv/inputs/
      employee-*.csv" />
    <property name="delegate" ref="flatFileItemReader" />
  </bean>

  <bean id="flatFileItemReader" class="org.springframework.batch
    .item.file.FlatFileItemReader">

    <property name="lineMapper">
    <bean class="org.springframework.batch.item.file
      .mapping.DefaultLineMapper">

      <property name="lineTokenizer">
```

```xml
    <bean class="org.springframework.batch.item.file.transform
      .DelimitedLineTokenizer">
      <property name="names" value="id, name" />
    </bean>
    </property>
    <property name="fieldSetMapper">
    <bean class="org.springframework.batch.item.file.mapping
      .BeanWrapperFieldSetMapper">
      <property name="prototypeBeanName" value="domain" />
    </bean>
    </property>
  </bean>
  </property>

</bean>

<bean id="flatFileItemWriter" class="org.springframework.batch
  .item.file.FlatFileItemWriter" >
  <!--create folder structure in the project root
    csv/outputs -->

  <property name="resource" value="file:csv/outputs/
    employee.all.csv" />
  <property name="appendAllowed" value="true" />
  <property name="lineAggregator">
  <bean class="org.springframework.batch.item.file
    .transform.DelimitedLineAggregator">
    <property name="delimiter" value="," />
    <property name="fieldExtractor">
    <bean class="org.springframework.batch.item.file
      .transform.BeanWrapperFieldExtractor">
      <property name="names" value="id, domain" />
    </bean>
    </property>
  </bean>
  </property>

</bean>
```

Create a few CSV files with the name `employee*.csv`, replacing the * with a different number for each file. Each file will have two values: `employeeId` and `name`.

The delimiter in the CSV file can also be configured in the XML, as shown in the following code:

```
<bean class="org.springframework.batch.item.file
  .transform.DelimitedLineAggregator">
<property name="delimiter" value="," />
<property name="fieldExtractor">
<bean class="org.springframework.batch.item.file
  .transform.BeanWrapperFieldExtractor">
  <property name="names" value="id, domain" />
</bean>
</property>
```

The values will be mapped with a **plain old java object (Pojo)**, `Employee.java`, and the output is processed. The file location is passed as input to the `MultiResourceItemReader` class.

In the next section, we shall see how we can schedule a batch job in Spring.

Spring Batch with a Spring scheduler

In this section, let's see how we can schedule a batch in Spring Batch framework. We shall see how we can configure the scheduler. This is a sample `jobproduct.xml` file that needs to be available in the classpath. If you are working on a Maven project, place it in the resource folder. You need to inject `joblauncher` with the intervals and method name `run()` to run the job at the scheduled time.

To use the scheduler, we need to configure the `job-product.xml` file. This file is also used in the next section to configure the external scheduler with the scheduler details.

To schedule running the task every 600 second interval:

```
<task:scheduled-tasks>
  <task:scheduled ref="MyJobScheduler" method="run"
    cron="*/600 * * * *" />
</task:scheduled-tasks>
```

Let's use the `@Component` and `@Autowired` annotations with `MyJobScheduler.class`.

```
@Component
public class MyJobScheduler {
  @Autowired
  private JobLauncher jobLauncher;
  @Autowired
  private Job job;
  public void run() {
```

```
try {
  String dateParam = new Date().toString();
  JobParameters param =
    new JobParametersBuilder().addString("date",
    dateParam).toJobParameters();
  JobExecution execution = jobLauncher.run(job, param);
  System.out.println("Exit Status  of the Job: " +
    execution.getStatus());

} catch (Exception e) {
e.printStackTrace();
}

}
}
```

Configuring Spring Batch with Quartz scheduler

The Spring Batch framework provides an option to configure an external scheduler into the application.

Let us integrate Quartz Scheduler with the Spring Batch application. Quartz is an open source Java-based scheduler. We shall make this application to read a file, but we shall integrate the Quartz scheduler to do the scheduling.

1. Create a simple Maven application with the name
   `SpringBatchQuartzExample`.

2. Use the same `pom.xml` file as in the previous application.

3. Add the Quartz JAR file to the dependencies in the `pom.xml` file.

4. Add these properties:

   `<quartz.version>1.8.6</quartz.version>`

5. Then, add these dependencies:

   ```
   <dependency>
     <groupId>org.quartz-scheduler</groupId>
     <artifactId>quartz</artifactId>
     <version>${quartz.version}</version>
   </dependency>
   ```

Let's create a file called `quartz-job.xml`. This should be present in the resource folder of the Maven project. To configure the batch to run every minute, use the following configuration in the code:

```
<bean class="org.springframework.scheduling.quartz
  .SchedulerFactoryBean">
  <property name="triggers">
  <bean id="cronTrigger" class="org.springframework.scheduling
    .quartz.CronTriggerBean">
  <property name="jobDetail" ref="jobDetail" />
  <property name="cronExpression" value="*/60 * * * ?" />
  </bean>
  </property>
</bean>
```

To integrate Spring Batch with Quartz Scheduler, use the following code:

```
<bean id="jobDetailBean" class="org.springframework.scheduling
  .quartz.JobDetailBean">
  <property name=" jobQuartzLauncherDetails "
    value="com.packt.quartz.JobQuartzLauncherDetails" />
  <property name="group" value="quartz-batch" />
  <property name="jobDataAsMap">
  <map>
    <entry key="jobName" value="reportJob" />
    <entry key="jobLocator" value-ref="jobRegistry" />
    <entry key="jobLauncher" value-ref="jobLauncher" />
    <entry key="param1" value="anjana" />
    <entry key="param2" value="raghu" />
  </map>
  </property>
</bean>
```

`JobQuartzLauncherDetails` is a bean that extends `QuartzJobBean`.

 QuartzJobBean is available in the package and can be found at `org.springframework.scheduling.quartz.QuartzJobBean`.

The class has setters for `JobLauncher` and `JobLocator`:

```
public class JobQuartzLauncherDetails extends QuartzJobBean {
  static final String JOB_NAME = "jobName";
  private JobLocator jobLocator;
  private JobLauncher jobLauncher;
  public void setJobLocator(JobLocator jobLocator) {
```

```
        this.jobLocator = jobLocator;
    }
    public void setJobLauncher(JobLauncher jobLauncher) {
        this.jobLauncher = jobLauncher;
    }
```

To read the `JobMapDetails` from the configuration, we have created another method as shown in the following code. We can see that different data types are handled here based on the values read from the map, and `JobParametersBuilder` is created.

```
    private JobParameters getJobParametersFromJobMap(Map<String,
        Object> jobDataMap) {
        JobParametersBuilder builder = new JobParametersBuilder();
        for (Entry<String, Object> entry : jobDataMap.entrySet()) {
            String key = entry.getKey();
            Object value = entry.getValue();
            if (value instanceof String && !key.equals(JOB_NAME)) {
                builder.addString(key, (String) value);
            } else if (value instanceof Float || value instanceof Double){
                builder.addDouble(key, ((Number) value).doubleValue());
            } else if (value instanceof Integer || value instanceof Long){
                builder.addLong(key, ((Number) value).longValue());
            } else if (value instanceof Date) {
                builder.addDate(key, (Date) value);
            } else {

            }
        }

        builder.addDate("run date", new Date());
        return builder.toJobParameters();
    }
```

As we know, `JobName` and `JobParamters` are required input for `JobLauncher` to run the job. In the preceding code snippet, we have got `JobParameters`. Next, we shall get `JobName` with the following code snippet using `JobExecutionContext`:

```
    protected void executeInternal(JobExecutionContext context) {
        Map<String, Object> jobDataMap = context.getMergedJobDataMap();
        String jobName = (String) jobDataMap.get(JOB_NAME);
        JobParameters jobParameters =
            getJobParametersFromJobMap(jobDataMap);

        try {
            jobLauncher.run(jobLocator.getJob(jobName), jobParameters);
        } catch (JobExecutionException e) {
            e.printStackTrace();
        }
    }
```

Product.java is a domain class that gets mapped to the values in the .csv file.

```java
public class Product {
  private int id;
  private String name;
  public int getId() {
    return id;
  }
  public void setId(int id) {
    this.id = id;
  }
  public String getName() {
    return name;
  }
  public void setName(String name) {
    name = name;
  }
  @Override
  public String toString() {
    return "Product [id=" + id + ", name=" + name + "]";
  }
}
```

The following is the code for CustomeItemWriter, which writes the product Pojo object values.

```java
public class CustomItemWriter implements ItemWriter<Product> {
  @Override
  public void write(List<? extends Product> items) throws
    Exception {
    System.out.println("writer..." + items.size());
    for(Product item : items){
      System.out.println(item);
    }
  }
}
```

Next, let's create the Main class to load the job-quartz.xml file and run the batch job every 60 seconds to read the CSV file and write using CustomItemWriter.

```java
import org.springframework.context.ApplicationContext;
import org.springframework.context.support
  .ClassPathXmlApplicationContext;
public class Main {
  public static void main(String[] args) {
    String springConfig = "spring/batch/jobs/job-quartz.xml";
    ApplicationContext context = new
      ClassPathXmlApplicationContext(springConfig);
  }
}
```

The Spring Batch framework uses Quartz Scheduler to run the batch job of reading a file, mapping the CSV values to product Pojo, and writing it using `CustomeItemWriter`.

In the next section, let's create a batch that reads a file and updates a database.

Using Spring Batch to read a file and update a MongoDB database

In this section, let's create a batch job that reads an XML file and writes to a MongoDB database. Think of a scenario where we keep getting an XML file from a source and that this file needs to be read and updated to a database.

1. The XML file structure is as shown here:

```xml
<?xml version="1.0" encoding="UTF-8" ?>
<Products>
  <product id="1">
    <categoryId>3</categoryId>
    <brandId>1</brandId>
    <name>computer</name>
    <price>15000</price>
  </product>
  <product id="2">
  <categoryId>4</categoryId>
  <brandId>1</brandId>
  <name>mouse</name>
  <price>250</price>
  </record>
  </ product>
  < product id="3">
    <categoryId>5</categoryId>
    <brandId>1</brandId>
    <name>mouse</name>
    <price>23000</price>
  </ product>
</Products>
```

2. Create a Maven Java-based project. In the `com.packt.model` package, add the corresponding product Pojo.

```java
public class Product {
  private int id;
  private int categoryId;
  private int brandId;
  private String name;
```

```
private int price;
public int getId() {
  return id;
}
public void setId(int id) {
  this.id = id;
}
public int getCategoryId() {
  return categoryId;
}
public void setCategoryId(int categoryId) {
  this.categoryId = categoryId;
}
public int getBrandId() {
  return brandId;
}
public void setBrandId(int brandId) {
  this.brandId = brandId;
}
public String getName() {
  return name;
}
public void setName(String name) {
  this.name = name;
}
public int getPrice() {
  return price;
}
public void setPrice(int price) {
  this.price = price;
}

}
```

3. Add the same dependencies as the ones shown in the previous section.

4. Update the `pom.xml` file.

5. Add the ORM and MongoDB database dependencies:

```xml
<dependency>
  <groupId>org.springframework</groupId>
  <artifactId>spring-oxm</artifactId>
  <version>${spring.version}</version>
</dependency>
<dependency>
```

```
<groupId>org.mongodb</groupId>
<artifactId>mongo-java-driver</artifactId>
<version>${mongodb.driver.version}</version>
</dependency>

<!-- Spring data mongodb -->
<dependency>
<groupId>org.springframework.data</groupId>
<artifactId>spring-data-mongodb</artifactId>
<version>${spring.data.version}</version>
</dependency>
```

6. Create a file named `mongodatabase.xml` and add the following configurations to it:

```
<mongo:mongo host="127.0.0.1" port="27017" />
<mongo:db-factory dbname="eshopdb" />

<bean id="mongoTemplate" class="org.springframework.data
.mongodb.core.MongoTemplate">
<constructor-arg name="mongoDbFactory"
  ref="mongoDbFactory" />
</bean>
```

7. Add the following configuration to the `job-product.xml` file.

   ° `StaxEventItemReader`: This is a class that reads the `products.xml` file. We need to provide the `rootElemenent` name to this class.

   ° `fragmentRootElementName`: This property accepts the string parameter which is the root element in the provided XML file.

We also need to provide the XML file name as a value to the resource property. The third property that needs to be passed is the `unmarshaller` reference. This class is available in the Spring OXM framework used for marshalling and unmarshalling the XML file.

```
<bean id="xmlItemReader" class="org.springframework.batch
  .item.xml.StaxEventItemReader">
  <property name="fragmentRootElementName" value="product" />
  <property name="resource" value="classpath:xml/product.xml" />
  <property name="unmarshaller" ref="productUnmarshaller" />
</bean>
```

The `XstreamMarshaller` accepts three properties to perform the unmarshalling process. It accepts a map with entry key and product Pojo as values, so that in the XML each product record is converted as a `Product` object and is stored in the map. The second property is again a bean created to convert the XML to POJO. This is named `ProductXMLConverter`.

```
<bean id="productUnmarshaller" class="org.springframework.oxm
  .xstream.XStreamMarshaller">

  <property name="aliases">
  <util:map id="aliases">
  <entry key="product" value="com.packt.model.Product" />
  </util:map>
  </property>
  <property name="converters">
  <array>
  <ref bean="productXMLConverter" />
  </array>
  </property>
</bean>


<bean id="productXMLConverter" class="com.packt.converter.
  ProductXMLConverter>
```

Let's look at the `ProductXMLConverter` class. This class implements the `converter` interface which is available in the `com.thoughtworks.xstream.converters.converter` package. The class overrides three methods defined in the interface:

- `public boolean canConvert(Class type)`
- `public void marshal(Object source, HierarchicalStreamWriter writer, MarshallingContext context)`
- `public Object unmarshal(HierarchicalStreamReader reader, UnmarshallingContext context)`

1. Since we shall be doing unmarshalling here, we shall clearly implement the `unmarshall` method.

   ```
   @Override
   public Object unmarshal(HierarchicalStreamReader reader,
     UnmarshallingContext context) {
     Product obj = new Product();
     obj.setId(Integer.valueOf(reader.getAttribute("id")));
     reader.moveDown(); //get id
     obj.setCategoryId(Integer.valueOf(reader.getAttribute(
       "categoryId")));
     reader.moveDown(); //get categoryId
   ```

```
obj.setBrandId(Integer.valueOf
  (reader.getAttribute("brandId")));
reader.moveDown(); //get brandId
obj.setName(String.valueOf(reader.getAttribute("name")));
reader.moveDown(); //get name
obj.setPrice(Integer.valueOf
  (reader.getAttribute("price")));
reader.moveDown(); //get name
return obj;
}
```

2. Configure `MongoDBItemWriter` to write to the Pojo object in the MongoDB database in `job-product.xml`:

```xml
<bean id="mongodbItemWriter"
  class="org.springframework.batch
  .item.data.MongoItemWriter">
  <property name="template" ref="mongoTemplate" />
  <property name="collection" value="product" />
</bean>
```

3. Configure the batch job in the `job-product.xml` file:

```xml
<batch:job id="productJob">
  <batch:step id="step1">
  <batch:tasklet>
  <batch:chunk reader="xmlItemReader"
    writer="mongodbItemWriter" commit-interval="1">
  </batch:chunk>
  </batch:tasklet>
  </batch:step>
</batch:job>
```

4. Write the `Main` class to run the batch job.

5. Load all the configuration files in the `Main` class:

```java
public class Main {
  public static void main(String[] args) {
    String[] springConfig =
      {"spring/batch/config/mongodatabase.xml",
      "spring/batch/config/context.xml",
      "spring/batch/jobs/job-product.xml"
    };

    ApplicationContext context =
      new ClassPathXmlApplicationContext(springConfig);
```

```
JobLauncher jobLauncher = (JobLauncher)
  context.getBean("jobLauncher");
Job job = (Job) context.getBean("productJob");

try {

  JobExecution execution = jobLauncher.run(job,
    new JobParameters());
  System.out.println("Exit Status of the ProductJOB: " +
    execution.getStatus());

  } catch (Exception e) {
    e.printStackTrace();
  }

  System.out.println("YES COMPLETED");

  }
}
```

So, when we run the Main class, the job gets instantiated and will run every 60 seconds. The job will read the XML and convert it into the Pojo product.java and will then insert it into the MongoDB database. The configurations are given in the MongoDB database XML file.

In the next section, we shall see how we can create a multithreaded environment to process multiple jobs.

Using Spring Batch with threads to partition jobs

In a Spring batch process, a single thread processes the requests sequentially. If we want to execute the batch job in parallel, we go in for a multithreaded environment.

Think of scenario where we are processing 1000 records in an employee table that is mapped with the Employee Pojo. We need to read 1000 records at a time and write to a CSV file.

A job is actually portioned into multiple subjobs, and a separate thread is assigned to process each subjob. So, if you have 1000 records to be read, this will take more time when done using a single thread. When we partition 1000 records into 100 subrecords, we can process them using 10 different threads running at the same time.

We can create a simple partitioner class by implementing the `Partitioner` interface. This partitioner will partition 1000 jobs into 100 subjobs. You will observe that we provided `start_range` and `end_range` variables in the partition range.

```
public class MyJobPartioner implements Partitioner {
  @Override
  public Map<String, ExecutionContext> partition(int gridSize) {
    Map<String, ExecutionContext> result = new HashMap<String,
      ExecutionContext>();
    int range = 100;
    int start_range = 1;
    int end_range = range;
    for (int i = 1; i <= gridSize; i++) {
      ExecutionContext execution_context = new ExecutionContext();
      System.out.println("\Name: Thread" + i+"start_range : " +
        start_range+"end_range", end_range);
      execution_context.putInt("start_range", start_range);
      execution_context.putInt("end_range", end_range);
      execution_context.putString("name", "Thread" + i);
      result.put("partition" + i, execution_context);
      start_range = end_range + 1;
      end_range += range;
    }
    return result;
  }

}
```

The `ExecutionContext` object used in the `Partitioner` class works with `ItemStream` and acts like a wrapper around the map. We can get two kinds of execution context objects in Spring Batch. One execution object works at the job level and another works at the step level. The job level execution context is used to share data or information among steps.

Let's implement an `ItemProcess` class that processes the partitioned records. Also observe that we are using the step execution context in the following code. The class overrides the `process` method.

1. This class is used for chunk processing the data.

```
@Component("itemProcessor")
@Scope(value = "step")
public class EmployeeProcessor implements ItemProcessor<Employee,
Employee> {
  @Value("#{stepExecutionContext[name]}")
  private String threadName;
  @Override
```

```
  public Employee process(Employee emp) throws Exception {
    System.out.println(threadName + " processing : " +
      emp.getId() + " : " + emp.getName());
    return emp;
  }
  public String getThreadName() {
    return threadName;
  }
  public void setThreadName(String threadName) {
    this.threadName = threadName;
  }

}
```

2. Let's configure the `job-partioner.xml` file.

```
<job id="partitionJob"
  xmlns="http://www.springframework.org/schema/batch">
  <step id="masterStep">
  <partition step="slave" partitioner="myJobPartioner">
  <handler grid-size="100" task-executor="taskExecutor" />
  </partition>
  </step>

</job>
<step id="slave"
  xmlns="http://www.springframework.org/schema/batch">
  <tasklet>
  <chunk reader="pagingItemReader"
    writer="flatFileItemWriter"
  processor="itemProcessor" commit-interval="1" />
  </tasklet>
</step>

<!—below is the configuration of MyJobPartioner bean-->

<bean id="myJobPartioner"
  class="com.packt.partition.MyJobPartioner" />
<bean id="taskExecutor" class="org.springframework.core
  .task.SimpleAsyncTaskExecutor" />

<!—below is the configuration of EmployeeProcesser bean-->

<bean id="itemProcessor" class="com.packt.processor
  .EmployeeProcessor" scope="step">
  <property name="threadName"
    value="#{stepExecutionContext[name]}" />
</bean>
```

Next, let's configure `pagingItemReader`, which acts in the same way as pagination. It fetches 100 records per page; this also connects with the data source using the JDBC information provided and executes a query to fetch a range of records, as specified. It will also sort the data based on the emp_id column.

```
<bean id="pagingItemReader" class="org.springframework
  .batch.item.database.JdbcPagingItemReader"
  scope="step">
  <property name="dataSource" ref="dataSource" />
  <property name="queryProvider">
  <bean class="org.springframework.batch.item
    .database.support.SqlPagingQueryProviderFactoryBean">
    <property name="dataSource" ref="dataSource" />
    <property name="selectClause" value="select emp_id,
      emp_name, emp_pass, emp_salary" />
    <property name="fromClause" value="from users" />
    <property name="whereClause" value="where emp_id &gt;=
      :fromId and id &lt;= :toId" />
    <property name="sortKey" value="emp_id" />
  </bean>
  </property>
  <!-- Inject via the ExecutionContext in MyJobPartioner -->
  <property name="parameterValues">
  <map>
    <entry key="fromId"
      value="#{stepExecutionContext[start_range]}" />
    <entry key="toId"
      value="#{stepExecutionContext[end_range]}" />
  </map>
  </property>
  <property name="pageSize" value="100" />
  <property name="rowMapper">
  <bean class="com.packt.EmployeeRowMapper" />
  </property>
  </bean>

<!--After reading it writes to  csv file using
  FlatfileItemwriter class-->

  <bean id="flatFileItemWriter" class="org.springframework
    .batch.item.file.FlatFileItemWriter" scope="step" >
    <property name="resource"
    value="file:csv/outputs/employee.processed#
      {stepExecutionContext[fromId]}-
      #{stepExecutionContext[toId]}.csv" />
```

```xml
<property name="appendAllowed" value="false" />
<property name="lineAggregator">
<bean class="org.springframework.batch.item.file
  .transform.DelimitedLineAggregator">
  <property name="delimiter" value="," />
  <property name="fieldExtractor">
  <bean class="org.springframework.batch.item.file
    .transform.BeanWrapperFieldExtractor">
    <property name="names" value="emp_id, emp_name,
      emp_pass, emp_salary" />
  </bean>
  </property>
</bean>
</property>
</bean>
</property>
</bean>
<!--Configuring FlatfileItemwriter class- ends-->
```

3. Let's write the `Main` class, which will load the configuration files, and then run the job.

```java
public class Main {
  public static void main(String[] args) {
    Main obj = new Main();
    obj.run();
  }
  private void run() {
    String[] springConfig = { "spring/batch/jobs/
      job-partitioner.xml" };
    ApplicationContext context = new
      ClassPathXmlApplicationContext(springConfig);
    JobLauncher jobLauncher = (JobLauncher)
      context.getBean("jobLauncher");
    Job job = (Job) context.getBean("partitionJob");
    try {
      JobExecution execution = jobLauncher.run(job, new
        JobParameters());
      System.out.println("Exit Status : " +
        execution.getStatus());
      System.out.println("Exit Status : " +
        execution.getAllFailureExceptions());
    } catch (Exception e) {
      e.printStackTrace();
    }
    System.out.println("COMPLETED");
  }

}
```

So, with the preceding configuration and classes, multiple threads get created to process 100 records per thread. The records are read from the database and are written to the CSV file.

In the next section, we shall use event listeners with Spring Batch.

Intercepting a Spring Batch job with listeners

Spring Batch comes with listeners. They intercept the job execution to perform certain tasks. StepListener is a super class for the following mentioned listeners:

- SkipListener: One of the most common use cases for SkipListener is to log out a skipped item so that another batch process, or even human process, can be used to evaluate and fix the issue leading to the skip. Because there are many cases in which the original transaction may be rolled back, Spring Batch makes two guarantees:

    - The appropriate skip method (depending on when the error happened) will only be called once per item.

    - The SkipListener will always be called just before the transaction is committed. This is to ensure that any transactional resources called by the listener are not rolled back by a failure within ItemWriter.

- ChunkListener: These listeners can be configured with a step, and if the step is of the type chunk-styled step, this will have both ItemReader and ItemWriter. The listener will intimate ItemWriter when ItemReader has completed its reading task.

```
public interface ChunkListener extends StepListener {
  void beforeChunk();
  void afterChunk();
}
<step id="step1">
  <tasklet>
  <chunk reader="reader" writer="writer"
    commit-interval="10"/>
  <listeners>
    <listener ref="chunkListener"/>
  </listeners>
  </tasklet>
</step>
```

- ItemWriterListener

- `ItemReaderListener`
- `ItemProcessListener`
- `StepExecutionListener`: It represents the most generic listener for step execution. It allows for notification before a step is started and after it has ended, whether it ended normally or failed.

You will observe that there is listener configured for each of the `ItemReader`, `ItemWriter`, `ItemProcess`, and `StepExecution` interfaces and classes.

Now we can have a look at how to configure listeners in the spring `batch.xml` file. Please have a look:

1. Create classes that implement the listeners and override their methods.

```
<bean id="packtStepListener"
  class="com.packt.listeners.PacktStepListener" />
<bean id="packtItemReaderListener"
  class="com.packt.listeners.PacktItemReaderListener" />
<bean id="packtItemWriterListener"
  class="com.packt.listeners.PacktItemWriterListener" />

<job id="readFileJob"
  xmlns="http://www.springframework.org/schema/batch">
  <step id="step1">
  <tasklet>
  <chunk reader="multiResourceReader"
    writer="flatFileItemWriter" commit-interval="1" />
  <listeners>
    <listener ref="packtStepListener" />
    <listener ref="packtItemReaderListener" />
    <listener ref="packtItemWriterListener" />
  </listeners>
  </tasklet>
  </step>
</job>
```

2. Let's see the `PacktItemReaderListener` and `PacktItemWriterListner` listeners. The `IteamReadListener` interface comes with three methods to be implemented:
   - `beforeRead()`
   - `afterRead()`
   - `onReadError()`

```
public class PacktItemReaderListener implements
  ItemReadListener<Product> {
```

```
@Override
public void beforeRead() {
  System.out.println("ItemReadListener - beforeRead");
}

@Override
public void afterRead(Product product) {
  System.out.println("ItemReadListener - afterRead");
}

@Override
public void onReadError(Exception ex) {
  System.out.println("ItemReadListener - onReadError");
}

}
```

3. Let us next look at `PackItemWriterListener`. The `ItemWriter` interface comes with three `abstract` methods:

   ° `beforeWrite`
   ° `afterWrite`
   ° `onWriteError`

```
public class PacktItemWriterListener implements
  ItemWriteListener<Product> {
  @Override
  public void beforeWrite(List<? extends Product> products)
    {
    System.out.println("ItemWriteListener - beforeWrite");
  }
  @Override
  public void afterWrite(List<? extends Product> products)
    {
    System.out.println("ItemWriteListener - afterWrite");
  }
  @Override
  public void onWriteError(Exception exception, List<?
    extends Product> products) {
    System.out.println("ItemWriteListener - onWriteError");
  }
}
```

So far, we have seen how to create custom listeners and listener configuration in `spring-job` file.

Now, let's try to integrate this with a scenario where we are reading multiple files in a directory and deleting the files.

1. We shall again consider product Pojo, with `id` and `name` as the instance variables with getters and setters.

```
public class Product {
  int id;
  String name;
  public int getId() {
    return id;
  }
  public void setId(int id) {
    this.id = id;
  }
  public String getName() {
    return name;
  }
  public void setName(String Name) {
    this.name = name;
  }
}
```

2. We need to define the Pojo in the XML as a bean.

```
<bean id="product" class="com.packt.Product" />
```

3. Next is the file deleting task class file. After the files are read, they need to be deleted from the directory.

```
<bean id="fileDeletingTasklet"
  class="com.packt.tasklet.FileDeletingTasklet" >
  <property name="directory" value="file:csv/inputs/" />
</bean>
```

4. Let's look at the `FileDeletingTasklet` class. This class implements the `TaskLet` interface. This will delete the files as per the specified directory.

```
public class FileDeletingTasklet implements Tasklet,
  InitializingBean {
  private Resource directory;
  @Override
  public void afterPropertiesSet() throws Exception {
    Assert.notNull(directory, "directory must be set");
  }

  @Override
```

```java
public RepeatStatus execute(StepContribution
  contribution, ChunkContext chunkContext) throws
  Exception {
  File dir = directory.getFile();
  Assert.state(dir.isDirectory());
  File[] files = dir.listFiles();
  for (int i = 0; i < files.length; i++) {
    boolean deleted = files[i].delete();
    if (!deleted) {
      throw new UnexpectedJobExecutionException("Could
        not delete file " + files[i].getPath());
    } else {
      System.out.println(files[i].getPath() + "
        is deleted!");
    }
  }
  return RepeatStatus.FINISHED;
}
public Resource getDirectory() {
  return directory;
}
public void setDirectory(Resource directory) {
  this.directory = directory;
}
}
```

5. The bean properties need to be set in the job configuration file created.

```xml
<bean id="fileDeletingTasklet"
  class="com.packt.tasklet.FileDeletingTasklet" >
  <property name="directory" value="file:csv/inputs/" />
</bean>
```

The next task would be to read the multiple files available in the directory. Since there are multiple resources that need to be read, we shall use a MultiResourceReader configuration in the bean.

```xml
<bean id="multiResourceReader" class=" org.springframework.batch
  .item.file.MultiResourceItemReader">
  <property name="resources" value="file:csv/inputs/
    product-*.csv" />
  <property name="delegate" ref="flatFileItemReader" />
</bean>
```

The `flatfileItemReader` maps the CSV values to the product Pojo. So, provide the following configuration to the `jobs.xml` file:

```xml
<bean id="flatFileItemReader" class="org.springframework
  .batch.item.file.FlatFileItemReader">
  <property name="lineMapper">
  <bean class="org.springframework.batch.item.file
    .mapping.DefaultLineMapper">
    <property name="lineTokenizer">
    <bean class="org.springframework.batch.item.file
      .transform.DelimitedLineTokenizer">
      <property name="names" value="id, name" />
    </bean>
    </property>
    <property name="fieldSetMapper">
    <bean class="org.springframework.batch.item.file
      .mapping.BeanWrapperFieldSetMapper">
      <property name="prototypeBeanName" value="product" />
    </bean>
    </property>
  </bean>
  </property>
</bean>
```

Then, after reading the CSV values and mapping them to Pojo from different CSV files, we can add the `writterListener` if we need to merge into a single CSV file.

```xml
<bean id="flatFileItemWriter" class="org.springframework.batch
  .item.file.FlatFileItemWriter">
  <property name="resource" value="file:csv/outputs/
    product.all.csv" />
  <property name="appendAllowed" value="true" />
  <property name="lineAggregator">
  <bean class="org.springframework.batch.item.file
    .transform.DelimitedLineAggregator">
    <property name="delimiter" value="," />
    <property name="fieldExtractor">
    <bean class="org.springframework.batch.item.file.transform
      .BeanWrapperFieldExtractor">
      <property name="names" value="id, name" />
    </bean>
    </property>
  </bean>
  </property>
</bean>
```

On running the `Main` class, all the beans configured in the XML file get instantiated for the batch job to run. The job does a chunk execution with `ItemReader` and `Writer`, as shown in the configuration of the `Main` class here:

```java
public class Main {
  public static void main(String[] args) {
    Main obj = new Main();
    obj.run();

  }

  private void run() {
    String[] springConfig = { "spring/batch/jobs/
      job-read-files.xml" };
    ApplicationContext context = new
      ClassPathXmlApplicationContext(springConfig);
    JobLauncher jobLauncher = (JobLauncher)
      context.getBean("jobLauncher");
    Job job = (Job) context.getBean("readMultiFileJob");

    try {
      JobExecution execution = jobLauncher.run(job, new
        JobParameters());
      System.out.println("Exit Status : " +
        execution.getStatus());
      System.out.println("Exit Status : " +
        execution.getAllFailureExceptions());
    } catch (Exception e) {
      e.printStackTrace();
    }
    System.out.println("COMPLTED CHECK THE OUTPUT DIRECTORY");
  }
}
```

In this section, we have learned about listeners and configuring listeners with the job.

In the next section, we shall see how we can do some unit testing on Spring Batch applications.

Unit testing Spring Batch applications

Let's demonstrate writing a test case for Spring Batch applications:

```xml
<dependency>
  <groupId>org.springframework.batch</groupId>
  <artifactId>spring-batch-test</artifactId>
  <version>2.2.0.RELEASE</version>
```

```
    </dependency>

    <!-- Junit -->
    <dependency>
      <groupId>junit</groupId>
      <artifactId>junit</artifactId>
      <version>4.11</version>
      <scope>test</scope>
    </dependency>
```

Let's create a simple `Test` class called `mport static org.junit.Assert.assertEquals`:

```
import org.junit.Test;
import org.junit.runner.RunWith;
import org.springframework.batch.core.BatchStatus;
import org.springframework.batch.core.JobExecution;
import org.springframework.batch.test.JobLauncherTestUtils;
import org.springframework.beans.factory.annotation.Autowired;
import org.springframework.test.context.ContextConfiguration;
import org.springframework.test.context
  .junit4.SpringJUnit4ClassRunner;
@RunWith(SpringJUnit4ClassRunner.class)
@ContextConfiguration(locations = {
  "classpath:spring/batch/jobs/job-report.xml",
  "classpath:spring/batch/config/context.xml",
  "classpath:spring/batch/config/database.xml",
  "classpath:spring/batch/config/test-context.xml"})
public class MainTest {
  @Autowired
  private JobLauncherTestUtils jobLauncherTestUtils;

  @Test
  public void launchJob() throws Exception {
    JobExecution jobExecution =
      jobLauncherTestUtils.launchStep("step1");

    assertEquals(BatchStatus.COMPLETED,
      jobExecution.getStatus());

  }
}
```

We have to create a file called `text-context.xml` to be available in the batch and configure the `JobLauncher` to be available in the XML file, and for the test package. In the `Test` class, use the `@Test annotation` method and call the `JobLauncher` to execute a step. We need to use `assertEquals` to check the status of the batch job against the `jobExecution` status.

Summary

In the chapter, we learned how to create Spring-based batch applications to read CSV files. We have also illustrated how Spring Batch can be used to read XML files. The most advanced topic was to partition the jobs and run the jobs into separate threads. We have also integrated Spring Batch with Quartz Scheduler.

We have demonstrated writing simple test cases using Spring Batch. We also used listeners to intercept a job defined to perform certain operations and have demonstrated certain configurations.

Spring Integration with FTP

5

FTP involves sending files over the Internet from one computer to another using a file transfer protocol. Spring Integration also provides support to the file transfer protocol. File transfer can be done via FTP or using SFTP (secure FTP).

Some of the abbreviations used in FTP scenarios are listed as follows:

- **FTP: File Transfer Protocol**.
- **FTPS: FTP Secure** is an extension to FTP that adds support for the **Transport Layer Security (TLS)** and **Secure Sockets Layer (SSL)** cryptographic protocols.
- **SFTP: SSH File Transfer Protocol**, that is, FTP over Secure Shell, protocol.

In a real scenario, a file server will have an FTP address, username and password. The clients connect to the server to transfer the files. We can either upload a file to a remote location download a file from a remote location using FTP.

Spring's integration package supports both sending and receiving files from the FTP or FTPS servers. It provides certain endpoints, and here are the endpoints/adapters available in Spring for FTP/FTPS:

- Inbound channel adapter
- Outbound channel adapter
- Outbound gateway

The channel adapters are nothing but message endpoints, which actually connect the message to a message channel. We can obviously see, send, and receive configurations and methods while dealing with the channel adapters.

In this chapter, we shall see what Spring enables us to do with FTP, and develop a sample application that demonstrates Spring's integration ability to support file transfer over this protocol. We shall also see the configurations that we need to write and how inbound and outbound adapters can be used to transfer files over FTP using Spring integration package.

Maven dependency

In order to create an FTP application using Spring integration framework, add the following dependency to the pom.xml file in your Maven project. The main packages are Spring Integration test and Spring Integration FTP. The libraries can be downloaded from the Maven repository or can be added to the project's pom.xml file.

Here are the Maven dependencies that need to be added to the pom.xml file to start developing applications with the Spring Integration FTP package:

```
<dependency>
  <groupId>org.springframework.integration</groupId>
  <artifactId>spring-integration-ftp</artifactId>
  <version>4.0.0.RELEASE</version>
  <scope>compile</scope>
</dependency>

<dependency>
  <groupId>org.springframework.integration</groupId>
  <artifactId>spring-integration-test</artifactId>
  <version>4.0.0.RELEASE</version>
  <scope>test</scope>
</dependency>

<dependency>
  <groupId>org.apache.ftpserver</groupId>
  <artifactId>ftpserver-core</artifactId>
  <version>1.0.6</version>
  <scope>compile</scope>
</dependency>
```

Spring's XSD for FTP

Let's look at the XSD that the Spring Integration package has provided for FTP. This has all the schema definitions and gives us all the configuration possibilities that are supported by Spring, so it becomes easier to configure the XML file.

The XSD (`http://www.springframework.org/schema/integration/ftp/spring-integration-ftp.xsd`) offers a lot of information about the Spring integration with FTP. It gives us information about configuring the channel adapters in the XML configuration files.

The inbound and outbound channel adapters are the two main elements in the XSD. Here is an extract from the XSD available at the link we just mentioned:

```
<xsd:element name="outbound-channel-adapter">...</xsd:element>
<xsd:element name="inbound-channel-adapter">...</xsd:element>
<xsd:complexType name="base-ftp-adapter-
  type">...</xsd:complexType>
</xsd:schema>
```

In the next sections, we shall see how we can configure each of the inbound and outbound channel adapters and configuration options supported by Spring integration for FTP.

Configuring an outbound channel adapter for FTP

Outbound channel adapter configuration is for the remote directory. It's meant to perform actions such as writing a file to the remote server (file upload), creating a new file, or adding a suffix on remote FTP servers. A few of the configurations that are available for outbound channel adapters from the XSD are listed here:

- It supports configuring the remote directory to write files using regular expression. The attribute used is as follows:

```
<xsd:attribute name="remote-directory-expression"
type="xsd:string">
```

- We can also configure to automatically create a directory in a remote location:

```
<xsd:attribute name="auto-create-directory"
  type="xsd:string" default="false">
```

- We can also configure to spring integration framework to work with FTP, to add a suffix to the file temporarily:

```
<xsd:attribute name="temporary-file-suffix"
  type="xsd:string">
```

- Another important configuration is to generate a filename in the remote location of the FTP server:

```
<xsd:attribute name="remote-filename-generator"
  type="xsd:string">
```

- The preceding feature is again advanced to support regular expressions:

```
<xsd:attribute name="remote-filename-generator-
  expression" type="xsd:string">
```

Configuring an inbound channel adapter for FTP

The inbound channel adapter configuration is for the local directory, that is, it is meant to perform actions such as writing a file from the remote server (file download), creating a new file, or adding a suffix on the local directory. The inbound channel adapter ensures that the local directory gets synchronized with the remote FTP directory.

A few of the configurations that are available for inbound channel adapters from the XSD are listed as follows:

- It provides configuration options to auto-create a local directory if it doesn't exist:

```
<xsd:attribute name="auto-create-local-directory"
  type="xsd:string">
  <xsd:annotation>
    <xsd:documentation>Tells this adapter if local
      directory must be auto-created if it doesn't exist.
      Default is TRUE.</xsd:documentation>
  </xsd:annotation>
</xsd:attribute>
```

- It provides an option to configure the remote server, and to delete the remote source file after copying it to the local directory:

```
<xsd:attribute name="delete-remote-files" type="xsd:string">
  <xsd:annotation>
    <xsd:documentation>Specify whether to delete the remote
      source file after copying. By default, the
      remote files will NOT be deleted.</xsd:documentation>
  </xsd:annotation>
</xsd:attribute>
```

- Ordering files in using the comparator configuration available:

```
<xsd:attribute name="comparator" type="xsd:string">
<xsd:annotation>
```

Specify a comparator to be used while ordering files. If none is provided, the order will be determined by the java.io file implementation:

```
</xsd:documentation>
  </xsd:annotation>
  </xsd:attribute>
```

- Configuring session caching using the following attribute:

```
<xsd:attribute name="cache-sessions" type="xsd:string"
  default="true">
  <xsd:annotation>
  <xsd:documentation>
<![CDATA[
```

Specify whether the sessions should be cached. The default value is `true`.

```
</xsd:documentation>
</xsd:annotation>
</xsd:attribute>
```

- The configuration that can be done using the XSD reference is as follows:

```
<int-ftp:inbound-channel-adapter id="ftpInbound"
                channel="ftpChannel"
                session-factory="ftpSessionFactory"
                charset="UTF-8"
                auto-create-local-directory="true"
                delete-remote-files="true"
                filename-pattern="*.txt"
                remote-directory="some/remote/path"
                local-directory=".">
  <int:poller fixed-rate="1000"/>
</int-ftp:inbound-channel-adapter>
```

FTPSessionFactory and FTPSSessionFactory

In this section, let's look at the two core classes for FTP using Spring integration, `FTPSessionFactory` and `FTPSSessionFactory`. These classes have lot of getters, setters, and instance variables, which give information about the data, file, and FTP mode. The instance variables and their usage are described as follows:

The class `org.springframework.integration.ftp.session.DefaultFtpSessionFactory` is used to configure the FTP details in the application. The class is configured as a simple bean in the configuration XML file .The class has getters and setters for the following:

- `Session`: This accepts session variables.

- `postProcessClientAfterConnect`: This handles additional initialization after the client connection action is performed.

- `postProcessClientBeforeConnect`: This handles additional initialization before the client connection action is performed.

- BufferSize: This defines the size of the buffered data that gets transferred over FTP.

- ClientMode: There are two modes supported by FTP. They are as follows:

  ○ **Active FTP mode**: This is specified in Spring FTP integration package as ACTIVE_LOCAL_DATA_CONNECTION_MODE. In active FTP mode, the server has to ensure that the random port 1023< communication channels are open. In active FTP mode, the client connects from a random unprivileged port (N > 1023) to the FTP server's command port, port 21. Then, the client starts listening to port N + 1 and sends the FTP command PORT N + 1 to the FTP server. The server will then connect back to the client's specified data port from its local data port, which is port 20.

  ○ **Passive FTP mode**: This is specified in Spring FTP integration package as PASSIVE_LOCAL_DATA_CONNECTION_MODE. In passive FTP mode, the client initiates both connections to the server, solving the problem of firewalls filtering the incoming data port connection to the client from the server. On opening an FTP connection, the client opens two random unprivileged ports locally (N > 1023 and N + 1). The first port contacts the server on port 21, but instead of then issuing a PORT command and allowing the server to connect back to its data port, the client will issue the PASV command. The result of this is that the server then opens a random unprivileged port (P > 1023) and sends P back to the client in response to the PASV command. The client then initiates the connection from port N + 1 to port P on the server to transfer data. The package DefaultFTPClientFactory has a setter method with a switch case to set the mode.

```
**
 * Sets the mode of the connection. Only local modes are
   supported.
 */
private void setClientMode(FTPClient client) {
  switch (clientMode ) {
    case FTPClient.ACTIVE_LOCAL_DATA_CONNECTION_MODE:
    client.enterLocalActiveMode();
    break;
    case FTPClient.PASSIVE_LOCAL_DATA_CONNECTION_MODE:
    client.enterLocalPassiveMode();
    break;
    default:
    break;
  }
}
```

- **Config**: This sets the FTP configuration object `org.apache.commons.net.` `ftp.FTPClientConfig config`

- **ConnectTimeout**: This specifies the connection timeout time after trying to connect to the client.

- **ControlEncoding**: This sets the encoding.

- **Data Timeout**: This sets the data timeout time during the file transfer.

- **Default Timeout**: This sets the socket timeout time.

- **File Type**: The FTP protocol supports several file types. They are listed as follows:

    ◦ **ASCII file type (default)**: The text file is transferred across the data connection in **Network Virtual Terminal (NVT)** ASCII. This requires the sender to convert the local text file into NVT ASCII and the receiver to convert NVT ASCII into the local text file type. The end of each line is transferred using the NVT ASCII representation of a carriage return followed by a linefeed. This means the receiver must scan every byte, looking for the CR, LF pair. (We saw the same scenario with TFTP's ASCII file transfer in Section 15.2.)

    ◦ **EBCDIC file type**: An alternative way of transferring text files when both ends are **Extended Binary Coded Decimal Interchange Code (EBCDIC)** systems.

    ◦ **Image file type**: This is also called the binary file type. The data is sent as a continuous stream of bits that are normally used to transfer binary files.

    ◦ **Local file type**: This is a way of transferring binary files between hosts with different byte sizes. The number of bits per byte is specified by the sender. For systems using 8-bits, a local file type with a byte size of eight is equivalent to the image file type. We should know that 8 bits make 1 byte.

Spring has the abstract class `AbstractFtpSessionFactory<T extends org.` `apache.commons.net.ftp.FTPClient>` which has defined the following parameters with static variables that can be used in the configuration of FTP:

```
public static final int ASCII_FILE_TYPE = 0;
public static final int EBCDIC_FILE_TYPE = 1;
public static final int BINARY_FILE_TYPE = 2;
public static final int LOCAL_FILE_TYPE = 3;
```

- **Host**: Specify the FTP host.

- **Password**: Specify the FTP password.

- `Port`: Specify the FTP port. There are two ports available, a data port and command port. The data port is configured as 20 and command port is configured as 21.
- `Username`: Specify the FTP username.

The following configuration shows the `DefaultFtpSessionFactory` class as a bean with bean ID `ftpClientFactory` and its property values set as per the FTP server credentials:

```xml
<bean id="ftpClientFactory" class="org.springframework
    .integration.ftp.session.DefaultFtpSessionFactory">
    <property name="host" value="localhost"/>
    <property name="port" value="22"/>
    <property name="username" value="anjana"/>
    <property name="password" value="raghu"/>
    <property name="clientMode" value="0"/>
    <property name="fileType" value="1"/>
</bean>
```

The `org.springframework.integration.ftp.session.
DefaultFtpsSessionFactory` class enables us to use FTPS connections. The class contains getters and setters for the following:

- `BufferSize`
- `clientMode`
- `config`
- `ControlEncoding`
- `DEFAULT_REMOTE_WORKING_DIRECTORY`
- `fileType`
- `host`
- `password`
- `port`
- `username`

The preceding fields are inherited from an abstract class named `AbstarctFtpSessionFactory`.

Here is a sample bean configuration of `DefaultFtpsClientFactory` and its properties that can be configured in the XML file:

```xml
<bean id="ftpClientFactory" class="org.springframework.integration
    .ftp.client.DefaultFtpsClientFactory">
```

```xml
        <property name="host" value="localhost"/>
        <property name="port" value="22"/>
        <property name="username" value="anju"/>
        <property name="password" value="raghu"/>
        <property name="clientMode" value="1"/>
        <property name="fileType" value="2"/>
        <property name="useClientMode" value="true"/>
        <property name="cipherSuites" value="a,b.c"/>
        <property name="keyManager" ref="keyManager"/>
        <property name="protocol" value="SSL"/>
        <property name="trustManager" ref="trustManager"/>
        <property name="prot" value="P"/>
        <property name="needClientAuth" value="true"/>
        <property name="authValue" value="anju"/>
        <property name="sessionCreation" value="true"/>
        <property name="protocols" value="SSL, TLS"/>
        <property name="implicit" value="true"/>
    </bean>
```

Spring FTP using an outbound channel example

In this section, lets look at a simple scenario of transferring files from Location1 to a remote location, Location2. For the sake of clarity, let's define them as follows:

- Location1: `d:\folder1`
- Location2: `d:\folder2`

Let's create a simple application in Spring with the Spring integration package, to accomplish the task of transferring files from Location1 to Location2. We need to have two main files to do this; the first one is the configuration file `applicationContext.xml` and the second is a Java class file that will intimate the Spring integration framework to upload the file to the remote location.

The `applicationContext.xml` file will have the entire necessary bean configuration with XMLNS required to use Spring integration package. The XMLNS that needs to be integrated is as follows:

```
xmlns:int="http://www.springframework.org/schema/integration"
xmlns:int-ftp="http://www.springframework.org/
   schema/integration/ftp"
```

We also need to configure DefaultFtpSessionFactory as a bean with FtpChannel
and FtpOutBoundAdpater. The DefaultFtpSessionFactory has setters for all
the FTP properties. FTPOutboundeAdapter will be configured with the remoteFTP
location and outboundchannel. Here is the complete configuration file:

```xml
<beans xmlns="http://www.springframework.org/schema/beans"
  xmlns:xsi="http://www.w3.org/2001/XMLSchema-instance"
  xmlns:int="http://www.springframework.org/schema/integration"
  xmlns:int-ftp="http://www.springframework.org/schema/
    integration/ftp"
  xsi:schemaLocation="http://www.springframework.org/
    schema/integration/ftp
    http://www.springframework.org/schema/integration/ftp/
    spring-integration-ftp.xsd
  http://www.springframework.org/schema/integration
    http://www.springframework.org/schema/
    integration/spring-integration.xsd
  http://www.springframework.org/schema/beans
    http://www.springframework.org/schema/beans/
    spring-beans.xsd">

  <bean id="ftpClientFactory" class="org.springframework
    .integration.ftp.session.DefaultFtpSessionFactory">
    <property name="host" value="localhost"/>
    <property name="port" value="21"/>
    <property name="username" value="myftpusername"/>
    <property name="password" value="myftppassword"/>
    <property name="clientMode" value="0"/>
    <property name="fileType" value="2"/>
    <property name="bufferSize" value="100000"/>
  </bean>

  <int:channel id="ftpChannel" />

  <int-ftp:outbound-channel-adapter id="ftpOutbound"
                  channel="ftpChannel"
                  remote-directory="D:/folder2"
                  session-factory="ftpClientFactory"/>

</beans>
```

Now let's create a simple Java class that intimates Spring to upload a file to Location2. This class will load the applicationContext.xml file and instantiate FTPChannel using the bean ID that is configured in the XML file using the context object. A file object is created with the filename that needs to be transferred to the remote location. This file object is sent to the Spring integration message, which in turn sends the message to the channel for the file to be delivered at the destination. Here is the sample code:

```
import org.springframework.context.ConfigurableApplicationContext;
import org.springframework.context.support
  .ClassPathXmlApplicationContext;
import org.springframework.integration.Message;
import org.springframework.integration.MessageChannel;
import org.springframework.integration.support.MessageBuilder;
import java.io.File;

public class SendFileSpringFTP {
  public static void main(String[] args)
    throws InterruptedException {
    ConfigurableApplicationContext ctx =
    new ClassPathXmlApplicationContext("/applicationContext.xml");
    MessageChannel ftpChannel = ctx.getBean("ftpChannel",
      MessageChannel.class);
    File file = new File("D:/folder2/report-Jan.txt");
    final Message<File> messageFile =
      MessageBuilder.withPayload(file).build();
    ftpChannel.send(messageFile);
    Thread.sleep(2000);
  }

}
```

Run the preceding class to see report-Jan.txt to be transferred to the remote location.

Configuring Spring FTP to read files in subfolders using the gateway

In this section, let's look at another configuration file that can be used to read subfolder reports.

We have used the expression attribute from the previous section dealing with FTP XSD. We shall further see how we can intimate the Spring integration FTP framework to trigger FTP commands with an expression attribute. Each of the commands executed in FTP will get a reply, usually three digits, for example:

- `125`: Data connection already open; transfer starting
- `200`: Command OK
- `214`: Help message (for human user)
- `331`: Username OK; password required
- `425`: Can't open data connection
- `452`: Error writing file
- `500`: Syntax error (unrecognized command)
- `501`: Syntax error (invalid arguments)
- `502`: Unimplemented mode type

The reply channels are created by gateways. In the following code, we have configured a reply channel for the splitters:

```
<int-ftp:outbound-gateway id="gatewayLS" cache-sessions="false"
    session-factory="ftpSessionFactory"
    request-channel="inbound"
    command="ls"
    command-options="-1"
    expression="'reports/*/*'"
    reply-channel="toSplitter"/>

<int:channel id="toSplitter" />

<int:splitter id="splitter" input-channel="toSplitter" output-
channel="toGet"/>

<int-ftp:outbound-gateway id="gatewayGET" cache-sessions="false"
    local-directory="localdir"
    session-factory="ftpSessionFactory"
    request-channel="toGet"
    reply-channel="toRemoveChannel"
    command="get"
    command-options="-P"
    expression="payload.filename"/>
```

With Spring integration support for FTP, we can also break the message into splits. This is configured using a `splitter` attribute (`AbstractMessageSplitter` `implements MessageHandler`) in the XML file, as follows:

```
<channel id="inputChannel"/>
<splitter id="splitter"
  ref="splitterBean"
  method="split"
  input-channel="inputChannel"
  output-channel="outputChannel" />
<channel id="outputChannel"/>
<beans:bean id="splitterBean" class="sample.PojoSplitter"/>
```

Logically, the `splitter` class has to split the messages and attach sequence numbers and size information to each split message, so that the sequence is not lost. The broken messages can be put together using aggregators and then sent across the channel.

Configuring Spring FTP in Java

In this section, let's see how we can configure FTP properties in a Java class by using annotations and creating an instance of the `DefaultFTPSession` factory and setting the properties using the setter methods available with the instance.

We can use the `@Configuration` annotation to configure the FTP properties as follows:

```
import org.springframework.integration.file.remote
  .session.SessionFactory;
import org.springframework.integration.ftp.session
  .DefaultFtpSessionFactory;
@Configuration
public class MyApplicationConfiguration {
  @Autowired
  @Qualifier("myFtpSessionFactory")
  private SessionFactory myFtpSessionFactory;
  @Bean
  public SessionFactory myFtpSessionFactory()
  {
    DefaultFtpSessionFactory ftpSessionFactory = new
      DefaultFtpSessionFactory();
    ftpSessionFactory.setHost("ftp.abc.org");
    ftpSessionFactory.setClientMode(0);
    ftpSessionFactory.setFileType(0);
    ftpSessionFactory.setPort(21);
    ftpSessionFactory.setUsername("anjju");
```

```
    ftpSessionFactory.setPassword("raghu");
    return ftpSessionFactory;
  }

}
```

Sending files over FTP using the Spring integration

Think of a scenario in which you are sending files over an FTP channel. Consider that there are two files, say `Orders.txt` and `vendors.txt`, that need to be sent over FTP to a remote location. To accomplish this, we need to follow these steps:

1. Create `FTPChannel`.
2. Make a directory in the base folder using `baseFolder.mkdirs()`.
3. Create two file objects at the base folder location.
4. Use `InputStream` and create two separate streams for orders and vendors.
5. Using the file utils available in Spring, copy the input streams to their specific files.
6. Using the `MessageBuilder` class, use the `withpayload()` method to convert the files into messages.
7. Lastly, send the message to the FTP channel and close the context.

Let's write some sample code to do this:

```
public void sendFilesOverFTP() throws Exception{

  ConfigurableApplicationContext ctx =
    new ClassPathXmlApplicationContext("META-INF/spring/
    integration/FtpOutboundChannelAdapterSample-context.xml");

  MessageChannel ftpChannel = ctx.getBean("ftpChannel",
    MessageChannel.class);

  baseFolder.mkdirs();
  final File fileToSendOrders = new File(baseFolder,
    "orders.txt");
  final File fileToSendVendors = new File(baseFolder,
    "vendore.txt");
```

```
final InputStream inputStreamOrders =
  FtpOutboundChannelAdapterSample.class.getResourceAsStream("/
  test-files/orders.txt");
final InputStream inputStreamVendors =
  FtpOutboundChannelAdapterSample.class.getResourceAsStream("/
  test-files/vendors.txt");
FileUtils.copyInputStreamToFile(inputStreamOrders,
  fileToSendOrders);
FileUtils.copyInputStreamToFile(inputStreamVendors,
  fileToSendVendors);
assertTrue(fileToSendOrders.exists());
assertTrue(fileToSendVendors.exists());
final Message<File> messageOrders =
  MessageBuilder.withPayload(fileToSendOrders).build();
final Message<File> messageVendors =
  MessageBuilder.withPayload(fileToSendVendors).build();
ftpChannel.send(messageOrders);
ftpChannel.send(messageVendors);
Thread.sleep(2000);
assertTrue(new File(TestSuite.FTP_ROOT_DIR + File.separator +
  "orders.txt").exists());
assertTrue(new File(TestSuite.FTP_ROOT_DIR + File.separator +
  "vendors.txt").exists());
LOGGER.info("Successfully transfered file 'orders.txt'
  and 'vendors.txt' to a remote FTP location.");
ctx.close();
}
```

FTP application using the Spring integration and Spring batch

In this section, we shall learn how to make FTP as a batch job. We shall create a configuration file in Java instead of XML. Here we shall set all the properties for a Spring batch database and tasklet using the @Configuration annotation. Then we have a properties file, which will set values to the instance variables in the ApplicationConfiguration.java file. The properties are loaded using the properties holder pattern available in Spring Framework.

1. We shall first update the configuration files. Here is a sample configuration file:

```
@Configuration
public class ApplicationConfiguration {
  //Below is the set of instance variables that will be
    configured.
  //configuring the jdbc driver
  @Value("${batch.jdbc.driver}")
```

```java
private String driverClassName;
//configuring the jdbc url
@Value("${batch.jdbc.url}")
private String driverUrl;

//configuring the jdbc username
@Value("${batch.jdbc.user}")
private String driverUsername;

//configuring the jdbc passowrd
@Value("${batch.jdbc.password}")
private String driverPassword;

//configuring the jobrepository autowiring the bean
@Autowired
@Qualifier("jobRepository")
private JobRepository jobRepository;

//configuring the  ftpsessionfactory
@Autowired
@Qualifier("myFtpSessionFactory")
private SessionFactory myFtpSessionFactory;

@Bean
public DataSource dataSource() {
  BasicDataSource dataSource = new BasicDataSource();
  dataSource.setDriverClassName(driverClassName);
  dataSource.setUrl(driverUrl);
  dataSource.setUsername(driverUsername);
  dataSource.setPassword(driverPassword);
  return dataSource;
}
//setting the ftp as a batch job
@Bean
@Scope(value="step")
public FtpGetRemoteFilesTasklet
  myFtpGetRemoteFilesTasklet(){
  FtpGetRemoteFilesTasklet  ftpTasklet = new
    FtpGetRemoteFilesTasklet();
  ftpTasklet.setRetryIfNotFound(true);
  ftpTasklet.setDownloadFileAttempts(3);
  ftpTasklet.setRetryIntervalMilliseconds(10000);
  ftpTasklet.setFileNamePattern("README");
  //ftpTasklet.setFileNamePattern("TestFile");
  ftpTasklet.setRemoteDirectory("/");
  ftpTasklet.setLocalDirectory(new
    File(System.getProperty("java.io.tmpdir")));
```

```
      ftpTasklet.setSessionFactory(myFtpSessionFactory);

      return ftpTasklet;
    }
    //setting the  ftp sessionfactory

    @Bean
    public SessionFactory myFtpSessionFactory() {
      DefaultFtpSessionFactory ftpSessionFactory = new
        DefaultFtpSessionFactory();
      ftpSessionFactory.setHost("ftp.gnu.org");
      ftpSessionFactory.setClientMode(0);
      ftpSessionFactory.setFileType(0);
      ftpSessionFactory.setPort(21);
      ftpSessionFactory.setUsername("anonymous");
      ftpSessionFactory.setPassword("anonymous");

      return ftpSessionFactory;
    }

    //Configuring the simple JobLauncher
    @Bean
    public SimpleJobLauncher jobLauncher() {
      SimpleJobLauncher jobLauncher = new
        SimpleJobLauncher();
      jobLauncher.setJobRepository(jobRepository);
      return jobLauncher;
    }

    @Bean
    public PlatformTransactionManager transactionManager() {
      return new DataSourceTransactionManager(dataSource());
    }

}
```

2. Let's use `property-placeholder` for further configuring the batch job.

3. Create a file named `batch.properties`:

```
batch.jdbc.driver=org.hsqldb.jdbcDriver
batch.jdbc.url=jdbc:hsqldb:mem:anjudb;sql
  .enforce_strict_size=true
  batch.jdbc.url=jdbc:hsqldb:hsql://localhost:9005/
  anjdb
batch.jdbc.user=anjana
batch.jdbc.password=raghu
```

4. Configure the application in the `context.xml` file or a separate file, the tasklet to run the FTP:

```xml
<batch:job id="ftpJob">
  <batch:step id="step1"  >
  <batch:tasklet
    ref="myApplicationFtpGetRemoteFilesTasklet" />
  </batch:step>
</batch:job>
```

5. Here is `MyApplicationFtpGetRemoteFilesTasklet`:

```java
public class MyApplicationFtpGetRemoteFilesTasklet
  implements Tasklet, InitializingBean {
  private File localDirectory;
  private AbstractInboundFileSynchronizer<?>
    ftpInboundFileSynchronizer;
  private SessionFactory sessionFactory;
  private boolean autoCreateLocalDirectory = true;
  private boolean deleteLocalFiles = true;
  private String fileNamePattern;
  private String remoteDirectory;
  private int downloadFileAttempts = 12;
  private long retryIntervalMilliseconds = 300000;
  private boolean retryIfNotFound = false;
  /**All the above instance variables have setters and
    getters*/

  /*After properties are set it just checks for certain
    instance variables for null values and calls the
    setupFileSynchronizer method.
    It also checks for local directory if it doesn't exits
    it auto creates the local directory.
  */
  public void afterPropertiesSet() throws Exception {
    Assert.notNull(sessionFactory, "sessionFactory
      attribute cannot be null");
    Assert.notNull(localDirectory, "localDirectory
      attribute cannot be null");
    Assert.notNull(remoteDirectory, "remoteDirectory
      attribute cannot be null");
    Assert.notNull(fileNamePattern, "fileNamePattern
      attribute cannot be null");

    setupFileSynchronizer();

    if (!this.localDirectory.exists()) {
      if (this.autoCreateLocalDirectory) {
```

```
      if (logger.isDebugEnabled()) {
        logger.debug("The '" + this.localDirectory +
          "' directory doesn't exist; Will create.");
      }
      this.localDirectory.mkdirs();
    }
    else
    {
      throw new FileNotFoundException(this
        .localDirectory.getName());
    }
  }
}
/*This method is called in afterpropertiesset() method. This
method checks if we need to transfer files using FTP or SFTP.
If it is SFTP then it initializes ftpInbounFileSynchronizer using
SFTPinbounfFileSynchronizer which has a constructor which takes
sessionFactory as the argument and has setter method to set file
Filter details with FileNamesPatterns.The method also sets the
remoteDirectory location..
*/
  private void setupFileSynchronizer() {
    if (isSftp()) {
      ftpInboundFileSynchronizer = new
        SftpInboundFileSynchronizer(sessionFactory);
      ((SftpInboundFileSynchronizer)
        ftpInboundFileSynchronizer).setFilter(new
        SftpSimplePatternFileListFilter(fileNamePattern));
    }
    else
    {
      ftpInboundFileSynchronizer = new
        FtpInboundFileSynchronizer(sessionFactory);
      ((FtpInboundFileSynchronizer)
        ftpInboundFileSynchronizer).setFilter(new
        FtpSimplePatternFileListFilter(fileNamePattern));
    }
    ftpInboundFileSynchronizer.setRemoteDirectory(
      remoteDirectory);
  }
/*This method is called during the file synchronization process
this will delete the files in the directory after copying..
*/
  private void deleteLocalFiles() {
    if (deleteLocalFiles) {
      SimplePatternFileListFilter filter = new
        SimplePatternFileListFilter(fileNamePattern);
```

```
      List<File> matchingFiles =
        filter.filterFiles(localDirectory.listFiles());
      if (CollectionUtils.isNotEmpty(matchingFiles)) {
        for (File file : matchingFiles) {
          FileUtils.deleteQuietly(file);
        }
      }
    }
  }
/*This is a batch execute method which operates with FTP ,it
synchronizes the local directory with the remote directory.
*/
  /* (non-Javadoc)
   * @see org.springframework.batch.core.step.tasklet
     .Tasklet#execute(org.springframework.batch
     .core.StepContribution, org.springframework.batch.core.
     scope.context.ChunkContext)
   */
  public RepeatStatus execute(StepContribution
    contribution, ChunkContext chunkContext)
    throws Exception {
    deleteLocalFiles();

    ftpInboundFileSynchronizer
      .synchronizeToLocalDirectory(localDirectory);

    if (retryIfNotFound) {
      SimplePatternFileListFilter filter = new
        SimplePatternFileListFilter(fileNamePattern);
      int attemptCount = 1;
      while (filter.filterFiles(localDirectory.listFiles())
        .size() == 0 && attemptCount <=
        downloadFileAttempts) {
        logger.info("File(s) matching " + fileNamePattern +
          " not found on remote site.  Attempt " +
          attemptCount + " out of " +
          downloadFileAttempts);
        Thread.sleep(retryIntervalMilliseconds);
        ftpInboundFileSynchronizer
          .synchronizeToLocalDirectory(localDirectory);
        attemptCount++;
      }

      if (attemptCount >= downloadFileAttempts &&
        filter.filterFiles(localDirectory.listFiles())
        .size() == 0) {
```

```
            throw new FileNotFoundException("Could not find
              remote file(s) matching " + fileNamePattern +
              " after " + downloadFileAttempts +
              " attempts.");
        }
    }

    return null;
}
```

Summary

In this chapter, we saw an overview of FTP and its abbreviations. We have seen different types of adapters, such as inbound and outbound adapters, with the outbound gateway and its configuration. We have also shown the springs-integration-ftp.xsd and have quoted various options available for each of the inbound and outbound adapters. We have also shown the libraries that are required to develop a maven application using the spring-integration-ftp package. Then we have looked at two important classes, FTPSessionFactory and FTPsSessionFactory, with getters and setters. We have also demonstrated an example of transferring files with SpringFTP using the outbound channel. We also demonstrated configuring FTP using Java via the @Configuration annotation. Lastly, we have demonstrated FTP as a tasklet. In the next chapter, we shall further look into Spring's integration with HTTP.

6

Spring Integration with HTTP

In this chapter, let us see how the Spring Integration package supports the HTTP protocol. We shall also look into HTTP and its features to get a better understanding of performing HTTP operations with the Spring framework.

HTTP stands for **Hyper Text Transfer Protocol**, which, in turn, stands for secure connection. This protocol comes under an application layer used for data transfer. It uses **Transmission Control Protocol/Internet Protocol (TCP/IP)** communication for data transfers. HTTP is a connectionless and stateless protocol, since the server and client are only aware of each other during request and response time. Any type of data can be sent across HTTP, as long as the server and client are able to handle it. The requests are sent via a web URL, that is a uniform resource locator. The URL contains the following parts: `http://www.domainname.com/path/?abc=xyz`

- Protocol: `http://` or `https://`
- Host: `www.domainname.com`
- Resource path: `path`
- Query: `abc=xyz`

HTTP methods and status codes

Let us look at the HTTP methods and status codes. The HTTP methods are a communication channel for performing operations on the HTTP protocol.

The following are the HTTP methods used:

- `GET`: This gets the existing resource for a given identifier.
- `PUT`: This puts a new resource.
- `POST`: This updates the existing resource.
- `DELETE`: This deletes the existing resource.

Status code is human readable diagnostic information about HTTP messages.

The following table shows all the available status codes and their meanings:

Status code	Meaning
200	The request has succeeded
201	The POST method was executed successfully
202	The request has been accepted for processing
203	No authorization for the information
204	No response from the server
301	The data requested is moved to a new URL
302	Forward action required for the request to be completely fulfilled
303	All the 3XX codes point to different URL for various actions like forwarding
304	Cache not modified properly
400	Bad syntax
401	Unauthorized request
402	Charge to header not matching
403	Forbidden request
404	Resource not found as per the provided URL
500	Unexpected error on the server
501	Server doesn't support the action
502	Too much load on the server
503	Gateway time out. Server is trying to access data from some other resource or service but it did not get the required response from it.

HTTP headers

These headers are found in the messages of HTTP request and response. They are just name value strings that are separated by a colon. Information like content type, caching, response types, can be directly given in the headers. Headers don't generally have any size limits but there are restrictions from the servers on the header size.

HTTP time-out

This is a 408 status code, which shows up on a webpage when the server is trying to access the data too many times and is not getting any response. This kind of error comes up, even when the servers are running slowly.

Timeouts can happen in two scenarios, one while interacting with the Spring Integration channels, which can be an inbound channel or an outbound channel, or while interacting with a HTTP server, which is in a remote location.

The time out support is done with the `RestTemplate` class available in the Spring Framework. Following is the sample configuration which can be used with Gateways and Outbound Adapters available with Spring Integration for HTTP.

```
<bean id="requestFactory"
      class="org.springframework.http.client.
SimpleClientHttpRequestFactory">
    <property name="connectTimeout" value="5000"/>
    <property name="readTimeout"    value="5000"/>
</bean>
```

HTTP proxy settings in Java

The proxy settings are supported by Java system properties. These properties can be set to use the server, which has proxy settings. The following are the properties that can be set:

- `http.proxyHost`: The host name of the proxy server.

- `http.proxyPort`: The port number, the default value being 80.

- `http.nonProxyHosts`: A list of hosts that should be reached directly, bypassing the proxy. This is a list of patterns separated by a | character. The patterns may start or end with a * character for wildcards. Any host matching one of these patterns will be reached through a direct connection instead of through a proxy.

The following are the proxy settings available for the secured HTTP:

- `https.proxyHost`: The host name of the proxy server.

- `https.proxyPort`: The port number, the default value being 80.

Proxy configuration support in Spring

Spring supports proxy configuration. We just need to configure the bean `SimpleClientHttpRequestFactory` which has a property proxy with `java.net.Proxy` bean. A sample configuration is shown in the following code:

```
<bean id="requestFactory" class="org.springframework.http
  .client.SimpleClientHttpRequestFactory">
  <property name="proxy">
  <bean id="proxy" class="java.net.Proxy">
    <constructor-arg>
    <util:constant static-field="java.net.Proxy.Type.HTTP"/>
    </constructor-arg>
    <constructor-arg>
    <bean class="java.net.InetSocketAddress">
      <constructor-arg value="123.0.0.1"/>
      <constructor-arg value="8080"/>
    </bean>
    </constructor-arg>
  </bean>
  </property>
</bean>
```

Spring Integration support for HTTP

Spring provides extended support to HTTP with adapters just like FTP, which consists of gateway implementation. Spring supports HTTP using the following two gateway implementations:

- `HttpInboundEndpoint`: To receive messages over HTTP we need to use either an adapter or an available gateway. The inbound adapter is called HTTP inbound adapter and the gateway is called HTTP inbound gateway. The adapter needs a servlet container, such as the Tomcat server or Jetty server. We need to make a web application with `web.xml`, with servlet configuration, and deploy it on the webserver. Spring itself provides a servlet called.

- `HttpRequestHandlerServlet`: This class extends a normal `HttpServlet`, and is available under the package `org.springframework.web.context. support.HttpRequestHandlerServlet`. Since it extends `HttpServlet`, it also overrides the `init()` and `service()` methods.

The following is the servlet configuration in a `web.xml` file:

```
<servlet>
  <servlet-name>inboundGateway</servlet-name>
```

```
    <servlet-class>o.s.web.context.support
       .HttpRequestHandlerServlet</servlet-class>
  </servlet>
```

The following is a gateway configuration for handling inbound HTTP requests. The gateway accepts a list of message converters, which will get converted from `HttpServletRequest` to message:

```
  <bean id="httpInbound" class="org.springframework.integration
     .http.inbound.HttpRequestHandlingMessagingGateway">
     <property name="requestChannel" ref="httpRequestChannel" />
     <property name="replyChannel" ref="httpReplyChannel" />
  </bean>
```

Spring Integration support for multipart HTTP requests

If the HTTP request is wrapped, the `MultipartHttpServletRequest` converters will convert the request to message payload, and this is nothing but a `MultiValueMap`. This map will have values, which are instances of Spring's multipart. The values are decided based on the content type. Values can also be byte arrays or strings. By default, if there is a bean by the name `MultipartResolver`, it gets recognized by the Spring's integration framework; if there is a bean with the name `multipartResolver`, it, in turn, enables the context. This will enable the inbound request mapper.

Spring Integration support for HTTP responses

Response to HTTP requests is usually sent with a 200Ok status code. To customize the response further, you can use the Spring MVC framework. In the Spring MVC application, we have an option to customize the response. We can provide a `viewName` to the response, which gets resolved by Spring MVC `ViewResolver`. We can configure the gateway to behave like a spring controller, which returns a view name as a response to the framework, and we can also configure the HTTP methods.

In the following configuration, you can see that we have used an integration package and have configured the `HttpRequestHandlingController` bean with the following properties:

- `HttpRequestChannel`
- `HttpReplyChannel`
- `viewName`
- `SupportedMedthodNames`

- The following code snippet shows the configuration for `HttpInbound` bean.
- We can also configure the supported HTTP Methods.

```xml
<bean id="httpInbound" class="org.springframework.integration.http
  .inbound.HttpRequestHandlingController">
  <constructor-arg value="true" /> <!-- indicates that a reply is
    expected -->
  <property name="requestChannel" ref="httpRequestChannel" />
  <property name="replyChannel" ref="httpReplyChannel" />
  <property name="viewName" value="jsonView" />
  <property name="supportedMethodNames" >
    <list>
      <value>GET</value>
      <value>DELETE</value>
    </list>
  </property>
</bean>
```

Configuring the outbound HTTP messages

Spring provides `HttpRequestExecutingMessageHandler`, which takes a string URL as a constructor argument. The class has a property called `ReponseChannel`, which also needs to be configured.

The bean will call the `RestTemplate` class by reading the URL configured in the constructor, which the `RestTemplate` calls `HttpMessageConverters`. The list of `HttpMessageConverters` are read and the `HttpRequest` body is generated.

The converter and `HttpRequestExecutingMessageHandler` are shown in the following code:

```xml
<bean id="httpOutbound" class="org.springframework.integration
  .http.outbound.HttpRequestExecutingMessageHandler">
  <constructor-arg value="http://localhost:8080/myweb" />
  <property name="outputChannel" ref="responseChannel" />
</bean>
```

OR

```xml
<bean id="httpOutbound" class="org.springframework.integration
  .http.outbound.HttpRequestExecutingMessageHandler">
  <constructor-arg value="http://localhost:8080/myweb" />
  <property name="outputChannel" ref="responseChannel" />
  <property name="messageConverters" ref="messageConverterList" />
  <property name="requestFactory" ref="customRequestFactory" />
</bean>
```

Configuring cookies with OutboundGateway

`OutboundGateway` has attribute transfer cookies, which accept Boolean values that are true or false. The header, in response, contains a set cookies parameter, which will convert the response to a cookie if the `transfer-cookie` attribute is set to `True`.

Configuring InboundGateway with both no response and with the response

Use the following code in order to configure an `InboundGateway` request with no response:

```
<int-http:inbound-channel-adapter id="httpChannelAdapter"
channel="requests"
    supported-methods="PUT, DELETE"/>
```

For the requests which need a response:

```
<int-http:inbound-gateway id="inboundGateway"
    request-channel="requests"
    reply-channel="responses"/>
```

RequestMapping support for an inbound channel adapter or a gateway

The `requestmapping` configuration can be done for an inbound channel adapter, or a gateway, as shown in the following code:

```
<inbound-gateway id="inboundController"
    request-channel="requests"
    reply-channel="responses"
    path="/foo/{fooId}"
    supported-methods="GET"
    view-name="foo"
    error-code="oops">
  <request-mapping headers="User-Agent"
<!--headers=""-->
    params="myParam=myValue"
    consumes="application/json"
    produces="!text/plain"/>
</inbound-gateway>
```

Based on this configuration, the namespace parser creates an instance of `IntegrationRequestMappingHandlerMapping` (if none exist yet), a `HttpRequestHandlingController` bean, and associated with it, an instance of `RequestMapping`, which, in turn, is converted to Spring MVC `RequestMappingInfo`.

With the path and supported method, the attributes of `<http:inbound-channel-adapter>`, or `<http:inbound-gateway>`, `<request-mapping>` translate directly into the respective options provided by the `org.springframework.web.bind.annotation.RequestMapping` annotation in Spring MVC.

The `<request-mapping>` subelement allows you to configure several Spring integration HTTP inbound endpoints to the same path (or even the same supported methods), and to provide different downstream message flows based on incoming HTTP requests.

Configuring the RequestMapping using the HTTP inbound endpoint

We can also declare just one HTTP inbound endpoint and apply routing and filtering logic within the Spring Integration flow to achieve the same result. This allows you to get the message into a flow as early as possible, for example:

```
<int-http:inbound-gateway request-channel="httpMethodRouter"
    supported-methods="GET,DELETE"
    path="/process/{entId}"
    payload-expression="#pathVariables.entId"/>
<int:router input-channel="httpMe
thodRouter" expression="headers.http_requestMethod">
    <int:mapping value="GET" channel="in1"/>
    <int:mapping value="DELETE" channel="in2"/>
</int:router>
<int:service-activator input-channel="in1" ref="service"
  method="getEntity"/>
<int:service-activator input-channel="in2" ref="service"
  method="delete"/>
```

Configuring the inbound channel adapter to read request information from the URL

We can also configure the inbound channel adapter to accept requests using the URI.

The URI can be `/param1/{param-value1}/param2/{param-value2}`. The URI template variables are mapped with a message payload by the payload expression attribute. Certain variables in the URI path can also be mapped with the header:

```
<int-http:inbound-channel-adapter id="inboundAdapterWithExpressions"
    path="/var-1/{phone}/var-2/{username}"
    channel="requests"
    payload-expression="#pathVariables.firstName">
    <int-http:header name="var-2" expression="#pathVariables.
username"/>
</int-http:inbound-channel-adapter>
```

The following is a list of payload expressions that can be used in a configuration:

- `#requestParams`: The `MultiValueMap` from the `ServletRequest` parameter map.
- `#pathVariables`: The map from URI template placeholders and their values.
- `#matrixVariables`: The map of `MultiValueMap`.
- `#requestAttributes`: The `org.springframework.web.context.request.RequestAttributes` associated with the current request.
- `#requestHeaders`: The `org.springframework.http.HttpHeaders` object from the current request.
- `#cookies`: The map `<String, Cookie>` of `javax.servlet.http.Cookies` from the current request.

Configuring the outbound gateway for HTTP responses

The outbound gateway or outbound channel adapter configuration is related to a HTTP response, and options to configure the response. The default response type for a HTTP request is null. The response method is usually POST. If the response type is null and the HTTP status code is null, then the reply message will have the `ResponseEntity` object. In the following sample configuration, we have configured the expected:

```
<int-http:outbound-gateway id="example"
    request-channel="requests"
    URL="http://localhost/test"
```

```
http-method="POST"
extract-request-payload="false"
expected-response-type="java.lang.String"
charset="UTF-8"
request-factory="requestFactory"
reply-timeout="1234"
reply-channel="replies"/>
```

Configuring the outbound adapter for different response types

We shall now show you two samples of configuring the outbound adapter with different response types.

Here, the expected response type expression is used with a value payload:

```
<int-http:outbound-gateway id="app1"
    request-channel="requests"
    URL="http://localhost/myapp"
    http-method-expression="headers.httpMethod"
    extract-request-payload="false"
    expected-response-type-expression="payload"
    charset="UTF-8"
    request-factory="requestFactory"
    reply-timeout="1234"
    reply-channel="replies"/>
```

Now, configure the outbound channel adapter to give a string response:

```
<int-http:outbound-channel-adapter id="app1"
    url="http://localhost/myapp"
    http-method="GET"
    channel="requests"
    charset="UTF-8"
    extract-payload="false"
    expected-response-type="java.lang.String"
    request-factory="someRequestFactory"
    order="3"
    auto-startup="false"/>
```

Mapping URI variables as subelement with an HTTP outbound gateway and an outbound channel adapter

In this section, we shall see the use of a URI variable, and URI variable expressions, as a subelement with the HTTP outbound gateway configuration.

If your URL contains URI variables, you can map them using the Uri-variable subelement. This subelement is available for the HTTP outbound gateway and the HTTP outbound channel adapter:

```
<int-http:outbound-gateway id="trafficGateway"
    url="http://local.yahooapis.com/trafficData?appid=YdnDemo&amp;zip=
  {zipCode}"
    request-channel="trafficChannel"
    http-method="GET"
    expected-response-type="java.lang.String">
    <int-http:uri-variable name="zipCode" expression="payload.
getZip()"/>
</int-http:outbound-gateway>
```

The Uri-variable subelement defines two attributes: name and expression. The name attribute identifies the name of the URI variable, while the expression attribute is used to set the actual value. Using the expression attribute, you can leverage the full power of **Spring Expression Language (SpEL)**, which gives you full dynamic access to the message payload and the message headers. For example, in the above configuration the getZip() method will be invoked on the payload object of the message, and the result of that method will be used as a value for the URI variable named zipCode.

Since Spring Integration 3.0, HTTP outbound endpoints support the Uri-variables-expression attributes to specify an Expression which should be evaluated, resulting in a map for all URI variable placeholders within the URL template. It provides a mechanism whereby different variable expressions can be used based on the outbound message. This attribute is mutually exclusive with the <Uri-variable/> subelement:

```
<int-http:outbound-gateway
    url="http://foo.host/{foo}/bars/{bar}"
    request-channel="trafficChannel"
    http-method="GET"
    Uri-variables-expression="@uriVariablesBean.populate(payload)"
    expected-response-type="java.lang.String"/>
```

Handling time-out with the HTTP outbound gateway and the HTTP inbound gateway

The following table shows the difference in handling the HTTP outbound and HTTP inbound gateway:

Time-out in HTTP outbound gateway	Time-Out in HTTP inbound gateway
ReplyTimeOut maps to sendTimeOut property of HttpRequestExecuting MessageHandler.	Here, we use the RequestTimeOut attribute which maps the requestTimeProperty of HttpRequestHandlingMessagingGateway class.
sendTimeOut default value is 1, which is sent to MessageChannel.	Default timeout properties in 1,000 ms. Timeout properties will be used set sendTimeOut parameter used in MessagingTemplate instance.

Spring support for header customizations

If we need to do further customization to the header, then the Spring Integration package provides us with complete support. If we explicitly specify the header names in the configuration with comma separated values, the default behavior will be overridden.

The following is the configuration for further header customization:

```
<int-http:outbound-gateway id="httpGateway"
    url="http://localhost/app2"
    mapped-request-headers="boo, bar"
    mapped-response-headers="X-*, HTTP_RESPONSE_HEADERS"
    channel="someChannel"/>

<int-http:outbound-channel-adapter id="httpAdapter"
    url="http://localhost/app2"
    mapped-request-headers="boo, bar, HTTP_REQUEST_HEADERS"
    channel="someChannel"/>
```

Another option is to use the header-mapper attribute, which takes the DefaultHttpHeaderMapper class configurations.

The class comes with factory methods that are static for inbound and outbound adapters.

The following is the configuration for the `header-mapper` attribute:

```
<bean id="headerMapper" class="o.s.i.http.support
  .DefaultHttpHeaderMapper">
  <property name="inboundHeaderNames" value="foo*, *bar, baz"/>
  <property name="outboundHeaderNames" value="a*b, d"/>
</bean>
```

Sending multipart HTTP requests using Spring's RestTemplate

Most of the time, we have implemented file upload functionality in our application. Files are sent over HTTP as a multipart request.

In this section, let us see how we can configure the inbound channel adapter using `RestTemplate` to send a file over HTTP request.

Let us configure the server with the inbound channel adapter and then write a client for it:

```
<int-http:inbound-channel-adapter id="httpInboundAdapter"
  channel="receiveChannel"
  name="/inboundAdapter.htm"
  supported-methods="GET, POST"/>
<int:channel id="receiveChannel"/>
<int:service-activator input-channel="receiveChannel">
  <bean class="org.springframework.integration.samples
    .multipart.MultipartReceiver"/>
</int:service-activator>
<bean id="multipartResolver" class="org.springframework.web
  .multipart.commons.CommonsMultipartResolver"/>
```

The `httpInboundAdapter` will receive the request and convert it to a message with a payload `LinkedMultiValueMap`. Then, we will be parsing that in the `multipartReceiver` service activator:

```
public void receive(LinkedMultiValueMap<String, Object>
  multipartRequest){
  System.out.println("### Successfully received multipart
    request ###");
  for (String elementName : multipartRequest.keySet()) {
    if (elementName.equals("company")){
      System.out.println("\t" + elementName + " - " +
        ((String[]) multipartRequest.getFirst("company"))[0]);
```

```
    }
    else if (elementName.equals("company-logo")){
      System.out.println("\t" + elementName + " - as
        UploadedMultipartFile: " + ((UploadedMultipartFile)
        multipartRequest.getFirst("company-logo"))
        .getOriginalFilename());
    }
  }
}
```

Now, let us write a client. By client, we mean creating a map and adding the file to it.

1. We shall now create a `MultiValueMap`:

    ```
    MultiValueMap map = new LinkedMultiValueMap();
    ```

2. The map can be populated with values, such as details of a person:

    ```
    Resource anjanapic = new
      ClassPathResource("org/abc/samples/multipart/anjana.png");
    map.add("username","anjana");
    map.add("lastname","mankale");
    map.add("city","bangalore");
    map.add("country","India");
    map.add("photo",anjana.png);
    ```

3. This step is to create headers and set the content type:

    ```
    HttpHeaders headers = new HttpHeaders();
    headers.setContentType(new MediaType("multipart",
      "form-data"));
    ```

4. We need to pass the `header` and `map` as a request to the `HttpEntity`:

    ```
    HttpEntity request = new HttpEntity(map, headers);
    ```

5. Let us use `RestTemplate` to pass the request:

    ```
    RestTemplate template = new RestTemplate();
    String Uri = "http://localhost:8080/multipart-
      http/inboundAdapter.htm";
    ResponseEntity<?> httpResponse = template.exchange(Uri,
      HttpMethod.POST, request, null
    ```

We should now get an output in which the photo is uploaded on the server.

Summary

In this chapter, we have learnt about HTTP and Spring Integration support for accessing HTTP methods and requests. We have also demonstrated multipart requests and responses, and have shown how to configure the inbound and outbound HTTP gateways and adapters.

We have learnt about sending multipart HTTP requests by configuring the Spring's inbound and outbound gateway. We have also demonstrated how we can use multi-value maps to populate the request and put the map in the HTTP header. Lastly, we have seen the list of payload expressions available.

In the next chapter, let us look at Spring's support to Hadoop.

7
Spring with Hadoop

Processing large chunks of data has been a major challenge in architecting modern day web applications. Hadoop is an open source framework from Apache that provides libraries to process and store large chunks of data. It offers a scalable, cost-effective, and fault-tolerant solution to store and process large chunks of data. In this chapter, let us demonstrate how the Spring Framework supports Hadoop. Map and Reduce, Hive, and HDFS are some of the Hadoop key terminology used with cloud-based technologies. Google has also come with its own Map and Reduce and distributed file system framework, apart from Apache Hadoop.

Apache Hadoop modules

Apache Hadoop consists of the following modules:

*   **Hadoop Common**: This is a common module used by other modules of Hadoop. It is like a utility package.
*   **Hadoop Distributed File System**: Hadoop Distributed File System can be considered when we have to store large amounts of data across various machines or machine clusters.
*   **Hadoop Yarn**: Think of a scenario where we have many servers on the cloud that need to be scheduled to restart or reboot at a particular time by sending an e-mail intimation to the tenants. Hadoop Yarn can be used for scheduling resources across computers or clusters.
*   **Hadoop Map and Reduce**: If we have to process a large set of data, we can break it into small clusters and process them as units and merge them back later. This can be done with the libraries provided in Apache map and reduce.

Spring namespace for Hadoop

Following is the namespace that needs to be used to integrate the Hadoop framework with Spring. `http://www.springframework.org/schema/hadoop/spring-hadoop.xsd` defines the XSD for Spring-Hadoop, which is normally used in the `application-context.xml` file. The XSD details how to configure Hadoop as jobs with Spring Framework.

```
<?xml version="1.0" encoding="UTF-8"?>
<beans xmlns="http://www.springframework.org/schema/beans"
    xmlns:xsi="http://www.w3.org/2001/XMLSchema-instance"
    xmlns:1hdp="2http://www.springframework.org/schema/hadoop"
    xsi:schemaLocation="
    http://www.springframework.org/schema/beans http://www.
springframework.org/schema/beans/spring-beans.xsd
    http://www.springframework.org/schema/hadoop http://www.
springframework.org/schema/hadoop/spring-hadoop.xsd">

    <bean id ... >

    4<hdp:configuration ...>
</beans>
```

Hadoop Distributed Files System

The **Hadoop Distributed File System (HDFS)** is used for storing large amounts of data on a distributed file system. HDFS stores metadata and application data separately on different servers. The servers used to store metadata are called `NameNode` servers. The servers used to store application data are called `DataNode` servers. The `NameNode` and `DataNodes` behave in a master-slave architecture. Usually, one `NameNode` will have many `DataNodes`. `NameNodes` stores the file's namespace, and the file will spilt it into many small chunks across `DataNodes`. `DataNodes` usually function as per the instruction from `NameNode` and per functions such as block creation, replication, and deletion. So, the major tasks with Hadoop will involve interacting with the file system. This may include creating files, parsing file for processes, or deleting files.

The Hadoop file system can be accessed in a number of ways. We have listed a few here:

- `hdfs`: It uses RPC for communication, and the protocol used is `hdfs://`. It requires the client, server, and clusters to have the same versions, else a serialization error will occur.

- hftp and hsftp: These are HTTP-based, version-independent protocols with the prefix hftp://.

- webhdfs: This is based on HTTP with REST API and is also version independent.

The abstract class org.apache.hadoop.fs.FileSystem behaves like an entry point into the Hadoop File System implementation. This class has been extended by Spring Framework with the subclass SimplerFileSystem. This subclass contains all the methods that serve file operations, such as copying from one location to another.

Spring Framework comes with a package in Hadoop to handle Hadoop Distributed File Systems. The package org.springframework.data.hadoop.fs has classes to handle the file resources.

HdfsResourceLoader is a class found in Sping's Hadoop File System package and is used to load the resources in Hadoop File System. It has constructors that take the configuration object as the input. The HdfsResourceLoader constructors are shown in the following code snippet. It also has methods to get the resource from a path specified and to close the file stream after use.

```
HdfsResourceLoader(Configuration config)
HdfsResourceLoader(Configuration config)
HdfsResourceLoader(Configuration config, URI uri)
HdfsResourceLoader(Configuration config, URI uri, String user)
HdfsResourceLoader(FileSystem fs)
```

Use the following command to configure Spring to use webhdfs:

```
<hdp:configuration>
  fs.default.name=webhdfs://localhost
  ...
</hdp:configuration>
```

To manually configure the URI and File System ID, the following configuration can be given:

```
<!-- manually creates the default SHDP file-system named 'hadoopFs'
-->
<hdp:file-system uri="webhdfs://localhost"/>

<!-- creates a different FileSystem instance -->
<hdp:file-system id="old-cluster" uri="hftp://old-cluster/"/>
```

Languages such as **Rhino** and **Groovy** have provided Java scripting or use Python to do the HDFS configuration. A sample one is shown in the following code. The scripts can be configured to run on start up or conditional start up. Two script variables that can be used for this configuration are `run-at-start-up` and `evaluate`. Scripts can also be configured to get started as tasklets (which means as a batch job).

```
<beans xmlns="http://www.springframework.org/schema/beans" ...>
<hdp:configuration .../>

<hdp:script id="inlined-js" language="javascript"
  run-at-startup="true">
  importPackage(java.util);
  name = UUID.randomUUID().toString()
  scriptName = "src/test/resources/test.properties"
  // fs - FileSystem instance based on 'hadoopConfiguration' bean
  // call FileSystem#copyFromLocal(Path, Path)
  fs.copyFromLocalFile(scriptName, name)
  // return the file length
  fs.getLength(name)
</hdp:script>

</beans>
```

Some of the implicit variables and classes associated with the implicit variables are shown here:

- `hdfsRL-org.springframework.data.hadoop.io.HdfsResourceLoader`: a HDFS resource loader (relies on `hadoop-resource-loader` or singleton type match, falls back to creating one automatically based on `'cfg'`).

- `distcp-org.springframework.data.hadoop.fs.DistributedCopyUtil`: Programmatic access to `DistCp`.

- `fs-org.apache.hadoop.fs.FileSystem`: a Hadoop File System (relies on `'hadoop-fs'` bean or singleton type match, falls back to creating one based on `'cfg'`).

- `fsh-org.springframework.data.hadoop.fs.FsShell`: a File System shell, exposing hadoop `fs` commands as an API.

HBase

Apache HBase is mainly the key value storage for Hadoop. It's actually a database that is easily scalable and can accommodate millions of rows and columns. It can be scaled across hardware and is similar to a NoSQL database. It integrates with Map and Reduce and works best with the RESTFUL API. HBase was derived from Google's bigdata. It has been used by Netflix, Yahoo, and Facebook. It is also memory intensive, since it's meant to handle large amounts of data and has to scale against hardware.

Let's create a simple employee table using Eclipse and Hadoop HBase. In Eclipse, just add the following JAR files, or if you are using Maven, ensure that the following JAR files are updated in Maven's `pom.xml` file:

- `hbase-0.94.8.jar`
- `commons-logging-1.1.1.jar`
- `log4j-1.2.16.jar`
- `zookeeper-3.4.5.jar`
- `hadoop-core-1.1.2.jar`
- `commons-configuration-1.6.jar`
- `common-lang-2.5.jar`
- `protobuf-java-2.4.0a.jar`
- `slf4j-api-1.4.3.jar`
- `slf4j-log4j12-1.4.3.jar`

Create a `Main` class to with the following code. This class will create an employee table with ID and Name as its two columns using the `HbaseAdmin` class. This class has methods for creating, modifying, and deleting tables in Hadoop.

```
import org.apache.hadoop.conf.Configuration;

import org.apache.hadoop.hbase.HBaseConfiguration;

import org.apache.hadoop.hbase.HColumnDescriptor;

import org.apache.hadoop.hbase.HTableDescriptor;

import org.apache.hadoop.hbase.client.HBaseAdmin;

public class HbaseTableCreation
{
  public static void main(String[] args) throws IOException {
    HBaseConfiguration hc = new HBaseConfiguration(new
    Configuration());

    HTableDescriptor ht = new HTableDescriptor("EmployeeTable");

    ht.addFamily( new HColumnDescriptor("Id"));

    ht.addFamily( new HColumnDescriptor("Name"));

    System.out.println( "connecting" );

    HBaseAdmin hba = new HBaseAdmin( hc );
```

```
        System.out.println( "Creating Table EmployeeTable" );

        hba.createTable( ht );

        System.out.println("Done....EmployeeTable..");
    }
}
```

HBase is supported by the Spring Framework, and `factoryBean` is also created in a Spring Hadoop package to support it. The `HbaseConfigurationFactoryBean` bean is available in the package `org.springframework.data.hadoop.hbase`. The `HBaseAccessor` class is an abstract class and has been extended by two subclasses, `HbaseTemplate` and `HbaseInterceptors`.

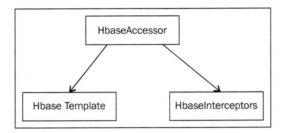

Spring offers a core class called `HBaseTemplate`. This class is the first point of contact for the application when HBase is implemented. This class has all the methods to access tables, such as `execute`, `find`, `find all`, and so on.

This class has the following constructor:

```
HbaseTemplate()
HbaseTemplate(Configuration configuration)
```

This is the HBase template configuration that can be used in the application's `context.xml` or `Hbasecontext.xml` files:

```
// default HBase configuration
<hdp:hbase-configuration/>

// wire hbase configuration (using default name
  'hbaseConfiguration') into the template
<bean id="htemplate" class="org.springframework.data.hadoop.hbase
  .HbaseTemplate" p:configuration-ref="hbaseConfiguration"/>
```

Let's also look at how `HBaseTemplate` is used for retrieving table information with a sample code snippet:

```
// writing to 'EmployeeTable'
template.execute("EmployeeTable", new TableCallback<Object>() {
  @Override
  public Object doInTable(HTable table) throws Throwable {
    Put p = new Put(Bytes.toBytes("Name"));
    p.add(Bytes.toBytes("Name"), Bytes.toBytes("SomeQualifier"),
      Bytes.toBytes("Anjana"));
    table.put(p);
    return null;
  }
});


// read each row from 'EmployeeTable'
List<String> rows = template.find("EmployeeTable", "Name", new
  RowMapper<String>() {
  @Override
  public String mapRow(Result result, int rowNum)
    throws Exception {
    return result.toString();
  }
}));
```

Spring also supports AOP integration with Hadoop HBase and has a package to handle all the AOP events using `HBaseInterceptors`. This class implements the following interfaces:

- `org.aopalliance.aop.Advice`
- `org.aopalliance.intercept.Interceptor`
- `org.aopalliance.intercept.MethodInterceptor`
- `InitializingBean`

`HBaseInterceptors` with `HBaseSynchronizationManager` can be used to bind an HBase table to a thread before a method call, or detach from it after a method call.

- This is Spring's Hadoop HBase configuration for creating an HBase configuration object to manage HBase configuration connections:

  ```
  <!-- default bean id is 'hbaseConfiguration' that uses the
  existing 'hadoopCconfiguration' object ->
  <hdp:hbase-configuration configuration-ref="hadoopCconfiguration"
  />
  ```

- This is Spring's Hadoop HBase configuration to manage proxies and connections when the application context is null or not available for some reason:

```
<!-- delete associated connections but do not stop the
  proxies -->
<hdp:hbase-configuration stop-proxy="false"
  delete-connection="true">
  toooo=baaaa
  property=value
</hdp:hbase-configuration>
```

- This is the configuration for a high performance coordination server called ZooKeeper which is used in Hadoop distributed systems:

```
<!-- specify ZooKeeper host/port -->
<hdp:hbase-configuration zk-quorum="${hbase.host}"
  zk-port="${hbase.port}">
```

We can also load the properties from the file as shown here:

```
<hdp:hbase-configuration properties-ref="some-props-bean"
  properties-location="classpath:/conf/testing/
  hbase.properties"/>
```

Map and Reduce

Map and Reduce is a programming approach that allows a lot of scalability. The term "Map and Reduce" implies that we will be using maps to process the data. We can see two steps here. The first one is map creation (a map is created with a key-value pair), and the second one is reduction, which reads the map created in the first step and breaks it into many smaller maps.

Let's think of a scenario that can be related to Map and Reduce—let's say that we need to get the population of tigers in India and do some work to enhance their living conditions so that they don't go extinct. We may have an average figure of the population of tigers. Say that we dispatch people to different states and they collect information like this: Karnataka (100), TamilNadu (150), and so on. We would then combine these figures into a single figure to get the total population of tigers. The mapping of population can be seen as a parallel process (mapping job), and combining the result can be seen as a reducing job.

Creating a configuration object in Spring for Map and Reduce

The configuration object holds information about the Map and Reduce job. The configuration object itself is a bean definition mapped to the class `ConfigurationFactoryBean`, with the default name `hadoopConfiguration`.

The configuration object can be simply configured as follows:

```
<hdp:configuration />
```

Here is another variation of configuring the configuration object:

```
<hdp:configuration resources="classpath:/custom-site.xml,
    classpath:/hq-site.xml">
```

Another variation is to configure Hadoop resources using `java.properties` directly in the `configuration` tag, like so:

```
<hdp:configuration>
        fs.default.name=hdfs://localhost:9000
        hadoop.tmp.dir=/tmp/hadoop
        electric=sea
    </hdp:configuration>
```

You can also use Spring's property placeholder to externalize the properties, as follows:

```
<hdp:configuration>
        fs.default.name=${hd.fs}
        hadoop.tmp.dir=file://${java.io.tmpdir}
        hangar=${number:18}
    </hdp:configuration>
        <context:property-placeholder location="classpath:hadoop.
properties" />
```

Map and Reduce jobs with Spring

Map and Reduce can be scheduled as a job using Spring Framework. Spring Framework comes with `spring-data-hadoop` package which supports Map and Reduce. With this, we need to ensure that we have the Apache Hadoop core package.

Let us implement a simple scenario of counting the occurrence of each word in the input file. Create a simple Maven Java project with the following mentioned dependencies.

Dependencies for Maven project

We need to add these dependencies in the `pom.xml` file:

```
< !-- Spring Data Apache Hadoop -- >
< dependency >
    < groupId > org.springframework.data </ groupId >
    < artifactId  > spring-data-hadoop </ artifactId >
    < version > 1.0.0.RELEASE </ version >
< /dependency >
< !-- Apache Hadoop Core -- >
< dependency >
    < groupId > org.apache.hadoop </ groupId >
    < artifactId > hadoop-core </ artifactId >
    < version > 1.0.3 </version >
</dependency>
```

Apache Hadoop Map and Reduce comes with a mapper class that can be used to create maps to solve the problem of reading the contents and storing the occurrence of the word with key-value pairs. Each line in the file will be broken into words to be stored in maps.

We can create a custom mapper by extending the `ApacheMapper` class and overriding the map method, as follows:

```
public class CustomWordMapper extends Mapper<LongWritable, Text,
  Text, IntWritable> {
  private Text myword = new Text();

  @Override
  protected void map(LongWritable key, Text value,
    Context context) throws IOException, InterruptedException {
    String line = value.toString();
    StringTokenizer lineTokenz = new StringTokenizer(line);
    while (lineTokenz.hasMoreTokens()) {
      String cleaned_data =
        removeNonLettersNonNumbers(lineTokenz.nextToken());
      myword.set(cleaned_data);
      context.write(myword, new IntWritable(1));
    }
  }

  /**
  * Replace all Unicode characters that are neither numbers nor
    letters with an empty string.
  * @param original, It is the original string
```

```
 * @return a string object that contains only letters and numbers
 */
private String removeNonLettersNonNumbers (String original) {
  return original.replaceAll("[^\\p{L}\\p{N}]", "");
}
}
```

The `CustomWordMapper` class does the following:

1. Creates an `myword` instance of the `Text()` class.

2. Overrides the `map` method of the super class `Mapper` and implements these steps:

    1. Text object is converted to string and assigned to string `line`.

    2. Line is a string object that is passed to string tokenizer.

    3. String tokenizer is looped using `while` and calls the `removeNonLettersNonNumbers` method. The returning string is assigned to a `myword` text instance.

    4. The `context.write(myword,newIntwritable(1))` method is called.

3. Has a method to remove non-letters and non-number that uses the `string.replaceAll()` method. It finally returns a string object which has only number and letters.

We shall next create a reducer component. The reducer component will do the following tasks:

1. Extend the `reducer` class.

2. Create a string attribute for the reducer class which accepts the string that needs to be searched and whose occurrence needs to be found.

3. Override the `reduce` method.

4. Remove unwanted key-value pairs.

5. Keep key-value pairs that are required.

6. Check whether the input key is already present. If it is present, it will get the occurrence and the latest value will be stored.

    ```
    import org.apache.hadoop.io.IntWritable;
    import org.apache.hadoop.io.Text;
    import org.apache.hadoop.mapreduce.Reducer;

    public class CustomWordReducer extends Reducer<Text, IntWritable,
    Text, IntWritable> {
        protected static final String MY_TARGET_TEXT = "SPRING";
    ```

```
@Override
 protected void reduce(Text keyTxt, Iterable<IntWritable> values,
Context context) throws IOException, InterruptedException {
        if (containsTargetWord(keyTxt)) {
            int wCount = 0;
            for (IntWritable value: values) {
                wCount += value.get();
            }
            context.write(key, new IntWritable(wCount));
        }
    }
    private boolean containsTargetWord(Text keyTxt) {
        return keyTxt.toString().equals(MY_TARGET_TEXT);
    }
}
```

7. Configure the `application.properties` file with HDFS ports and input and output file paths.

8. Here is the sample `application.properties` file:

   fs.default.name=hdfs://localhost:9000

   mapred.job.tracker=localhost:9001

   input.path=/path/to/input/file/

   output.path=/path/to/output/file

   Once the properties are configured, it should be available in the Spring context. So, configure the properties file in Spring's `application-context.xml` file using `property-placeholder`. This is the configuration snippet that needs to be added in the `application-conext.xml` file.

   ```
   <context:property-placeholder
     location="classpath:application.properties" />
   ```

   You can directly configure Apache Hadoop in the `application-context.xml` file or use the properties file and read the key-value pair from the properties file. Since we have used the properties file, we shall read the values from the properties file. The following code snippet shows that `${mapred.job.tracker}` is a key in the properties file. You can see that the default name is also configured from the properties file using the key `${fs.default.name}`. Configure Apache Hadoop in the `application-context.xml` file as follows:

   ```
   <hdp:configuration>
     fs.default.name=${fs.default.name}
     mapred.job.tracker=${mapred.job.tracker}
   </hdp:configuration>
   ```

9. Next, we need to configure Hadoop as a job in Spring:

    1. Provide a job ID.

    2. Specify the input path; it will be read from the properties file.

    3. Specify the output path; it will be read from the properties file.

    4. Jar-by class.

    5. Mapper class-reference to the custom mapper class.

    6. Reducer class-reference to the custom reducer class.

10. This is the configuration snippet that needs to be available in the `application-xccontext.xml` file. Configure the Hadoop job in the `application-context.xml` file, as follows:

```
<hdp:job id="wordCountJobId"
input-path="${input.path}"
output-path="${output.path}"
jar-by-class="net.qs.spring.data.apachehadoop.Main"
mapper="com.packt.spring.data.apachehadoop
  .CustomWordMapper"
reducer="com.packt.spring.data.apachehadoop
  .CustomWordReducer"/>
```

11. Lastly, we need to configure the job runner in the `application-context.xml` file. The job runner configuration tells Spring Framework when to start the job. Here we have configured the job runner to start `wordcountjob` on start up.

12. Here is the configuration snippet for job runner. Configure the `application-context.xml` file to run the Hadoop job.

```
<hdp:job-runner id="wordCountJobRunner"
  job-ref="wordCountJobId" run-at-startup="true"/>
```

Since this is a standalone Spring application, we do not have a web module that will invoke the application context. The context needs to be loaded in a class file. So, let's create a `Main` class with a `static` method to load the `application-context.xml` file.

We can create a class that loads the `application-context.xml` file on start up, as follows:

```
import org.springframework.context.ApplicationContext;
importorg.springframework.context.support
  .ClassPathXmlApplicationContext;

public class Main {
  public static void main(String[] arguments) {
```

```
        ApplicationContext ctx = new
          ClassPathXmlApplicationContext("application-context.xml");
      }
    }
```

Let's create a file named `myinput.txt` with content, as follows:

```
SPRING IS A SEASON. SPRING IS A FRAMEWORK IN JAVA. ITS SPRING IN
   INDIA. SPRING IS GREEEN. SPRING SPRING EVERY WHERE
```

Next, we need to give an input file to HDFS by executing this command:

```
hadoop dfs -put myinput.txt /input/myinput.txt
hadoop dfs -ls /input
```

Run the `Main` class to see the output.

Map and Reduce jobs using Hadoop streaming and Spring DataApache Hadoop

In this section, we shall demonstrate Map and Reduce data streaming with Unix shell commands. Since this is related to Hadoop streaming, we shall set up a Hadoop instance on the Unix system. A Hadoop instance is always is run on a Unix machine for production mode, while for development, a Windows Hadoop instance is used.

1. These are the requirements to set up the requirement:
    ○ JAVA 1.7.x
    ○ SSH must be installed

2. Download the latest Apache Hadoop Distribution Binary Package.

3. Unzip and extract the package into a folder.

4. Set up the following environment variables:
    ○ JAVA_HOME
    ○ HADOOP_HOME
    ○ HADOOP_LOG_DIR
    ○ PATH

    We also need to configure the files that are present in the `conf` folder of the Hadoop installation directory:
    ○ Core-site.xml
    ○ Hdfs-site.xml
    ○ Mapred-site.xml

We need to set a default Hadoop file system.

5. To configure a default Hadoop file system, provide setting information in the core-site.xml file.

    ```
    <configuration>
      <property>
      <name>fs.default.name</name>
      <value>hdfs://localhost:9000</value>
      </property>
    </configuration>
    ```

6. Also configure the replication factor. Replication factor configuration ensures that a copy of the file gets stored in the Hadoop file system. A property dfs.replication and its value is set in the hdfs-site.xml file.

    ```
    <configuration>
      <property>
        <name>dfs.replication</name>
        <value>1</value>
      </property>
    </configuration>
    ```

7. Lastly, configure the job tracker; this configuration is done in the mapred-site.xml file.

    ```
    <configuration>
      <property>
        <name>mapred.job.tracker</name>
        <value>localhost:9001</value>
      </property>
    </configuration>
    ```

8. To run Hadoop in pseudo distributed mode, we just need the format; in the bin folder, there are start and stop Hadoop instance commands.

Next, we shall demonstrate how to integrate Python with Apache Hadoop data.

We shall create a simple project using Maven. These are the dependencies:

```
<!-- Spring Data Apache Hadoop -->
<dependency>
  <groupId>org.springframework.data</groupId>
  <artifactId>spring-data-hadoop</artifactId>
  <version>1.0.0.RC2</version>
</dependency>
<!-- Apache Hadoop Core -->
<dependency>
```

```
    <groupId>org.apache.hadoop</groupId>
    <artifactId>hadoop-core</artifactId>
    <version>1.0.3</version>
</dependency>
<!-- Apache Hadoop Streaming -->
<dependency>
    <groupId>org.apache.hadoop</groupId>
    <artifactId>hadoop-streaming</artifactId>
    <version>1.0.3</version>
</dependency>
```

We need a mapper and reducer Python script. A mapper script in Python should be implemented to do the following:

- The script should read from a standard input stream, read the input one line at time, and convert it into UTF-8

- The words in the line have to be split into words

- The special characters from the line need to be replaced with blank characters, and then get a key value pair as a tab; they are delimited to standard output

Here is the mapper script in Python:

```python
#!/usr/bin/python
# -*- coding: utf-8 -*-
import sys
import unicodedata


# Removes punctuation characters from the string
def strip_punctuation(word):
    return ''.join(x for x in word if unicodedata.category(x) !=
      'Po')


#Process input one line at the time
for line in sys.stdin:
    #Converts the line to Unicode
    line = unicode(line, "utf-8")
    #Splits the line to individual words
    words = line.split()
    #Processes each word one by one
    for word in words:
        #Removes punctuation characters
```

```
word = strip_punctuation(word)
#Prints the output
print ("%s\t%s" % (word, 1)).encode("utf-8")
```

The Reducer script in Python should be implemented to do the following:

1. The script should read the key-value pair output generated from the `mapper` class. Then, count the occurrence of keywords.

```
#!/usr/bin/python
# -*- coding: utf-8 -*-s
import sys
wordCount = 0
#Process input one line at the time
for line in sys.stdin:
    #Converts the line to Unicode
    line = unicode(line, "utf-8")
    #Gets key and value from the current line
    (key, value) = line.split("\t")
    if key == "Amily":
        #Increase word count by one
        wordCount = int(wordCount + 1);
#Prints the output
print ("Watson\t%s" % wordCount).encode("utf-8")
```

2. Once the Python script is ready, we need to provide the mapper and reducer class names and configurations in the properties files. This is the `.properties` file:

```
#Configures the default file system of Apache Hadoop
fs.default.name=hdfs://localhost:9000

#The path to the directory that contains our input files
input.path=/input/

#The path to the directory in which the output is written
output.path=/output/

#Configure the path of the mapper script
mapper.script.path=pythonmapper.py

#Configure the path of the reducer script
reducer.script.path=pythonreducer.py
```

3. We also need to configure `property-placeholder` and Apache Hadoop in the `context.xml` file. Here is the configuration:

```
<context:property-placeholder
  location="classpath:application.properties" />
<hdp:configuration>
  fs.default.name=${fs.default.name}
</hdp:configuration>
```

4. Lastly, we need to configure the Hadoop job and assign the job to job runner, which will initialize the job.

```
<hdp:configuration>
  fs.default.name=${fs.default.name}
</hdp:configuration>
<hdp:streaming id="streamingJob"
  input-path="${input.path}"
  output-path="${output.path}"
  mapper="${mapper.script.path}"
  reducer="${reducer.script.path}"/>
<hdp:job-runner id="streamingJobRunner" job-
  ref="streamingJob" run-at-startup="true"/>
```

5. Now, we need to invoke the configuration using the application context, so that the application context is loaded with all the configurations in the Spring Framework.

```
import org.springframework.context.ApplicationContext;
import org.springframework.context.support
  .ClassPathXmlApplicationContext;

public class Main {
  public static void main(String[] arguments) {
    ApplicationContext ctx = new
      ClassPathXmlApplicationContext(
      "applicationContext.xml");
  }
}
```

6. Run the following command in Command Prompt to provide an input file. Let the file be placed in a folder named `input`:

```
hadoop dfs -put MILLSANDBOON.txt /input/ MILLSANDBOON.txt
```

7. The output is made available in the output directory, which can be read using the following commands:

```
hadoop dfs -rmr /output
hadoop dfs -cat /output/part-00000
```

You should see an output that shows the occurrence of the word "Amily" in the provided text.

Summary

So far, we have seen how Spring integrates with Apache Hadoop and provides a Map and Reduce process to search and count data. We have also discussed the integration of Python with Apache Hadoop. We have demonstrated how we can configure Hadoop jobs in Spring Framework, and have also seen HDFS configurations.

Hadoop is vast concept. For further information, refer to `http://docs.spring.io/spring-hadoop/docs/current/reference/html/` and `https://github.com/spring-projects/spring-hadoop-samples`.

We have demonstrated how we can install a Hadoop instance on Unix machines. In the next chapter, we shall see how to use Spring Dynamic Modules with OSGI.

8
Spring with OSGI

OSGI is a short form **Open Service Gateway Intiative**. It's a specification consisting of a modular system and service platform for the dynamic deployment of modules. As per the specification, the application can be broken down into modules and deployed independently. When we think of developing an OSGI application, it means that we need to use the OSGI API available to develop the application. The second step would be to deploy it in the OSGI container. So, while developing applications in OSGI, we can break the application into modules and independently deploy them, and then uninstall; we can also have various versions of the application running in parallel. In this chapter, we shall see how Spring supports the OSGI bundled development and the deployment of its application. We shall first start with OSGI and then gradually move over to Springs's support.

OSGI containers

OSGI containers must implement a set of services, and a contract is established between the OSGI container and application. All the following mentioned OSGI containers are open source:

- **KnoplerFish**: The Knopler framework can be easily installed and it is easier to bundle and deploy modules in the container. The Bundle applications need a `.manifest` file and build `.xml` file. It's mandatory to have the framework. JAR file should be available in the Java build path. The Bundle that needs to be deployed in the KnoplerFish container will have a class that implements the `BundleActivator` interface. The interface comes with `start()` and `stop()` methods that needs to be implemented. Usually a thread class is also created, and the thread is started in the `BundleActivator` interface implementation class's start method, and stopped in the stop method. You can also create an OSGI service by creating an interface and implementation class. The service can be registered in the `BundleActivator` class' `start()` method. That is the class that implements the `BundleActivator` interface. There are `ServiceListeners` and `ServiceTrackers` to monitor the OSGI services in the container.

- **Equinox**: This is an implementation of the core OSGI framework. It provides various optional OSGI services. Eclipse offers an OSGI plugin to develop OSGI bundled applications. Eclipse offers a JAR file which can be easily installed, using Eclipse's install start, stop command.

- **Apache Felix**: Apache Felix is another OSGI container from Apache projects. Felix has various subprojects which can be plugged in. It also supports a similar way of application development, as explained under Knoplerfish. It also has a Maven bundle plugin.

OSGI usage

Let us list the key usages of OSGI framework:

- The framework offers modularity of the application

- The framework implements bundle based architecture

- Multiple versions of the same project can be made to run in parallel

- We can also integrate the OSGI applications and OSGI bundles into web containers

- There are also a few challenges of making it work with the front end of web applications

- There are lot of frameworks, at least four frameworks, available for developing POJO applications on top of OSGI specification

- The size of the OSGI bundle is relatively small

Spring integration with OSGI

Spring provides complete support for OSGI development. The OSGI module support was called Spring OSGI, and it is presently updated with a new set of libraries and versions called Spring Dynamic Modules. A Spring Dynamic Module allows you to write Spring applications on top of an OSGI framework. One of its challenges is to make simple POJOs to seamlessly work with the OSGI framework and to integrate Spring Beans as an OSGI service. Spring Beans can be exported as an OSGI services

```
<bean name="authorService"
 class="com.packt.osgi.authorservice.impl.AuthorServiceImpl"/>
<osgi:service id="auhtorServiceOsgi"
 ref="authorService"
 interface="com.packt.osgi.authorservice.AuthorService"/>
```

The Spring dynamic programming model provides API programming and Spring Beans are visible across bundles. The Spring dynamic model provides us with the dependency injection across bundles, and with all the support for OSGI from the Spring dynamic service, handling has become easier.

Every bundle will ideally have a separate application context. The application context is created and destroyed with the start and stop of the bundle. These context files are present under META-INF.

A typical bundle structure is depicted in the following image:

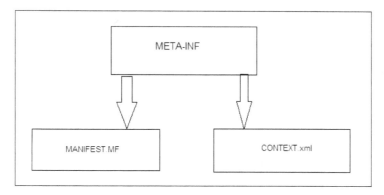

The following image depicts how OSGI modules can be part of web applications and how each bundle interacts with the OSGI framework. You can also see that there are many web applications on the web container which access the application bundles as services using the OSGI framework.

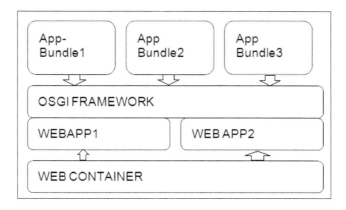

Spring Dynamic Modules and OSGI

Let us look at how Spring Dynamic Modules work. Spring comes with its OSGI integration framework, which has a class called `extender`. This checks for all existing bundles and marks the bundles which are powered by Spring. The extender marks a bundle as Spring compatible only if it has Spring context manifest header or an XML file in `META-INF/spring` folder. All the preceding steps are triggered on start up and the extender package is available on `org.springframeork.osgi.bundle.extender`. Now, we have to know why Spring dynamic modules mark the Spring powered bundles. The bundles with Spring configuration files are further converted to an application-context object. The extender not only marks the Spring powered bundles to create an application-context object, but also checks if the bundle is importing any OSGI services. If any such bundle is found exporting an external service, then such beans are moved to the OSGI shared service registry. The extender registers bundles that export OSGI services with a listener and events. OSGI is also tested with Equinox, Felix and KnoplerFish.

The following are the steps to be followed when setting up Spring DM in Eclipse IDE:

1. Download Spring DM; look out for the latest Spring OSGI DM.

2. Extract the ZIP file into the local directory; call it `c:\OSGI-SPRING`.

3. Create a new workspace while starting Eclipse.

4. Import all the necessary JAR files and all the Spring DM JAR files by choosing the **Plugin Development** option, or the **Install plug-in** option in Java. Ensure that you have all the following mentioned plugins in the Eclipse environment.

   ° `org.springframeork.osgi.bundle.core`

   ° `org.springframeork.osgi.bundle.extender`

   ° `org.springframeork.osgi.bundle.io`

   ° `org.springframeork.bundle.spring.aop`

   ° `org.springframeork.bundle.spring.beans`

   ° `org.springframeork.bundle.spring.context`

   ° `org.springframeork.bundle.spring.core`

   ° `org.springframeork.bundle.spring.jdbc`

   ° `org.springframeork.bundle.spring.tx`

   ° `org.springframeork.osgi.aopalliance.osgi`

Simple applications with OSGI

In this section, let us first develop a simple OSGI application. We shall create two bundles—one which provides the service to print a string and another bundle which would consume the service at an equal interval of time.

1. Following is the first bundle:

```
package com.packt.osgi.provider.able;

public interface MySimpleOSGIService {
  void mysimplemethod();
}
package com.packt.osgi.provider.impl;

import com.bw.osgi.provider.able.MySimpleOSGIService;

public class MySimpleOSGIServiceImpl implements
  MySimpleOSGIService {
  @Override
  void mysimplemethod(){
    System.out.println("this my simple method which is
      the implementation class");
  }
}
```

2. Exporting the service using activator:

```
package com.packt.osgi.provider;
import org.osgi.framework.BundleActivator;
import org.osgi.framework.BundleContext;
import org.osgi.framework.ServiceRegistration;
import com.bw.osgi.provider.able.MySimpleOSGIService;
import com.bw.osgi.provider.impl.MySimpleOSGIServiceImpl;

public class MyProviderActivator implements BundleActivator
  {
  private ServiceRegistration registration;

  @Override
  public void start(BundleContext bundleContext)
    throws Exception {
    registration = bundleContext.registerService(
      MySimpleOSGIService.class.getName(),
      new MySimpleOSGIServiceImpl(),
      null);
  }
```

```
@Override
public void stop(BundleContext bundleContext)
  throws Exception {
  registration.unregister();
}
}
```

3. Now, we have the first bundle ready and we shall use Maven to build it. We also need the Maven bundle plugin to build the XML file.

```xml
?xml version="1.0" encoding="UTF-8"?>

<project xmlns="http://maven.apache.org/POM/4.0.0"
  xmlns:xsi="http://www.w3.org/2001/XMLSchema-instance"
  xsi:schemaLocation="http://maven.apache.org/POM/4.0.0
  http://maven.apache.org/xsd/maven-4.0.0.xsd">
  <modelVersion>4.0.0</modelVersion>

  <groupId>OSGiDmMySimpleProvider</groupId>
  <artifactId>OSGiDmMySimpleProvider</artifactId>
  <version>1.0</version>

  <dependencies>
    <dependency>
    <groupId>org.apache.felix</groupId>
    <artifactId>org.osgi.core</artifactId>
    <version>1.4.0</version>
    </dependency>
  </dependencies>

  <build>
    <plugins>
      <plugin>
      <groupId>org.apache.maven.plugins</groupId>
      <artifactId>maven-compiler-plugin</artifactId>
      <version>2.0.2</version>
      <configuration>
        <source>1.6</source>
        <target>1.6</target>
      </configuration>
      </plugin>

      <plugin>
        <groupId>org.apache.felix</groupId>
        <artifactId>maven-bundle-plugin</artifactId>
        <extensions>true</extensions>
        <configuration>
          <instructions>
```

```
        <Bundle-SymbolicName>OSGiDmMySimpleProvider</
          Bundle-SymbolicName>
        <Export-Package>com.packt.osgi.provider.able</
          Export-Package>
        <Bundle-Activator>com.packt.osgi.provider
          .MyProviderActivator</Bundle-Activator>
        <Bundle-Vendor>PACKT</Bundle-Vendor>
        </instructions>
        </configuration>
      </plugin>
    </plugins>
  </build>
</project>
```

4. To build it, a simple `mvn install` command is sufficient.

5. Next, let us try to consume the service:

```
package com.packt.osgi.consumer;
import javax.swing.Timer;
import java.awt.event.ActionEvent;
import java.awt.event.ActionListener;
import com.packt.osgi.provider.able.MySimpleOSGIService;
public class MySimpleOSGIConsumer implements
  ActionListener {
  private final MySimpleOSGIService service;
  private final Timer timer;
  public MySimpleOSGIConsumer(MySimpleOSGIService
    service) {
    super();
    this.service = service;
    timer = new Timer(1000, this);
  }

  public void startTimer(){
    timer.start();
  }

  public void stopTimer() {
    timer.stop();
  }

  @Override
  public void actionPerformed(ActionEvent e) {
    service.mysimplemethod();
  }
}
```

6. Now, we must again create an activator for the consumer:

```
package com.packt.osgi.consumer;

import org.osgi.framework.BundleActivator;
import org.osgi.framework.BundleContext;
import org.osgi.framework.ServiceReference;
import com.packt.osgi.provider.able.MySimpleOSGIService;

public class MySimpleOSGIActivator implements
  BundleActivator {
  private MySimpleOSGIConsumer consumer;

  @Override
  public void start(BundleContext bundleContext)
    throws Exception {
    ServiceReference reference = bundleContext
      .getServiceReference(
      MySimpleOSGIService.class.getName());

    consumer = new MySimpleOSGIConsumer((
      MySimpleOSGIService)
      bundleContext.getService(reference));
    consumer.startTimer();
  }

  @Override
  public void stop(BundleContext bundleContext)
    throws Exception {
    consumer.stopTimer();
  }
}
```

Integrating Spring Dynamic Modules with OSGI

In this section, let us demonstrate how we can integrate Spring Dynamic Modules to work with an OSGI application. Spring Dynamic Modules (Spring DM) makes the development of OSGI-based applications a lot easier. We can easily inject the services like any other Spring beans.

We shall look at the following dependencies required to integrate Spring Dynamic Modules:

- OSGI services
- The `BundleActivator` class
- The `Context.xml` file configuration to inject in the service

The following is the list of dependencies that needs to be made available in the application classpath:

- `com.springsource.net.sf.cglib-2.1.3.jar`
- `com.springsource.org.aopalliance-1.0.0.jar`
- `log4j.osgi-1.2.15-SNAPSHOT.jar`
- `com.springsource.slf4j.api-1.5.0.jar`
- `com.springsource.slf4j.log4j-1.5.0.jar`
- `com.springsource.slf4j.org.apache.commons.logging-1.5.0.jar`
- `org.springframework.aop-3.x.jar`
- `org.springframework.beans-3.x.jar`
- `org.springframework.context-3.x.jar`
- `org.springframework.core-3.x.jar`
- `spring-osgi-core-1.2.1.jar`
- `spring-osgi-extender-1.2.1.jar`
- `spring-osgi-io-1.2.1.jar`

So, let us create a simple `HelloWorldService` interface class:

```
package com.packt.osgi.provider.able;
public interface HelloWorldService {
  void hello();
}
```

Next, we shall implement the `service` class. This is class does a simple

```
package com.packt.osgi.provider.impl;
import com.packt.osgi.provider.able.HelloWorldService;
public class HelloWorldServiceImpl implements HelloWorldService {
  @Override
  public void hello(){
    System.out.println("Hello World !");
  }
}
```

We shall write an activator class which needs to activate the service `BundleActivator`. The `ProviderActivator` class that we need to call is `HelloWorldService`. We are actually registering the service. However, using the Spring DM integration makes things simple for us with a configuration. We don't need this integration class.

```
package com.packt.osgi.provider;
import org.osgi.framework.BundleActivator;
import org.osgi.framework.BundleContext;
import org.osgi.framework.ServiceRegistration;
import com. packt.osgi.provider.able.HelloWorldService;
import com. packt.osgi.provider.impl.HelloWorldServiceImpl;

public class ProviderActivator implements BundleActivator {
  private ServiceRegistration registration;

    @Override
    public void start(BundleContext bundleContext)
      throws Exception {
      registration = bundleContext.registerService(
                  HelloWorldService.class.getName(),
                  new HelloWorldServiceImpl(),null);
    }

    @Override
    public void stop(BundleContext bundleContext) throws Exception {
      registration.unregister();
    }
}
```

We just have to create a `provider-context.xml` file in the folder `META-INF/spring`. This is a simple context in XML file, but we use a new namespace to register the service - `http://www.springframework.org/schema/osgi`. So, let us start:

```
<?xml version="1.0" encoding="UTF-8"?>
<beans xmlns="http://www.springframework.org/schema/beans"
  xmlns:xsi="http://www.w3.org/2001/XMLSchema-instance"
  xmlns:osgi="http://www.springframework.org/schema/osgi"
  xmlns:context="http://www.springframework.org/schema/context"
  xsi:schemaLocation="
    http://www.springframework.org/schema/beans
    http://www.springframework.org/schema/beans/
      spring-beans-3.0.xsd
    http://www.springframework.org/schema/osgi
    http://www.springframework.org/schema/osgi/spring-osgi.xsd">
    <bean id="helloWorldService" class="com.packt.osgi.provider
      .impl.HelloWorldServiceImpl"/>
    <osgi:service ref="helloWorldService"
      interface="com.packt.osgi.provider.able.HelloWorldService"/>
</beans>
```

The only thing specific to OSGI is the osgi:service declaration. This line indicates that we need to register the HelloWorldService as an OSGI service, using the interface HelloWorldService as the name of the service.

If you put the context file in the META-INF/spring folder, it will be automatically detected by the Spring Extender and an application context will be created.

1. We can now go to the consumer bundle. In the first phase, we created that consumer:

```java
package com.packt.osgi.consumer;
import javax.swing.Timer;
import java.awt.event.ActionEvent;
import java.awt.event.ActionListener;
import com.bw.osgi.provider.able.HelloWorldService;
public class HelloWorldConsumer implements ActionListener {
  private final HelloWorldService service;
  private final Timer timer;
  public HelloWorldConsumer(HelloWorldService service) {
    super();
    this.service = service;
    timer = new Timer(1000, this);
  }
  public void startTimer(){
    timer.start();
  }
  public void stopTimer() {
    timer.stop();
  }
  @Override
  public void actionPerformed(ActionEvent e) {
    service.hello();
  }
}
```

2. Next, let us write the BundleActivator class:

```java
package com.packt.osgi.consumer;
import org.osgi.framework.BundleActivator;
import org.osgi.framework.BundleContext;
import org.osgi.framework.ServiceReference;
import com. packt.osgi.provider.able.HelloWorldService;
public class HelloWorldActivator implements
BundleActivator {
  private HelloWorldConsumer consumer;
  @Override
```

```
public void start(BundleContext bundleContext)
  throws Exception {
  ServiceReference reference =
    bundleContext.getServiceReference(
    HelloWorldService.class.getName());
  consumer = new HelloWorldConsumer((HelloWorldService)
    bundleContext.getService(reference));
  consumer.startTimer();
}
@Override
public void stop(BundleContext bundleContext)
  throws Exception {
  consumer.stopTimer();
}
}
```

The injection is not necessary anymore. We can keep the start of the timer here, but, once again, we can use the features of the framework to start and stop the timer.

3. So, let us delete the activator and create an application context to create the consumer and start it automatically, and put it in the META-INF/spring folder:

```
<?xml version="1.0" encoding="UTF-8"?>
<beans xmlns="http://www.springframework.org/schema/beans"
  xmlns:xsi="http://www.w3.org/2001/XMLSchema-instance"
  xmlns:osgi="http://www.springframework.org/schema/osgi"
  xmlns:context="http://www.springframework.org/
    schema/context"
  xsi:schemaLocation="
    http://www.springframework.org/schema/beans
    http://www.springframework.org/schema/beans/
      spring-beans-3.0.xsd
    http://www.springframework.org/schema/osgi
    http://www.springframework.org/schema/osgi/
      spring-osgi.xsd">

  <bean id="consumer" class="com.packt.osgi.consumer
    .HelloWorldConsumer" init-method="startTimer"
    destroy-method="stopTimer" lazy-init="false" >
    <constructor-arg ref="eventService"/>
  </bean>

  <osgi:reference id="eventService" interface="com.packt
    .osgi.provider.able.HelloWorldService"/>
</beans>
```

We used the `init` method and `destroy` method attributes to start and stop the time with the framework, and we use the `constructor-arg` to inject the reference in to the service. The reference to the service is obtained using the `osgi:reference` field and using the interface as a key to the service.

That's all we have to do with this bundle. A lot more simple than the first version isn't it? And more than the simplification, you can see that the sources aren't depending on either OSGI or Spring Framework; this is plain Java and is a great advantage.

The Maven POM files are the same as in the first phase, except that we can cut the dependency to OSGI.

The provider:

```
<?xml version="1.0" encoding="UTF-8"?>

<project xmlns="http://maven.apache.org/POM/4.0.0"
  xmlns:xsi="http://www.w3.org/2001/XMLSchema-instance"
  xsi:schemaLocation="http://maven.apache.org/POM/4.0.0
    http://maven.apache.org/xsd/maven-4.0.0.xsd">
  <modelVersion>4.0.0</modelVersion>
  <groupId>OSGiDmHelloWorldProvider</groupId>
  <artifactId>OSGiDmHelloWorldProvider</artifactId>
  <version>1.0</version>
  <packaging>bundle</packaging>

  <build>
    <plugins>
      <plugin>
        <groupId>org.apache.maven.plugins</groupId>
        <artifactId>maven-compiler-plugin</artifactId>
        <version>2.0.2</version>
        <configuration>
          <source>1.6</source>
          <target>1.6</target>
        </configuration>
      </plugin>

      <plugin>
        <groupId>org.apache.felix</groupId>
        <artifactId>maven-bundle-plugin</artifactId>
        <extensions>true</extensions>
        <configuration>
          <instructions>
            <Bundle-SymbolicName>OSGiDmHelloWorldProvider</Bundle-
              SymbolicName>
```

```
        <Export-Package>com.bw.osgi.provider.able</Export-
            Package>
        <Bundle-Vendor>Baptiste Wicht</Bundle-Vendor>
      </instructions>
    </configuration>
  </plugin>
 </plugins>
 </build>
</project>
```

The consumer:

```
<?xml version="1.0" encoding="UTF-8"?>

<project xmlns="http://maven.apache.org/POM/4.0.0"
  xmlns:xsi="http://www.w3.org/2001/XMLSchema-instance"
  xsi:schemaLocation="http://maven.apache.org/POM/4.0.0
    http://maven.apache.org/xsd/maven-4.0.0.xsd">
  <modelVersion>4.0.0</modelVersion>
  <groupId>OSGiDmHelloWorldConsumer</groupId>
  <artifactId>OSGiDmHelloWorldConsumer</artifactId>
  <version>1.0</version>
  <packaging>bundle</packaging>

  <dependencies>
    <dependency>
      <groupId>OSGiDmHelloWorldProvider</groupId>
      <artifactId>OSGiDmHelloWorldProvider</artifactId>
      <version>1.0</version>
    </dependency>
  </dependencies>

  <build>
    <plugins>
      <plugin>
        <groupId>org.apache.maven.plugins</groupId>
        <artifactId>maven-compiler-plugin</artifactId>
        <version>2.0.2</version>
        <configuration>
          <source>1.6</source>
          <target>1.6</target>
        </configuration>
      </plugin>

      <plugin>
        <groupId>org.apache.felix</groupId>
        <artifactId>maven-bundle-plugin</artifactId>
```

```
      <extensions>true</extensions>
      <configuration>
        <instructions>
          <Bundle-SymbolicName>OSGiDmHelloWorldConsumer</Bundle-
            SymbolicName>
          <Bundle-Vendor>Baptiste Wicht</Bundle-Vendor>
        </instructions>
      </configuration>
    </plugin>
  </plugins>
</build>
</project>
```

And we can build the two bundles using the Maven install. So, let us test our stuff in Felix:

```
Welcome to Apache Felix Gogo
g! install file:../com.springsource.slf4j.org
  .apache.commons.logging-1.5.0.jar
Bundle ID: 5
g! install file:../com.springsource
  .slf4j.log4j-1.5.0.jar
Bundle ID: 6
g! install file:../com.springsource
  .slf4j.api-1.5.0.jar
Bundle ID: 7
g! install file:../log4j.osgi-1.2.15-SNAPSHOT.jar
Bundle ID: 8
g! install file:../com.springsource.net.sf.cglib-2.1.3.jar
Bundle ID: 9
g! install file:../com.springsource.org.aopalliance-1.0.0.jar
Bundle ID: 10
g! install file:../org.springframework.core-2.5.6.SEC01.jar
Bundle ID: 11
g! install file:../org.springframework.context-2.5.6.SEC01.jar
Bundle ID: 12
g! install file:../org.springframework.beans-2.5.6.SEC01.jar
Bundle ID: 13
g! install file:../org.springframework.aop-2.5.6.SEC01.jar
Bundle ID: 14
g! install file:../spring-osgi-extender-1.2.1.jar
Bundle ID: 15
g! install file:../spring-osgi-core-1.2.1.jar
Bundle ID: 16
g! install file:../spring-osgi-io-1.2.1.jar
Bundle ID: 17
```

```
g! start 5 7 8 9 10 11 12 13 14 15 16 17
log4j:WARN No appenders could be found for logger
    (org.springframework.osgi.extender.internal.activator
    .ContextLoaderListener).
log4j:WARN Please initialize the log4j system properly.
g! install file:../OSGiDmHelloWorldProvider-1.0.jar
Bundle ID: 18
g! install file:../OSGiDmHelloWorldConsumer-1.0.jar
Bundle ID: 19
g! start 18
g! start 19
g! Hello World !
Hello World !
Hello World !
Hello World !
Hello World !
Hello World !
Hello World !
Hello World !
stop 19
g!
```

In conclusion, Spring DM really makes the development with OSGI easier. With Spring DM, you can also start bundles. It also allows you to make web bundles and to use the services of the OSGI compendium easily.

Summary

In this chapter, we have developed a simple OSGI application. We also demonstrated how Spring DM supports the OSGI development, reduces the creation of files, and makes things easier with configuration.

Bootstrap your Application with Spring Boot

9

In this chapter, we shall see another Spring package—Spring Boot, which allows users to quickly get started with the Spring Framework. Applications that make use of **Spring Boot Abstraction Layer** are called **Spring Boot Applications**. Spring has come up with a Spring intializer web application, which has a web interface, in which we can select the kind of application we would need to get started.

If you have ever run with different application servers, new developers typically have to configure many settings just to get up and run. The Spring Boot approach allows developers to get up and run right out of the box, allowing them to focus on developing code and not configuring application servers.

Spring has also come up with a command line interface to help us quickly start with Spring development. In this chapter, let's dive into Spring Boot and see what it offers.

Setting up Spring Boot

The Spring Boot application can be set up in the following mentioned ways:

- Use `http://start.spring.io/`
  - ° Use Maven to download the dependency from repository
  - ° Use Gradle
- Download source code from Spring guide repo
- Download Spring STS and use the starter project

Spring Gradle MVC application

Gradle is similar to Maven; it helps in building the applications. We need to provide all the dependency information in the `build.gradle` file. Spring boot also has a Gradle plugin. The Gradle plugin helps in placing all the dependencies JAR files on the classpath and finally builds into a single runnable JAR file. The runnable JAR file will have an `application.java` file; this class will have a `public static void main()` method. This class will be flagged as a runnable class.

A sample Gradle file is shown here:

```
buildscript {
  repositories {
    maven { url "http://repo.spring.io/libs-milestone" }
    mavenLocal()
  }
  dependencies {
    classpath("org.springframework
      .boot:spring-boot-gradle-plugin:1.1.3.RELEASE")
  }
}

apply plugin: 'java'
apply plugin: 'war'
apply plugin: 'spring-boot'
jar {
  baseName = PacktSpringBootMVCDemo '
  version =  '1.0'
}
repositories {
  mavenCentral()
  maven { url "http://repo.spring.io/libs-milestone" }
}

configurations {
  providedRuntime
}
dependencies {
  compile ("org.springframework.boot:spring-boot-starter-web")
  providedRuntime("org.apache.tomcat.embed:tomcat-embed-jasper")

}
task wrapper(type: Wrapper) {
  gradleVersion = '2.0'
}
```

If you are using an Eclipse as IDE, STS has come up with Gradle pulgins for Eclipse (`http://gradle.org/docs/current/userguide/eclipse_plugin.html`) which can be downloaded and installed from `https://www.gradle.org/tooling`. Gradle also comes with a similar set up to clean and build the application.

The next step is to define the application context root in the properties file. A Gradle project structure is similar to a Maven project structure. Place the `application.properties` file in the `resources` folder. We need to provide the server context path and server context port. Following is the sample properties file:

```
server.contextPath=/PacktSpringBootMVCDemo
server.port=8080
```

1. Let us create a simple package: `com.packt.controller`
2. Create a simple Spring controller class in the package and use the @ Controller annotations.
3. Let us create a method with `@Request` mapping annotations. The `@RequestMapping` annotations maps send a request to a JSP page. In this method, we are mapping the request to the methods. The methods return a string variable or a model view object.

```
package com.packt.controller;
import org.springframework.stereotype.Controller;
import org.springframework.web.bind
  .annotation.RequestMapping;
import org.springframework.web.bind
  .annotation.RequestMethod;
import org.springframework.web
  .servlet.ModelAndView;
@Controller
public class PacktController{
  @RequestMapping(value = "/saygoodmorning  method =
    RequestMethod.GET)
  public ModelAndView getGoodmorning() {
    return new ModelAndView("greet").addObject("greet",
      "goodmorning");
  }
  @RequestMapping(value = "/saygoodafternoon  method =
    RequestMethod.GET)
  public ModelAndView getGoodmorning() {
    return new ModelAndView("greet").addObject("greet ",
      "goodafternoon");
  }
  @RequestMapping(value = "/saygoodnight  method =
    RequestMethod.GET)
```

```
  public ModelAndView getGoodmorning() {
    return new ModelAndView("greet").addObject("greet ",
      "goodnight");
  }
}
```

4. Create a Spring MVC configuration file as follows using @Configuration
    and @WebMVC annotation. We have also configured the internal view
    resolver for the application file.

```
package com.packt.config;
import org.springframework.context.annotation.Bean;
import org.springframework.context.annotation
  .Configuration;
import org.springframework.web.servlet.config
  .annotation.DefaultServletHandlerConfigurer;
import org.springframework.web.servlet
  .config.annotation.EnableWebMvc;
import org.springframework.web.servlet
  .config.annotation.WebMvcConfigurerAdapter;
import org.springframework.web.servlet.view
  .InternalResourceViewResolver;

@Configuration
@EnableWebMvc
public class ApplicationConfigurerAdapter extends
  WebMvcConfigurerAdapter{
  @Override
  public void configureDefaultServletHandling(
    DefaultServletHandlerConfigurer configurer) {
    configurer.enable();
  }

  @Bean
  public InternalResourceViewResolver viewResolver() {
    InternalResourceViewResolver resolver = new
      InternalResourceViewResolver();
    resolver.setPrefix("WEB-INF/jsp/");
    resolver.setSuffix(".jsp");
    return resolver;
  }

}
```

Let us create a simple JSP page named `greet.jsp`:

```
<html>
  <head><title>Hello world Example</title></head>
  <body>
    <h1>Hello ${name}, How are you?</h1>
  </body>
</html>
```

Next create a simple application class with annotations `@EnableAutoConfiguration` and `@ComponentScan` annotations. The `@ComponenetScan` annotation indicates that the Spring Framework core should search for all of the classes under the package. The `@EnableAutoConfiguration` annotation is used instead of configuring dispatcher servlet in `web.xml` file.

Following is the sample file:

```
import org.springframework.boot.SpringApplication;
import org.springframework.boot.autoconfigure
  .EnableAutoConfiguration;
import org.springframework.context.annotation.ComponentScan;
import org.springframework.context.annotation.Configuration;

@Configuration
@EnableAutoConfiguration
@ComponentScan
public class Application {
  public static void main(String[] args) {
    SpringApplication.run(Application.class, args);
  }

}
```

Access the following URLs:

- `http://localhost:8080/PacktSpringBootMVCDemo/saygoodmorning`
- `http://localhost:8080/PacktSpringBootMVCDemo/saygoodafternoon`
- `http://localhost:8080/PacktSpringBootMVCDemo/saygoodnight`

Hot swapping with Spring Boot

Hot swapping or hot deployment means that you can make changes to the class file or any file in the application, and see the changes reflected in the running application immediately. We may need to reload the application on the web browser or just refresh the page. Spring Loaded is a dependency JAR file that supports hot deployment. Let us look at hot swapping in the Spring Boot application.

Let's create a simple Spring MVC application with the Thymeleaf template engine:

1. First, we need to download the Spring Loaded JAR from GitHub repositories. Check the following URL for the latest version:

    `https://github.com/spring-projects/spring-loaded.`

2. Ensure that you have all the mentioned dependencies in a `pom.xml` file or explicitly add them to your project:

    ```xml
    <dependency>
        <groupId>org.apache.tomcat.embed</groupId>
        <artifactId>tomcat-embed-jasper</artifactId>
        <scope>provided</scope>
    </dependency>
    <dependency>
        <groupId>javax.servlet</groupId>
        <artifactId>jstl</artifactId>
    </dependency>
    <dependency>
        <groupId>org.springframework.boot</groupId>
        <artifactId>spring-boot-starter-actuator</artifactId>
    </dependency>
    ```

3. The next step is to add the downloaded Spring loaded JAR to the Eclipse or Eclipse STS environment. Follow the given steps to add Spring loaded JAR as a run time configuration:

    1. Create a `PacktSpringBootThymeLeafExample` project in Eclipse.
    2. Right Click on your project.
    3. Search for **Run As**.
    4. Click on **Run Configuration**.
    5. Click on Java Application.
    6. Click on Project Name.
    7. Select **Arguments** in the **VM Argument** section; add the following command:

        ```
        - javaagent:/<provide the path to the jar>/springloaded-
        1.2.0.RELEASE.jar -noverify
        ```

    8. Click on **Apply** and **Run**.

We also need to configure the `application.properties` file, so that any modifications done to **Thymeleaf** pages don't need a server restart:

```
spring.thymeleaf.cache: false.
```

We can use the Spring STS starter project and create a Spring Boot class. Spring Eclipse STS will give us the following two classes:

- `Application.java`
- `ApplicationTest.java`

The `Application.java` is the main class for Spring Boot, as it has the public static void main method in it. In this method, `ApplicationContext` is initialized in it using `SpringApplication` class. The `SpringApplication` class has some of the following annotations:

- `@ConditionalOnClass`
- `@ConditionalOnMissingBean`

These are executed to check the list of beans available on the classpath. If you would like to see the beans placed under the classpath by the framework, make a slight modification to the generated `Application.java` file as follows:

```java
@ComponentScan
@EnableAutoConfiguration
public class Application {
  public static void main(String[] args) {
    ApplicationContext ctx =
      SpringApplication.run(Application.class, args);
    System.out.println("--------------------------LIST BEANS
      PROVIDED BY SPRING BOOT_---------------------");
    String[] beanNames = ctx.getBeanDefinitionNames();
    Arrays.sort(beanNames);
    for (String beanName : beanNames) {
      System.out.println(beanName);
    }

  }
}
```

Output:

```
--------------------------LIST BEANS PROVIDED BY SPRING BOOT_-------
--------------
JSPController
application
applicationContextIdFilter
auditEventRepository
auditListener
autoConfigurationAuditEndpoint
```

```
basicErrorController
beanNameHandlerMapping
beanNameViewResolver
....
mappingJackson2HttpMessageConverter
messageConverters
messageSource
tomcatEmbeddedServletContainerFactory
traceEndpoint
traceRepository
viewControllerHandlerMapping
viewResolver
webRequestLoggingFilter
```

The SpringApplication class is found in the package org.springframework.
boot.SpringApplication.

A simple illustration of SpringApplication class is shown here, where the static run
method of the SpringApplication class is shown:

```
@Configuration
@EnableAutoConfiguration
public class MyPacktApplication {

  // ... Bean definitions

  public static void main(String[] args) throws Exception {
    SpringApplication.run(MyPacktApplication.class, args);
  }
```

Look at another illustration here, where a SpringApplication class is first
initialized and then the .run method is called:

```
@Configuration
@EnableAutoConfiguration
public class MyPacktApplication {
  // ... Bean definitions
  public static void main(String[] args) throws Exception {
    SpringApplication app = new
      SpringApplication(MyPacktApplication.class);
    // ... customize app settings here
    app.run(args)
  }
}
```

The following are the constructors available for the `SpringApplication` class:

- `SpringApplication(Object... sources)`
- `SpringApplication(ResourceLoader resourceLoader, Object... sources)`

1. Let us create a Simple Controller class with the `@RestController` annotation that is available in Spring's latest version 4.x.

```
@RestController
public class MyPacktController {

  @RequestMapping("/")
  public String index() {
    return "Greetings ";
  }

  @RequestMapping("/greetjsontest")
  public @ResponseBody Map<String, String>
    callSomething () {

    Map<String, String> map = new HashMap<String,
      String>();
    map.put("afternoon", " Good afternoon");
    map.put("morning", " Good Morning");
    map.put("night", " Good Night");
    return map;
  }
}
```

2. Next, we shall configure Spring Boot to process JSP pages; by default Spring Boot doesn't configure the JSP, so we shall create a JSP controller as shown in the following code snippet:

```
@Controller
public class SpringBootJSPController {
  @RequestMapping("/calljsp")
  public String test(ModelAndView modelAndView) {

    return "myjsp";
  }
}
```

3. Configure the properties files as follows:

```
spring.view.prefix: /WEB-INF/jsp/
spring.view.suffix: .jsp
```

4. Let us create a JSP file `myjsp`:

```jsp
<%@ page language="java" contentType="text/html;
  charset=UTF-8" pageEncoding="UTF-8"%>
<!DOCTYPE html PUBLIC "-//W3C//DTD HTML 4.01
  Transitional//EN" "http://www.w3.org/TR/html4/loose.dtd">
<html>
  <head>
    <meta http-equiv="Content-Type" content="text/html;
      charset=UTF-8">
    <title>Insert title here</title>
  </head>
  <body>
    <h1>Hello world</h1>
  </body>
</html>
```

Following is the implementation class of `EmbededServletContainerCustomizer`, which actually embeds the web server container in the application. It invokes the server and deploys the application into it.

```java
@ComponentScan
@EnableAutoConfiguration

public class Application implements
  EmbeddedServletContainerCustomizer {
  @Value("${someproperty:webapp/whereever }")
  private String documentRoot;
  @Override
  public void customize(
    ConfigurableEmbeddedServletContainerFactory factory) {
    factory.setDocumentRoot(new File(documentRoot));
  }
}
```

Integrating Spring Boot with Spring Security

In this section, we shall see how we can integrate Spring boot with Spring security using annotations. We can easily integrate Spring security with Spring boot.

1. Let us first embed a tomcat server in Spring boot to accept a request; following is the code we need to create a key store file to make it more secure:

```java
@Bean
EmbeddedServletContainerCustomizer containerCustomizer (
  @Value("${https.port}") final int port,
  @Value("${keystore.file}") Resource keystoreFile,
```

```java
@Value("${keystore.alias}") final String alias,
@Value("${keystore.password}") final String keystorePass,
@Value("${keystore.type}") final String keystoreType)
  throws Exception {
  final String absoluteKeystoreFile =
    keystoreFile.getFile().getAbsolutePath();
  return new EmbeddedServletContainerCustomizer() {
    public void
      customize(ConfigurableEmbeddedServletContainer
      container) {
      TomcatEmbeddedServletContainerFactory tomcat =
        (TomcatEmbeddedServletContainerFactory)
        container;
      tomcat.addConnectorCustomizers(new
        TomcatConnectorCustomizer() {
        public void customize(Connector connector) {
          connector.setPort(port);
          connector.setSecure(true);
          connector.setScheme("https");
          Http11NioProtocol proto = (Http11NioProtocol)
            connector.getProtocolHandler();
          proto.setSSLEnabled(true);
          proto.setKeystoreFile(absoluteKeystoreFile);
          proto.setKeyAlias(alias);
          proto.setKeystorePass(keystorePass);
          proto.setKeystoreType(keystoreType);
        }
      });
    }
  };
}
```

2. Let us also create a Simple Security Configuration file in java using @
   Configuration and @EnableWebMVCSecurity annotations. The security
   configuration file extends WebSecurityConfigurerAdapter.

```java
@Configuration
@EnableWebMvcSecurity
public class WebSecurityConfig extends
WebSecurityConfigurerAdapter {

  @Value("${ldap.domain}")
  private String DOMAIN;

  @Value("${ldap.url}")
  private String URL;
```

```
@Value("${http.port}")
private int httpPort;

@Value("${https.port}")
private int httpsPort;

@Override
protected void configure(HttpSecurity http)
  throws Exception {
  /*
  * Set up your spring security config here. For
    example...
  */
  http.authorizeRequests().anyRequest().authenticated()
    .and().formLogin().loginUrl("/login").permitAll();
    /*
    * Use HTTPs for ALL requests
    */
    http.requiresChannel().anyRequest().requiresSecure();
    http.portMapper().http(httpPort).mapsTo(httpsPort);
}

@Override
protected void configure(AuthenticationManagerBuilder
  authManagerBuilder) throws Exception {
authManagerBuilder.authenticationProvider(
  activeDirectoryLdapAuthenticationProvider())
  .userDetailsService(userDetailsService());
}

@Bean
public AuthenticationManager authenticationManager() {
  return new ProviderManager(
  Arrays.asList(
  activeDirectoryLdapAuthenticationProvider()));
}
@Bean
public AuthenticationProvider
  activeDirectoryLdapAuthenticationProvider() {
  ActiveDirectoryLdapAuthenticationProvider provider =
    new ActiveDirectoryLdapAuthenticationProvider(
    DOMAIN, URL);
    provider.setConvertSubErrorCodesToExceptions(true);
    provider
      .setUseAuthenticationRequestCredentials(true);
    return provider;
  }
}
```

Cloud Foundry support for Eclipse Spring Boot

In this section, let's see how we can develop applications on Cloud Foundry using Spring boot. **Cloud Foundry** is a platform that is used as a service cloud application. It is an open Paas. Paas makes it feasible to run deploy, and run an application on cloud.

Refer to the following link, which gives the complete information of the Spring platform that is available as service and how we can configure Spring to work with Cloud Foundry. You will see that it offers Platform as a service from MongoDB to RabbitMQ Messaging Server.

```
http://docs.cloudfoundry.org/buildpacks/java/spring-service-bindings.
html
```

Eclipse has also come up with a plugin for cloud foundry which can be downloaded and installed from the following given location. The plugin supports Spring boot and grails application. You can also create a server instance to a private cloud that uses a self signed certificate.

```
https://github.com/cloudfoundry/eclipse-integration-cloudfoundry
```

All that we need to do is develop a simple boot application, and drag and drop it into the cloud foundry server, then restart the server.

RestfulWebService using Spring Boot

In this section, let's develop a simple restful service and bootstrap the application using `SpringBoot`. We will also create a simple restful service that will store the product information into the database.

The Product creation scenario should satisfy the following mentioned use cases:

- Given that no product with the same `Product_id` exists, it should store a new product in the database and immediately return the stored object.
- Given there exist a product with the same `Product_id`, it should not store, but return an error status with the relevant message.
- Given there are previously stored products, it should be able to retrieve the list of them.

Following is the of `pom.xml` file, for the dependency reference used in the application. You can see that we have used the parent Spring boot reference here, so that we can resolve all the dependency references. We have also set that Java version as 1.7 in the `pom.xml` file.

```xml
<project xmlns:xsi="http://www.w3.org/2001/XMLSchema-instance"
  xmlns="http://maven.apache.org/POM/4.0.0"
  xsi:schemaLocation="http://maven.apache.org/POM/4.0.0
    http://maven.apache.org/maven-v4_0_0.xsd">
  <modelVersion>4.0.0</modelVersion>

  <groupId>com.packt.restfulApp</groupId>
  <artifactId>restfulSpringBootApp</artifactId>
  <version>1.0-SNAPSHOT</version>
  <packaging>jar</packaging>

  <parent>
    <groupId>org.springframework.boot</groupId>
    <artifactId>spring-boot-starter-parent</artifactId>
    <version>1.0.1.RELEASE</version>
  </parent>

  <name>Example Spring Boot REST Service</name>

  <properties>
    <java.version>1.7</java.version>
    <guava.version>16.0.1</guava.version>
    <project.build.sourceEncoding>UTF-8
      </project.build.sourceEncoding>
    <project.reporting.outputEncoding>UTF-8
      </project.reporting.outputEncoding>
  </properties>

</project>
```

Let's see the dependencies used in the `pom.xml` file. Following is the Spring boot dependencies used. Also, observe that the version information is not specified, since it is managed by the previously mentioned `spring-boot-starter-parent`.

```xml
<dependencies>
  <!-- Spring Boot -->
  <dependency>
    <groupId>org.springframework.boot</groupId>
    <artifactId>spring-boot-starter</artifactId>
  </dependency>

  <dependency>
```

```xml
      <groupId>org.springframework.boot</groupId>
      <artifactId>spring-boot-starter-test</artifactId>
      <scope>test</scope>
   </dependency>

   <dependency>
      <groupId>org.springframework.boot</groupId>
      <artifactId>spring-boot-starter-web</artifactId>
   </dependency>

   <dependency>
      <groupId>org.springframework.boot</groupId>
      <artifactId>spring-boot-starter-data-jpa</artifactId>
   </dependency>

   <!-- Hibernate validator -->

   <dependency>
      <groupId>org.hibernate</groupId>
      <artifactId>hibernate-validator</artifactId>
   </dependency>

   <!-- HSQLDB -->

   <dependency>
      <groupId>org.hsqldb</groupId>
      <artifactId>hsqldb</artifactId>
      <scope>runtime</scope>
   </dependency>

   <!-- Guava -->

   <dependency>
      <groupId>com.google.guava</groupId>
      <artifactId>guava</artifactId>
      <version>${guava.version}</version>
   </dependency>

   <!-- Java EE -->

   <dependency>
      <groupId>javax.inject</groupId>
      <artifactId>javax.inject</artifactId>
      <version>1</version>
   </dependency>
</dependencies>
```

We shall also see why these dependencies are used for Spring boot. When it comes to Spring boot, its functions are spread between the starter modules:

- `spring-boot-starter`: This is the main core module of Spring boot
- `spring-boot-starter-test`: This has some tools for unit testing, including JUnit4 and Mockito
- `spring-boot-starter-web`: This pulls Spring MVC dependencies, but also Jackson which will be used for JSON, and most importantly Tomcat, which acts as an embedded Servlet container
- `spring-boot-starter-data-jpa`: This is used for setting up Spring Data JPA, and comes bundled with Hibernate
- `Guava`: It uses `@Inject` annotation instead of `@Autowired`

Lastly, add a Spring boot Maven plugin as follows. The functionalities of the `spring-boot-maven` plugin are, as follows:

- It provides a `spring-boot:run` goal for Maven, so the application can be easily run without packaging.
- It hooks into a package goal to produce an executable JAR file with all the dependencies included, similar to a `maven-shade` plugin, but in a less messy way.

```
<build>
  <plugins>

  <!-- Spring Boot Maven -->

    <plugin>
      <groupId>org.springframework.boot</groupId>
      <artifactId>spring-boot-maven-plugin</artifactId>
    </plugin>

  </plugins>
</build>
```

So far, we have looked at the dependencies and its functions, now let us start framing the application.

Bean Class or Entity Class:

1. Let us create a simple `Product.java` file as follows:

```
@Entity
public class Product {
  @Id
```

```
@Column(name = "id", nullable = false, updatable = false)
@NotNull
private Long product_id;
@Column(name = "password", nullable = false)
@NotNull
@Size(max = 64)
private String product_name;

public Action(Long product_id, String product_name) {

  this. produc_id = product_id;
  this. produc_name = produc_name;
}
```

2. Next create a `Jparepository` subinterface; we do not need to provide any implementation for this, since it gets handled by Spring JPA data:

```
public interface ProductRepository extends JpaRepository<Product,
String>{

}
```

Service class:

1. Let's create a service interface which handles the save.

```
public interface ProductService {

Product save(Product product);

}
```

2. We should also create an implementation class for the service interface:

```
@Service
public class ProductServiceImpl implements ProductService {

  private final ProductRepository repository;

  @Inject
  public ProductServiceImpl(final ProductRepository
    repository) {
    this.repository = repository;
  }

  @Override
  @Transactional
  public Product save(final Product product) {
```

```
        Product existing = repository.findOne(Product.getId());
        if (existing != null) {
          throw new ProductAlreadyExistsException(
            String.format("There already exists a Product with
            id=%s", product.getId()));
        }
        return repository.save(product);
      }
```

3. In the next step, we shall also create a test class for the service `Impl` as follows:

```
@RunWith(MockitoJUnitRunner.class)
public class ProductControllerTest {

  @Mock
  private ProductService ProductService;

  private ProductController ProductController;

  @Before
  public void setUp() {
    ProductController = new
      ProductController(ProductService);
  }

  @Test
  public void shouldCreateProduct() throws Exception {
    final Product savedProduct =
      stubServiceToReturnStoredProduct();
    final Product Product = new Product();
    Product returnedProduct =
      ProductController.createProduct(Product);
    // verify Product was passed to ProductService
    verify(ProductService, times(1)).save(Product);
    assertEquals("Returned Product should come from the
      service", savedProduct, returnedProduct);
  }

  private Product stubServiceToReturnStoredProduct() {
    final Product Product = new Product();
    when(ProductService.save(any(Product.class)))
      .thenReturn(Product);
    return Product;
  }
```

4. Let's create a controller using the @RestController annotations; also observe that we used the @Inject annotation:

   ○ @RestController: The difference between this and the @Controller annotation is that the former also implies @ResponseBody on every method, which means that there is less to write, since from a restful web service we are returning JSON objects anyway.

   ○ @RequestMapping: This maps the createProduct() to the POST request on the /Product URL. The method takes the product object as a parameter. It is created from the body of the request thanks to @RequestBody annotation. It is then validated, which is enforced by @Valid.

   ○ @Inject: The ProductService will be injected to the constructor, and the product object is passed to its save() method for storage. After storing, the stored product object will be returned. Spring will convert it back to JSON automatically, even without @ResponseBody annotation, which is default for @RestController.

```
@RestsController
public class ProductController {
  private final ProductService ProductService;
  @Inject
  public ProductController(final ProductService
    ProductService) {
    this.ProductService = ProductService;
  }
  @RequestMapping(value = "/Product", method =
    RequestMethod.POST)
  public Product createProduct(@RequestBody @Valid final
    Product Product) {
    return ProductService.save(Product);
  }
}
```

5. Let's create a Main class with public static void main(). Let us also use these annotations:

   ○ @Configuration - This tells the Spring Framework that it is a configuration class

   ○ @ComponentScan - This enables the scanning of packages and subpackages for Spring Components

   ○ @EnableAutoConfiguration

   The class further extends SpringBootServletInitializer, which will configure the dispatcher servlet for us and override the configure method.

The following is the Main class:

```
@Configuration
@EnableAutoConfiguration
@ComponentScan
public class Application extends SpringBootServletInitializer {

  public static void main(final String[] args) {
    SpringApplication.run(Application.class, args);
  }

  @Override
  protected final SpringApplicationBuilder configure(final
    SpringApplicationBuilder application) {
    return application.sources(Application.class);
  }
}
```

6. Now, let's run the application using Maven and Bootstrap:

```
mvn package
java -jar target/restfulSpringBootApp.jar
```

Having done that now you can:

```
curl -X POST -d '{ "id": "45", "password": "samsung" }' http://
localhost:8080/Product
```

And see whether the response from http://localhost:8080/ will be like:

```
{ "id": "45", "password": "samsung" }
```

Summary

In this chapter, we have demonstrated the process of using Spring boot to Bootstarp applications. We started with setting up a simple Spring boot project. We have also created a simple MVC application with Gradle support. Next, we discussed hot swapping java files using Spring boot.

We have also given information as to how Spring boot supports the cloud foundry server and helps to deploy applications on cloud. Lastly, we have demonstrated a restful application with Spring boot.

In the next chapter, we will talk about Spring caching.

10
Spring Cache

Spring cache has come into action since the Spring 3.1 versions. Spring has also added annotations to support the caching mechanism. The caching abstraction layer provides a lot of support to use different caching solutions. In this chapter, we shall explore Spring caching. We shall see how to set up a Spring cache. You can ideally tie your caching code with a business logic.

Caching avoids re-computing. Ideally, you don't have to repeat the same process again to fetch the same values. Cache stores the values in the memory. You can always choose what you would like to cache and what you don't like to. It's a part of architectural design. Once the data is cached, it's retrieved from the cached memory, thus saving computational time.

Spring annotations for caching

Spring has come up with two main annotations for caching; we will be using these throughout the chapter. The following are the two annotations:

- `@Cacheable`: This can be used to mark the method and return values that will be stored in the cache. This can be applied at the method or type level.
    - When applied at the method level, the annotated method's return value is cached
    - When applied at type level, the return value of every method is cached

- `@CacheEvict`: This is used for releasing objects from cache memory.

@Cacheable usage

Let us look at small implementation of using `@Cacheable` annotations applied at type level. We are thinking of simple DAO class, with two methods with different names. We have used the `@Cacheable` annotation, which takes three arguments:

- Value
- Key
- Condition

No we can implement it:

```
@Cacheable(value = "product")
public class ProductDAO {

    public Product findProduct(String Name, int price) {

        return new Product(Name,price);
    }
    public Product findAnotherProduct(String Name, int price) {

        return new Product(Name,price);
    }
}
```

In the preceding code, Spring cache by default will assign a cache key, with an annotated signature.

We can also provide a customized key. Using SpEL expressions, the following is the demonstration for providing custom keys for cache:

```
public class ProductDAO {

    public Product findProduct(String productName, int price) {

        return new Product(productName,price);
    }

@Cacheable(value = "product" ,key="#productName")
    public Product findAnotherProduct(String productName, int price) {

        return new Product(productName,price);
    }
}
```

We can also perform conditional caching. Let us do conditional caching of products with a price greater than 1000:

```
@Cacheable(value = "product", condition = "#price>1000")
  public Product findProductByPrice(String productName, int price) {

    return new Product(String productName, int price);
  }
```

The @CacheEvict usage

Let us look at using @CacheEvict for flushing single objects and multiple objects from the cache. The productId will have new cached values every time and the user adds a rating. The previous rating will get evicted:

```
@Transactional
@CacheEvict(value="products", key="#rating.producttId")
public ItemRatingResponse addRatingForproduct(Rating rating, Integer
currentNumberOfRatings, Float currentRating) {
  return addRatingForItem(rating, currentNumberOfRatings,
    currentRating);
}
```

The following is the @CacheEvict usage for flushing all the cached objects. You can see that multiple objects are flushed at one time.

```
@Caching(evict = {
    @CacheEvict(value="referenceData", allEntries=true),
    @CacheEvict(value="product", allEntries=true),
    @CacheEvict(value="searchResults", allEntries=true),
    @CacheEvict(value="newestAndRecommendedproducts",
      allEntries=true),
    @CacheEvict(value="randomAndTopRatedproducts",
      allEntries=true)
  })
public void flushAllCaches() {
  LOG.warn("All caches have been completely flushed");
}
```

Spring caching repository

The cache repository is where the actual objects are saved. Spring supports two types of repositories:

Using `ConcurrentMap` is also an option for implementing caching in the application. The repository has little (if any) effect on the code, and switching between repositories should be very easy. Our objects will be cached within a ConcurrentMap.

We can configure the ConcurrentMap as shown in the following code:

```
<bean id="cacheManager" class="org.springframework.cache.support.
SimpleCacheManager">
    <property name="caches">
     <set>
       <bean class="org.springframework.cache.concurrent.
         ConcurrentMapCacheFactoryBean" p:name="task" />
     </set>
    </property>
      </bean>
```

The Ehcache popular library

This cache is used by a lot of popular frameworks to handle caching in an application. The ehcache is used by a hibernate framework to handle caching in the DAO (Date access) layer of the application.

We can have more than one repository. Note that, the name of this repository must be same as the name used in the annotation.

Spring CacheManager

Let's look at the core interfaces and implementation classes that are used for configuring caching in a Spring caching framework. Spring CacheManager is actually an interface in the Spring's caching framework. The following is the list of classes that implement the CacheManager interface:

- `AbstractCacheManager`: This abstract class implements the `CacheManager` interface. It is useful for static environments, where the backing caches do not change.

- `CompositeCacheManager`: This is the composite `CacheManager` implementation that iterates over a given collection of `CacheManager` instances. It allows `NoOpCacheManager` to be automatically added to the list for handling the cache declarations without a backing store.

- `ConcurrentMapCacheManager`: This is the `CacheManager` implementation that lazily builds `ConcurrentMapCache` instances for each `getCache(java. lang.String)` request. It also supports a static mode where the set of cache names is predefined through `setCacheNames(java.util.Collection)`, with no dynamic creation of further cache regions at runtime.

- `ehCacheCacheManager`: `CacheManager` backed by an EhCache `CacheManager`.

- `NoOpCacheManager`: A basic, no operation CacheManager implementation suitable for disabling caching, typically used for backing cache declarations without an actual backing store. It will simply accept any items into the cache, without actually storing them.

- `SimpleCacheManager`: The Simple CacheManager works against a given collection of caches. This is useful for testing or simple caching declarations.

Maven dependency for Spring with caching

If you are using Maven as a build tool, ensure that you add the ehcache dependency in the `pom.xml` file. Below is the Maven dependency for using cache with spring's caching framework:

```
<groupId>net.sf.ehcache</groupId>
<artifactId>ehcache</artifactId>
<version>2.7.4</version>
</dependency>
```

Declarative configuration of ehcache

In the following section, we can see how we can configure the cache storage declaratively. The `ecache.xml` file is as follows:

```
<ehcache
  xsi:noNamespaceSchemaLocation="ehcache.xsd"
  updateCheck="true"
  monitoring="autodetect"
  dynamicConfig="true"
  maxBytesLocalHeap="150M"
  >
  <diskStore path="java.io.tmpdir"/>

  <cache name="searchResults"
      maxBytesLocalHeap="100M"
      eternal="false"
      timeToIdleSeconds="300"
      overflowToDisk="true"
      maxElementsOnDisk="1000"
      memoryStoreEvictionPolicy="LRU"/>
```

```
<cache name="Products"
    maxBytesLocalHeap="40M"
    eternal="false"
    timeToIdleSeconds="300"
    overflowToDisk="true"
    maxEntriesLocalDisk="1000"
    diskPersistent="false"
    diskExpiryThreadIntervalSeconds="120"
    memoryStoreEvictionPolicy="LRU"/>

<cache name="referenceData"
    maxBytesLocalHeap="5M"
    eternal="true"
    memoryStoreEvictionPolicy="LRU">
    <pinning store="localMemory"/>
</cache>

<cache name="newestAndRecommendedProducts"
        maxBytesLocalHeap="3M"
    eternal="true"
    memoryStoreEvictionPolicy="LRU">
    <pinning store="localMemory"/>
</cache>

<cache name="randomAndTopRatedProducts"
        maxBytesLocalHeap="1M"
    timeToLiveSeconds="300"
    memoryStoreEvictionPolicy="LRU">
  </cache>

</ehcache>
```

Let's also look at what each of the following properties used in the echace.xml mean, so that it will aid in their proper usage:

- `maxBytesLocalHeap`: This defines how many bytes the cache may use from the VM's heap. If a CacheManager `maxBytesLocalHeap` has been defined, this cache's specified amount will be subtracted from the CacheManager. Other caches will share the remainder. This attribute's values are given as `<number>k|K|m|M|g|G` for kilobytes (k | K), megabytes (m | M), and gigabytes (g | G). For example, `maxBytesLocalHeap="2g"` allots 2 gigabytes of heap memory. If you specify a `maxBytesLocalHeap`, you can't use the `maxEntriesLocalHeap` attribute. `maxEntriesLocalHeap` can't be used if a CacheManager `maxBytesLocalHeap` is set.

Set at the highest level, this property defines the memory allocated for all the defined caches. You have to divide it afterwards with the individual caches.

- `eternal`: This sets whether the elements are eternal. If eternal, timeouts are ignored and the element is never expired.

- `timeToIdleSeconds`: This sets the time to idle for an element before it expires. That is, the maximum amount of time between accesses before an element expires. It is only used if the element is not eternal. Optional attribute. A value of `0` means that an element can idle for infinity. The default value is `0`.

- `timeToLiveSeconds`: This sets the time to live for an element before it expires which is the maximum time between creation time and when an element expires. It is only used if the element is not eternal. Optional attribute. A value of `0` means that an element can live for infinity. The default value is 0.

- `memoryStoreEvictionPolicy`: The policy would be enforced upon reaching the `maxEntriesLocalHeap` limit. The default policy is **Least Recently Used (LRU)**.

 If you want take some load off your database, you could also use the `localTempSwap` persistence strategy, and in that case, you can use `maxEntriesLocalDisk` or `maxBytesLocalDisk` at either the cache or CacheManager level to control the size of the disk tier.

Two of the configured caches, reference Data and `newestAndRecommendedPodcasts` are pinned in the local memory (`<pinning store="localMemory"/>`), which means that the data will remain in the cache at all times. To unpin the data from the cache you have to clear the cache.

Spring MVC with caching

In this section, let us develop a simple MVC application to demonstrate simple spring caching. Let us start with the configuration.

To enable caching, we need to add the following configuration to the application `context.xml` file:

```
<beans xmlns="http://www.springframework.org/schema/beans"
xmlns:xsi="http://www.w3.org/2001/XMLSchema-instance"
xmlns:cache="http://www.springframework.org/schema/cache"
xsi:schemaLocation="http://www.springframework.org/schema/beans
http://www.springframework.org/schema/beans/spring-beans.xsd
```

```
http://www.springframework.org/schema/cache http://www.
springframework.org/schema/cache/spring-cache.xsd">
<cache:annotation-driven />
//your beans
</beans>
```

`<cache:annotation-driven />` will recognize the spring cache annotations `@Cacheable` and `@CacheEvict`.

Let us demonstrate an application `context.xml` file with a simple caching configuration:

```
<?xml version="1.0" encoding="UTF-8"?>
<beans xmlns="http://www.springframework.org/schema/beans"
xmlns:xsi="http://www.w3.org/2001/XMLSchema-instance"
xmlns:p="http://www.springframework.org/schema/p"
xmlns:context="http://www.springframework.org/schema/context"
xmlns:cache="http://www.springframework.org/schema/cache"
xsi:schemaLocation="
 http://www.springframework.org/schema/beans
 http://www.springframework.org/schema/beans/spring-beans.xsd
http://www.springframework.org/schema/cache
http://www.springframework.org/schema/cache/spring-cache.xsd
http://www.springframework.org/schema/context
http://www.springframework.org/schema/context/spring-context.xsd">
<!-- Scans within the base package of the application for @Components
to configure as beans -->
<context:component-scan base-package="com" />
<!-- Process cache annotations -->
<cache:annotation-driven />

<!-- Configuration for using Ehcache as the cache manager-->
<bean id="cacheManager" p:cache-manager-ref="ehcache"/>
<bean id="ehcache" p:config-location="classpath:ehcache.xml"/>
<bean id="author" class="com.packt.model.Author"/>
</beans>
```

Next let us demonstrate the `ehchace.xml` file:

```
<ehcache>
<diskStore path="java.io.tmpdir"/>
<cache name="authorCache"
maxElementsInMemory="10000"
eternal="false"
timeToIdleSeconds="120"
timeToLiveSeconds="120"
```

```
overflowToDisk="true"
maxElementsOnDisk="10000000"
diskPersistent="false"
diskExpiryThreadIntervalSeconds="120"
memoryStoreEvictionPolicy="LRU"/>
</ehcache>
```

Next, we shall see a simple POJO class `Author.java`:

```
package com.packt.model;
import org.slf4j.Logger;
import org.slf4j.LoggerFactory;
import org.springframework.cache.annotation.Cacheable;

public class Author {
 Logger logger = LoggerFactory.getLogger(getClass());
 @Cacheable(value="authorCache", key = "#id")
public String getAuthor(Integer id){
logger.info("get author called");
return "author"+id;
}
}
```

Next, we shall write a simple controller with the injected Author pojo:

```
package com.packt.web;
import java.util.HashMap;
import org.springframework.beans.factory.annotation.Autowired;
import org.springframework.stereotype.Controller;
import org.springframework.web.bind.annotation.RequestMapping;
import org.springframework.web.bind.annotation.RequestParam;
import com.packt.model.Author;
@Controller
public class WebController {

@Autowired
Author author;
@RequestMapping("/index.htm")
public String authorPage(@RequestParam(required= false) Integer
  id, HashMap<String, String> map){
map.put("message", author.getAuthor(id));
return "index";
}
}
```

Lastly, we shall write a `.jsp` file:

```
<%@ page language="java" contentType="text/html; charset=ISO-8859-
    1"
pageEncoding="ISO-8859-1"%>

<%@taglib prefix="c" uri="http://java.sun.com/jsp/jstl/core" %>
<!DOCTYPE html PUBLIC "-//W3C//DTD HTML 4.01 Transitional//EN"
    "http://www.w3.org/TR/html4/loose.dtd">
<html>
<head>
<meta http-equiv="Content-Type" content="text/html; charset=ISO-
    8859-1">
<title>Cache Example</title>
</head>
<body>
<h1>This is ${message }</h1>
</body>
</html>
```

When we run the application with `http://localhost:8080/springcachedemo/ index.htm?id=1`, the data gets cached and the second time we access the URL you will be able to observe that the value is retrieved from cache.

Now update the ID in the URL `id=2. Access http://localhost:8080/ springcachedemo/index.htm?id=2`, the data is not retrieved from cache, but it gets cached.

Implementing your own caching algorithm

In this section, let us start by implementing a simple cache algorithm and see its draw backs, and then show how spring caching can be used to solve the problems.

Let's draw a simple flow chart to look at the caching scenario:

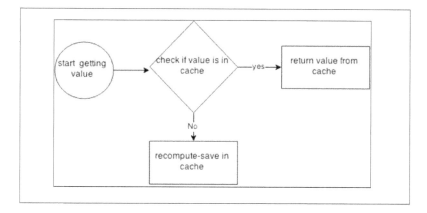

Let's see how we can implement caching in a simple way. Think of generating a Fibonacci number. A Fibonacci number is generated by adding its previous two Fibonacci numbers. So we can compute a simple class in java and see how we can use caching here.

Let's create a map to cache the objects:

```java
import java.util.HashMap;
import java.util.Map;
public class FibonacciCache {
  private Map<Long, Long> cachemap = new HashMap<>();
  public FibonacciCache() {
    // The base case for the Fibonacci Sequence
    cachemap.put(0L, 1L);
    cachemap.put(1L, 1L);
  }
  public Long getNumber(long index) {
    // Check if value is in cache
    if (cachemap.containsKey(index)) {
     return cachemap.get(index);
    }

    // Compute value and save it in cache
    long value = getNumber(index - 1) + getNumber(index - 2);
    cachemap.put(index, value);
    return value;
  }
}
```

This approach is not thread safe and the same value is computed more than once. When two threads run over the class, they end up caching the same value.

We can overcome this by implementing concurrent hash maps. The preceding code can be rewritten as follows:

```java
import java.util.HashMap;
import java.util.Map;

public class FibonacciConncurentCache {
  private Map<Long, Long> concurrent_cachemap = new
    ConcurrentHashMap<>();
  public FibonacciCache() {
    // The base case for the Fibonacci Sequence
   concurrent_cachemap.put(0L, 1L);
    concurrent_cachemap.put(1L, 1L);
  }
  public Long getNumber(long index) {
    // Check if value is in cache
    if (concurrent_cachemap.containsKey(index)) {
      return concurrent_cachemap.get(index);
    }
    // Compute value and save it in concurrent_cachemap
    long value = getNumber(index - 1) + getNumber(index - 2);
    concurrent_cachemap.put(index, value);
    return value; }}
```

The preceding code will make the algorithm thread safe, preventing the re-computation of the same values. But this design cannot be used for other algorithms. If we have to find whether the next Fibonacci number is odd or prime, this wouldn't be supported.

Let us tackle this using Future, Callable ExecutorService, and Concurrent HashMap. We will also see what Future callable and executor Service means.

ExecutorService provides options to create thread pool. ExecutorService is an interface in concurrency package. `ThreadPoolExecutor` and `ScheduledThreadPoolExecutor` are the two classes that implement the `ExecutorService`.

There are a few different ways to delegate tasks for execution to a `ExecutorService`:

- execute (Runnable)
- submit (Runnable)
- submit (Callable)
- invokeAny (...)
- invokeAll (...)

Callable is an interface similar to Runnable. It is a task that returns a result and may throw an exception. Implementors define a single method with no arguments called `call`.

The Callable interface is similar to Runnable, in that, both are designed for classes whose instances are potentially executed by another thread. A Runnable, however, does not return a result and cannot throw a checked exception.

The Executors class contains utility methods to convert from other common forms to Callable classes.

Let us create a generic class; `MyCache`, this class instance accepts the Key and Value pair. It uses a concurrent `HashMap`.

1. Let's call the `getter` and `setter` methods on condition; if the value is already in the cache, then just get the value, and set it only if it is absent.

```java
import java.util.concurrent.Callable;
import java.util.concurrent.ConcurrentHashMap;
import java.util.concurrent.ConcurrentMap;
import java.util.concurrent.ExecutionException;
import java.util.concurrent.Future;
import java.util.concurrent.FutureTask;

public class MyCache<K, V> {

  private final ConcurrentMap<K, Future<V>> cache = new
    ConcurrentHashMap<>();

  private Future<V> createFutureIfAbsent(final K key, final
    Callable<V> callable) {
    Future<V> future = cache.get(key);
    if (future == null) {
      final FutureTask<V> futureTask = new
        FutureTask<V>(callable);
      future = cache.putIfAbsent(key, futureTask);
      if (future == null) {
        future = futureTask;
        futureTask.run();
      }
    }
    return future;
  }

  public V getValue(final K key, final Callable<V>
    callable) throws InterruptedException,
    ExecutionException {
    try {
```

```
          final Future<V> future = createFutureIfAbsent(key,
            callable);
          return future.get();
        } catch (final InterruptedException e) {
          cache.remove(key);
          throw e;
        } catch (final ExecutionException e) {
          cache.remove(key);
          throw e;
        } catch (final RuntimeException e) {
          cache.remove(key);
          throw e;
        }
      }
      public void setValueIfAbsent(final K key, final V value) {
        createFutureIfAbsent(key, new Callable<V>() {
          @Override
          public V call() throws Exception {
            return value;
          } });
  }}
```

2. The next step is to use the cache algorithm in our Fibonacci series code:

```
import java.util.concurrent.Callable;
import org.slf4j.Logger;
import org.slf4j.LoggerFactory;

public class MyFibonacci {

  private static final Logger LOGGER =
    LoggerFactory.getLogger(MyFibonacci.class);

  public static void main(final String[] args) throws
    Exception {
    final long index = 12;
    final MyFibonacci myfibi = new MyFibonacci();
    final long fn = myfibi.getNumber(index);
    MyFibonacci.LOGGER.debug("The {}th Fibonacci number is:
      {}", index, fn);
  }

  private final MyCache<Long, Long> cache = new
    MyCache<>();

  public MyFibonacci() {
    cache.setValueIfAbsent(0L, 1L);
```

```
            cache.setValueIfAbsent(1L, 1L);
        }

        public long getNumber(final long index) throws Exception {
            return cache.getValue(index, new Callable<Long>() {
                @Override
                public Long call() throws Exception {
                    MyFibonacci.LOGGER.debug("Computing the {}
                        MyFibonacci number", index);
                    return getNumber(index - 1) + getNumber(index - 2);
                }
            });
        }
    }
```

As you can see in the preceding example, the modifications required were minimal. All caching code is encapsulated within the caching algorithm and our code simply interacts with it. The caching algorithm is thread safe and since all the state is saved by the caching algorithm, our class is inherently thread safe. Using this new approach, we can have this class (MyFibonacci) focusing on its business logic, that is, computing the Fibonacci sequence. Each Fibonacci number is evaluated only once. All the other times, this was retrieved from the cache. In the following example, we will see how to use the same cache algorithm in another context. Think of a long learning task which needs to use a cache. We shall use a Spring Stop Watch class found in the org.spring.framework.util.StopWatch package. The class has two constructors:

- StopWatch(): This constructs a new stop watch

- StopWatch(String id): This constructs a new stop watch with the given ID

The simple stop watch allows for timing a number of tasks, exposing a total running time, and giving a running time for each named task. It conceals the use of System.currentTimeMillis(), improving the readability of the application code, and reducing the likelihood of calculation errors.

 Note that this object is not designed to be thread safe, and does not use synchronization or threading. Therefore it is safe to invoke it from EJBs.

This class is normally used to verify performance during proof of concepts and in development, rather than as part of production applications.

Let's look at the code:

```
import java.util.concurrent.Callable;
import org.slf4j.Logger;
import org.slf4j.LoggerFactory;
```

```
mport org.springframework.util.StopWatch;

public class LongRunningTaskExample {

  private static final Logger LOGGER =
  public static void main(final String[] args) throws Exception {
    final LongRunningTaskExample task = new
      LongRunningTaskExample();

    final StopWatch stopWatch = new StopWatch(" Long Running
      Task");
    stopWatch.start("First Run");
    task.computeLongTask("a");
    stopWatch.stop();

    stopWatch.start("Other Runs");
    for (int i = 0; i < 100; i++) {
      task.computeLongTask("a");
    }
    stopWatch.stop();

    LongRunningTaskExample.LOGGER.debug("{}", stopWatch);
  }

  private final MyCache<String, Long> cache = new MyCache<>();

  public long computeLongTask(final String key) throws Exception {
    return cache.getValue(key, new Callable<Long>() {
      @Override
      public Long call() throws Exception {
        FictitiousLongRunningTask.LOGGER.debug("Computing  Long
          Running Task: {}", key);
        Thread.sleep(10000); // 10 seconds
        return System.currentTimeMillis();
      }
    });
  }
}
```

Output for the preceding code:

```
[main] DEBUG LongRunningTask.java:36 - Computing  Long Running Task: a

[main] DEBUG LongRunningTask.java:27 - StopWatch ' Long Running Task':
running time (millis) = 10006; [First Run] took 10005 = 100%; [Other
Runs] took 1 = 0%
```

No changes were required to the caching algorithm and implementing it was quite easy. The preceding code will produce something similar to the following code. As shown in the preceding output, once the first value is computed and saved in cache, all other retrievals happen instantly without introducing any noticeable delays.

Let's go further and implement the preceding log running task and cache the computational value using spring cache.

We will create two simple classes: `Worker` and `Main`. The `Worker` class has two methods which are called from the `main` class:

```java
Import org.springframework.context.support.
  ClassPathXmlApplicationContext;
public class Main {
  public static void main(final String[] args) {
    final String xmlFile = "META-INF/spring/app-context.xml";
    try (ClassPathXmlApplicationContext context = new
      ClassPathXmlApplicationContext(xmlFile)) {
      final Worker worker = context.getBean(Worker.class);
      worker.longTask(1);
      worker.longTask(1);
      worker.longTask(1);
      worker.longTask(2);
      worker.longTask(2);
    }
  }
}

import org.springframework.stereotype.Component;
@Component
public class Worker {
  public String longTask(final long id) {
    System.out.printf("Running long task for id: %d...%n", id);
    return "Long task for id " + id + " is done";
  }
  public String shortTask(final long id) {
    System.out.printf("Running short task for id: %d...%n", id);
    return "Short task for id " + id + " is done";
  }
}
```

You can observe that the Longtask has passed the same value to be recomputed. We can tackle this with the @Cacheable annotation. The preceding code can be rewritten, as follows. This will prevent the recompilation of Longtask for the same value.

```
import org.springframework.stereotype.Component;
@Component
public class Worker {
@Cacheable("task")
  public String longTask(final long id) {
    System.out.printf("Running long task for id: %d...%n", id);
    return "Long task for id " + id + " is done";
  }
  public String shortTask(final long id) {
    System.out.printf("Running short task for id: %d...%n", id);
    return "Short task for id " + id + " is done";
  }
}
```

Summary

In this chapter, we saw how we can implement our own caching algorithm and how to make a generic algorithm. We looked at Spring support for caching, and different kinds of caching repositories in the Spring caching framework. We have demonstrated how caching can be used with annotations in the Spring MVC application. We have also discussed the scenario of removing cache and when is it ideal to opt for caching. Lastly, we also discussed the classes and interface that supports the caching mechanism in Spring framework.

In the next chapters, we shall look at Spring with the thymeleaf framework integration and Spring Webservices.

11
Spring with Thymeleaf Integration

Thymeleaf is a template engine that is completely written in Java. It supports XML/ XHTML/HTML5, and that means we can develop templates using XML or XHTML or HTML5 using the Thymeleaf template engine library. It provides an optional module for Spring MVC and Spring Web Flow integration. Template engines help us to create reusable components in the UI. Template usually by convention consists of a header, menu, message, body, content and footer components. The content part is loaded dynamically with messages. We can create different layouts with a template.

Thymeleaf can be used instead of JSP. We have so far used tiles with JSP for making templates with custom tags. Thymeleaf templates are XHTML, XML, HTML5 template engines. Even web designers can easily interact with it. The expression language used is very much advanced compared to the JSP expression language.

In this chapter, we shall demonstrate how to integrate Spring MVC with the Thymeleaf template. We shall see how to get started with Spring Thymeleaf with available dependency.

Thymeleaf attributes

Let's look at some of the basic attributes that Thymeleaf provides for designing a page. We shall also look at the how it interacts with Java object and loops. Thymeleaf uses a lot of attributes.

- To display a message:
  ```
  <p th:text="#{msg.greet}">Helloo Good Morning!</p>
  ```

- To display a loop, we have `th:each`:

```
<li th:each="product : ${products}"
  th:text="${product.title}">XYZLLDD</li>
```

- Now, lets look at a form submit action:

```
<form th:action="@{/buyBook}">
```

- If we have to button submit, then add:

```
<input type="button" th:value="#{form.submit}" />
```

Spring Thymeleaf dependency

To get started with the Thymeleaf template engine, we need to add the following dependency in the `pom.xml` file:

- The Thyemleaf library:
  - ○ groupId: `org.thymeleaf`
  - ○ artifactId: `thymeleaf`
  - ○ version: 2.1.4 Release

- The Spring-Thymeleaf plugin library:
  - ○ groupId: `org.thymeleaf`
  - ○ artifactId: `thymeleaf-spring4`
  - ○ version: 2.1.4. Release

For testing the framework (the note version does not necessarily match that of the core), Thymeleaf requires Java SE 5.0 or newer. Besides, it depends on the following libraries:

- unbescape 1.1.0 or later
- ONGL 3.0.8 or later
- Javassist 3.16.1-GA or later
- slf4j 1.6.6 or later
- Additionally, if you use the LEGACYHTML5 template mode, you will need the NekoHTML 1.9.21 or later

Spring MVC and Thymeleaf

In this section, let's look at configuring Thymeleaf in a Spring MVC framework. We can also use the `SpringContext.xml` file for Thymeleaf configuration, but since we have seen a lot of such examples in which have performed a configuration in an XML file, we shall look at adding configuration in a Java file using Spring annotations. Let us create a simple class `CustomPacktConfiguration` and use `@Configuration` annotation for the class, which tells the framework that this class has the configurations.

In the configuration class, set the template mode to the format used in the application, that is whether it is XHTML or XML template. Then we need to set the template configuration to the `thymeleafviewResolver` object and also we need to actually pass the `templateResolver` class.

```
@Configuration
@ComponentScan(basePackageClasses = PacktController.class)
public class CutomPacktConfiguration {
  @Bean public ViewResolver viewResolver() {
    ClassLoaderTemplateResolver templateResolver = new
      ClassLoaderTemplateResolver();
    templateResolver.setTemplateMode("XHTML");
    templateResolver.setPrefix("views/");
    templateResolver.setSuffix(".html");
    SpringTemplateEngine engine = new SpringTemplateEngine();
    engine.setTemplateResolver(templateResolver);
    ThymeleafViewResolver thymeleafviewResolver = new
      ThymeleafViewResolver();
    thymeleafviewResolver.setTemplateEngine(engine);
    return thymeleafviewResolver;
    }
  }


@Controller
public class MyPacktControllerController {
  @Autowired private PacktService packtService;
  @RequestMapping("/authors")
  public String authors(Model model) {
    model.addAttribute("authors",packtService.getAuthors));
    return "authors";
  }

}
```

MVC with Spring Thymeleaf

In this section, we will go deeper into Thymeleaf integration in the Spring application, and develop a simple MVC application that lists authors and allows the user to add, edit and delete authors. An advantage of having done the configuration in a Java file rather than in an XML file is the code security. Your XML can easily be changed, but in case of configuration in the Java file, we may have to deploy the class file on to the server to see the changes. In this example, let us use `JavaConfig` approach to configure the beans. We can omit the XML configuration files.

1. Let us first start with the controller, it has methods to insert and list the authors available in the database.

```java
package demo.packt.thymeleaf.controller;
import org.springframework.beans.factory
    .annotation.Autowired;
import org.springframework.stereotype.Controller;
import org.springframework.ui.Model;
import org.springframework.web.bind
    .annotation.ExceptionHandler;
import org.springframework.web.bind
    .annotation.ModelAttribute;
import org.springframework.web.bind
    .annotation.PathVariable;
import org.springframework.web.bind
    .annotation.RequestMapping;
import org.springframework.web.bind
    .annotation.RequestMethod;
import org.springframework.web
    .servlet.ModelAndView;
import demo.packt.thymeleaf.exception.AuthorFoundException;
import demo.packt.thymeleaf.model.Author;
import demo.packt.thymeleaf.model.AuthorData;
import demo.packt.thymeleaf.service.AuthorService;

@Controller
public class AuthorController {
  private static final String HOME_VIEW = "home";
  private static final String RESULTS_FRAGMENT = "results
    :: resultsList";

  @Autowired
  private AuthorService authorService;

  @ModelAttribute("author")
  public Author prepareAuthorModel() {
    return new Author();
```

```
    }

    @ModelAttribute("authorData")
    public AuthorData prepareAuthorDataModel() {
      return authorService.getAuthorData();
    }

    @RequestMapping(value = "/home", method =
      RequestMethod.GET)
    public String showHome(Model model) {
      prepareAuthorDataModel();
      prepareAuthorModel();
      return HOME_VIEW;
    }


    @RequestMapping(value = "/authors/{surname}", method =
      RequestMethod.GET)
    public String showAuthorListwithSurname(Model model,
      @PathVariable("surname") String surname) {
      model.addAttribute("authors",
        authorService.getAuthorsList(surname));
      return RESULTS_FRAGMENT;
    }

    @RequestMapping(value = "/authors", method =
      RequestMethod.GET)
    public String showAuthorList(Model model) {
      model.addAttribute("authors",
        authorService.getAuthorsList());
      return RESULTS_FRAGMENT;
    }

    @RequestMapping(value = "/authors/insert", method =
      RequestMethod.POST)
    public String insertAuthor(Author newAuthor, Model model)
      {
      authorService.insertNewAuthor(newAuthor);
      return showHome(model);
    }

    @ExceptionHandler({AuthorFoundException.class})
    public ModelAndView
      handleDatabaseError(AuthorFoundException e) {
      ModelAndView modelAndView = new ModelAndView();
      modelAndView.setViewName("home");
```

```
    modelAndView.addObject("errorMessage",
      "error.user.exist");
    modelAndView.addObject("Author", prepareAuthorModel());
    modelAndView.addObject("authorData",
      prepareAuthorDataModel());

    return modelAndView;
  }
}
```

2. Next define the custom `RuntimeException` by extending the `RuntimeException` class:

```java
package demo.packt.thymeleaf.exception;
public class AuthorFoundException extends RuntimeException
  {
  private static final long serialVersionUID =
    -3845574518872003019L;
  public AuthorFoundException() {
    super();
  }
  public AuthorFoundException(String message) {
    super(message);
  }
}
```

3. In this step, we will start with the Thymeleaf service, and write an interface and implementing class.

   ° The interface depicts the methods used in the interface:

```java
package demo.packt.thymeleaf.service;
import java.util.List;
import demo.packt.thymeleaf.model.Author;
import demo.packt.thymeleaf.model.AuthorData;
public interface AuthorService {
  HotelData getAuthorData();
  List<Author> getAuthorsList();
  List<Author> getAuthorList(String surname);
  void insertNewAuthor(Author newAuthor);
}
```

   ° Next we shall implement the interface:

```java
package demo.packt.thymeleaf.service;
import java.util.List;
import org.springframework.beans.factory.annotation.Autowired;
import org.springframework.stereotype.Service;
```

```
import demo.packt.thymeleaf.exception.AuthorFoundException;
import demo.packt.thymeleaf.model.Author;
import demo.packt.thymeleaf.model.AuthorData;
import demo.packt.thymeleaf.repository.AuthorRepository;

@Service("authorServiceImpl")
public class AuthorServiceImpl implements AuthorService {
  @Autowired
  AuthorRepository authorRepository;
  @Override
  public AuthorData getAuthorData() {
    AuthorData data = new AuthorData();
    data.setAddress("RRNAGAR, 225");
    data.setName("NANDA");
    return data;
  }
  @Override
  public List<Author> getAuthorsList() {
    return authorRepository.findAll();
  }
  @Override
  public List<Author> getAuthorsList(String surname) {
    return authorRepository.findAuthorsBySurname(surname);
  }

  @Override
  public void insertNewGuest(Author newAuthor) {
    if (authorRepository.exists(newAuthor.getId())) {
      throw new AuthorFoundException();
    }
    authorRepository.save(newAuthor);
  }
}
```

4. Let us implement the repository class used in the application service implementation class:

```
package demo.packt.thymeleaf.repository;
import java.util.List;
import org.springframework.data.mongodb
  .repository.MongoRepository;
import org.springframework.data.mongodb.repository.Query;
import demo.packt.thymeleaf.model.Guest;
public interface AuthorRepository extends
  MongoRepository<Author, Long> {
```

```
@Query("{ 'surname' : ?0 }")
List<Author> findAuthorsBySurname(String surname);
}
```

5. Next implement the Model class (`Author` and `AuthorData`) in the application.

   ° Let's implement the `Author` class first:

```
package demo.packt.thymeleaf.model;
import java.io.Serializable;
import org.springframework.data.annotation.Id;
import org.springframework.data.mongodb
  .core.mapping.Document;
@Document(collection = "authors")
public class Author implements Serializable {
  private static final long serialVersionUID = 1L;
  @Id
  private Long id;
  private String name;
  private String surname;
  private String country;

  /**
   * @return the name
   */
  public String getName() {
    return name;
  }
  /**
   * @param name the name to set
   */
  public void setName(String name) {
    this.name = name;
  }
  /**
   * @return the surname
   */
  public String getSurname() {
    return surname;
  }
  /**
   * @param surname the surname to set
   */
  public void setSurname(String surname) {
    this.surname = surname;
  }
  /**
   * @return the id
```

```
*/
public Long getId() {
  return id;
}
/**
 * @param id the id to set
 */
public void setId(Long id) {
  this.id = id;
}
/**
 * @return the country
 */
public String getCountry() {
  return country;
}
/**
 * @param country the country to set
 */
public void setCountry(String country) {
  this.country = country;
}
}
```

  ° Next, let us implement the `AuthorData` class:

```
package demo.packt.thymeleaf.model;
import java.io.Serializable;
public class AuthorData implements Serializable {
  private static final long serialVersionUID = 1L;
  private String name;
  private String address;
  public String getName() {
    return name;
  }
  public void setName(String name) {
    this.name = name;
  }
  public String getAddress() {
    return address;
  }
  public void setAddress(String address) {
    this.address = address;
  }
}
```

6. In this step, we will create the configuration class; as discussed earlier, we are not using XML for configuration. We have two configuration files—we are using MongoDB for database configuration and the other is the component scan configuration file:

```
import org.springframework.context.annotation
  .Configuration;
import org.springframework.data.mongodb.config
  .AbstractMongoConfiguration;
import org.springframework.data.mongodb.repository
  .config.EnableMongoRepositories;
import com.mongodb.Mongo;
@Configuration
@EnableMongoRepositories(«demo.packt.thymeleaf.repository»)
public class MongoDBConfiguration extends
  AbstractMongoConfiguration {
  @Override
  protected String getDatabaseName() {
    return "author-db";
  }
  @Override
  public Mongo mongo() throws Exception {
    return new Mongo();
  }
}
```

This class is an important class that marks the beginning of the application instantiation. Here, we have also configured the Thymeleaf template view resolver and provided the component scan information. The template and view resolver have also been configured in the class:

```
package demo.packt.thymeleaf.configuration;

import org.springframework.context.annotation.Bean;
import org.springframework.context.annotation.ComponentScan;
import org.springframework.context.annotation.Configuration;
import org.springframework.context.annotation.Description;
import org.springframework.context.annotation.Import;
import org.springframework.context.support
  .ResourceBundleMessageSource;
import org.springframework.web.servlet.config
  .annotation.EnableWebMvc;
import org.springframework.web.servlet.config
  .annotation.ResourceHandlerRegistry;
import org.springframework.web.servlet.config
  .annotation.WebMvcConfigurerAdapter;
```

```
import org.thymeleaf.spring3.SpringTemplateEngine;
import org.thymeleaf.spring3.view.ThymeleafViewResolver;
import org.thymeleaf.templateresolver
  .ServletContextTemplateResolver;

@EnableWebMvc
@Configuration
@ComponentScan("demo.packt.thymeleaf")
@Import(MongoDBConfiguration.class)
public class WebAppConfiguration extends
  WebMvcConfigurerAdapter {

  @Bean
  @Description("Thymeleaf template resolver serving HTML
    5")
  public ServletContextTemplateResolver templateResolver()
    {
    ServletContextTemplateResolver templateResolver = new
      ServletContextTemplateResolver();
    templateResolver.setPrefix("/WEB-INF/html/");
    templateResolver.setSuffix(".html");
    templateResolver.setTemplateMode("HTML5");

    return templateResolver;
  }

  @Bean
  @Description("Thymeleaf template engine with Spring
    integration")
  public SpringTemplateEngine templateEngine() {
    SpringTemplateEngine templateEngine = new
      SpringTemplateEngine();
    templateEngine.setTemplateResolver(templateResolver());

    return templateEngine;
  }

  @Bean
  @Description("Thymeleaf view resolver")
  public ThymeleafViewResolver viewResolver() {
    ThymeleafViewResolver viewResolver = new
      ThymeleafViewResolver();
    viewResolver.setTemplateEngine(templateEngine());

    return viewResolver;
  }
```

```
@Bean
@Description("Spring message resolver")
public ResourceBundleMessageSource messageSource() {
  ResourceBundleMessageSource messageSource = new
    ResourceBundleMessageSource();
  messageSource.setBasename("i18n/messages");

  return messageSource;
}

@Override
public void addResourceHandlers(ResourceHandlerRegistry
  registry) {
  registry.addResourceHandler("/resources/**")
    .addResourceLocations("/WEB-INF/resources/");
}
}
```

7. The next step is to create HTML files under the `WEB-INF` folder create a `home.html` file as follows:

```
<!DOCTYPE html>
<html xmlns="http://www.w3.org/1999/xhtml"
      xmlns:th="http://www.thymeleaf.org" lang="en">

<head>
<meta charset="UTF-8"/>
<title>Thymeleaf example</title>
<link rel="stylesheet"
  th:href="@{/spring/resources/css/styles.css}"
  type="text/css" media="screen"/>
<script th:src="@{/spring/resources/js/functions.js}"
  type="text/javascript"></script>
<script th:src="@{/spring/resources/js/jquery-min-
  1.9.1.js}" type="text/javascript"></script>
</head>

<body>
<div style="width:800px; margin:0 auto;">

<h1 th:text="#{home.title}">Thymeleaf example</h1>

<div class="generic-info">
  <h3 th:text="#{author.information}">Author
    Information</h3>

  <span th:text="${authorData.name}">Author name</span><br
    />
```

```
      <span th:text="${authorData.address}">Author
        address</span><br />
  </div>


  <div class="main-block">
    <!-- Insert new Author -->
    <span class="subtitle">Add Author form</span>
    <form id="guestForm" th:action="@{/spring/authors/
      insert}" th:object="${Author}" method="post">
      <div class="insertBlock">
      <span class="formSpan">
      <input id="authorId" type="text" th:field="*{id}"
        required="required"/>
      <br />
      <label for="authorId"
        th:text="#{insert.id}">id:</label>
      </span>
      <span class="formSpan" style="margin-bottom:20px">
      <input id="authorName" type="text" th:field="*{name}"
        required="required"/>
        <br />
        <label for="authorName"
          th:text="#{insert.name}">name:</label>
      </span>

      <span class="formSpan">
      <input id="authorSurname" type="text"
        th:field="*{surname}" required="required"/>
      <br />
      <label for="authorSurname"
        th:text="#{insert.surname}">surname:</label>
      </span>
      <span class="formSpan" style="margin-bottom:20px">
      <input id="authorCountry" type="text"
        th:field="*{country}" required="required"/>
      <br />
      <label for="authorCountry"
        th:text="#{insert.country}">country:</label>
      </span>

      <input type="submit" value="add"
        th:value="#{insert.submit}"/>
      <span class="messageContainer"
        th:unless="${#strings.isEmpty(errorMessage)}"
        th:text="#{${errorMessage}}"></span>
      </div>
    </form>
```

```html
<!-- Guests list -->
<form>
  <span class="subtitle">Author list form</span>
  <div class="listBlock">
  <div class="search-block">
  <input type="text" id="searchSurname"
    name="searchSurname"/>
  <br />
  <label for="searchSurname"
  th:text="#{search.label}">Search label:</label>

  <button id="searchButton" name="searchButton"
    onclick="retrieveAuthors()" type="button"
    th:text="#{search.button}">Search button</button>
  </div>

  <!-- Results block -->
  <div id="resultsBlock">

  </div>
  </div>

  </form>
</div>

</div>
</body>
</html>
```

8. Lastly, create a simple `results.html` file:

```html
<!DOCTYPE html>
<html xmlns="http://www.w3.org/1999/xhtml"
  xmlns:th="http://www.thymeleaf.org" lang="en">
<head>
</head>
<body>
  <div th:fragment="resultsList"
    th:unless="${#lists.isEmpty(authors)}"
    class="results-block">
  <table>
  <thead>
  <tr>
  <th th:text="#{results.author.id}">Id</th>
  <th th:text="#{results.author.surname}">Surname</th>
  <th th:text="#{results.author.name}">Name</th>
```

```
<th th:text="#{results.author.country}">Country</th>
</tr>
</thead>
<tbody>
<tr th:each="author : ${authors}">
<td th:text="${author.id}">id</td>
<td th:text="${author.surname}">surname</td>
<td th:text="${author.name}">name</td>
<td th:text="${author.country}">country</td>
</tr>
</tbody>
</table>
</div>
</body>
</html>
```

This would give the user a list of authors and a form for inserting author information into the MongoDB database, using the Thymeleaf template.

Spring Boot with Thymeleaf and Maven

In this section, we will see how we can use Spring boot to create a Spring with Thymeleaf application.

The pre-requisite for this operation is Maven, which should be installed. To check if Maven is installed, type the following command in to the Command Prompt:

```
mvn -version
```

1. Use the archetype to generate a Spring boot with a `thymeleaf` project:

    ```
    mvn archetype:generate -DarchetypeArtifactId=maven-archetype-
    quickstart -DgroupId=com.packt.demo -DartifactId=spring-boot-
    thymeleaf -interactiveMode=false
    ```

    The preceding command will create a `spring-boot-thymeleaf` directory. This can be imported into Eclipse IDE.

2. You will open the `pom.xml` file and add a `parent` project:

    ```
    <parent>
      <groupId>org.springframework.boot</groupId>
      <artifactId>spring-boot-starter-parent</artifactId>
      <version>1.1.8.RELEASE</version>
    </parent>
    ```

3. Start adding a dependency to the `pom.xml` file:

```
<dependencies>
  <dependency>
  <groupId>org.springframework.boot</groupId>
  <artifactId>spring-boot-starter-web</artifactId>
  </dependency>
  <dependency>
  <groupId>org.springframework.boot</groupId>
  <artifactId>spring-boot-starter-thymeleaf</artifactId>
  </dependency>
</dependencies>
```

4. Lastly add the Spring boot plugin:

```
<build>
  <plugins>
  <plugin>
  <groupId>org.springframework.boot</groupId>
  <artifactId>spring-boot-maven-plugin</artifactId>
  </plugin>
  </plugins>
</build>
```

Let us start modifying the web. But wait a moment — this is not the web application!

1. So, let's modify the `App` class so that it is the entry point to the Spring Boot application:

```
package com.packt.demo
import org.springframework.boot.SpringApplication;
import org.springframework.boot.autoconfigure
  .EnableAutoConfiguration;
import org.springframework.context
  .annotation.ComponentScan;
import org.springframework.context
  .annotation.Configuration;

@EnableAutoConfiguration
@Configuration
@ComponentScan
public class App {
  public static void main(String[] args) {
    SpringApplication.run(App.class);
  }
}
```

2. Next, let's configure the Thymeleaf template. To configure it we need to add templates under the `src/main/resources/templates` directory:

```html
<!DOCTYPE html>
<html>
<head>
  <title>Hello Spring Boot!</title>
  <meta http-equiv="Content-Type" content="text/html;
    charset=UTF-8"/>
</head>
<body>
<p>Hello Spring Boot!</p>
</body>
<html>
```

3. You can upgrade the Thymeleaf template by adding CSS and JavaScript reference as follows:

```html
<!DOCTYPE html>
<html>
<head>
  <title>Hello Spring Boot!</title>
  <meta http-equiv="Content-Type" content="text/html;
    charset=UTF-8"/>
  <link href="../static/css/core.css"
    th:href="@{/css/core.css}"
    rel="stylesheet" media="screen" />
</head>
<body>
<p>Hello Spring Boot!</p>
</body>
</html>
```

4. Spring boot supports WebJars out of the box. Add the following dependencies to the `pom.xml` file.

```xml
<dependency>
  <groupId>org.webjars</groupId>
  <artifactId>bootstrap</artifactId>
  <version>3.2.0</version>
</dependency>
<dependency>
  <groupId>org.webjars</groupId>
  <artifactId>jquery</artifactId>
  <version>2.1.1</version>
</dependency>
```

And reference the libraries in the templates as follows:

```
<link href="http://cdn.jsdelivr.net/webjars/bootstrap/
  3.2.0/css/bootstrap.min.css"
  th:href="@{/webjars/bootstrap/3.2.0/
    css/bootstrap.min.css}"
  rel="stylesheet" media="screen" />

<script src="http://cdn.jsdelivr.net/
  webjars/jquery/2.1.1/jquery.min.js"
  th:src="@{/webjars/jquery/2.1.1/jquery.min.js}"></script>
```

As you can see, for static prototyping, libraries are downloaded from the CDN, converting the packaging from JAR to WAR

It is fairly easy with Spring boot to run this project as a plain web application. Firstly, we need to convert the type of packaging in pom.xml from JAR to WAR (the packaging element). Secondly, make sure that Tomcat is a provided dependency:

```
<packaging>war</packaging>
```

We also need to create a controller to handle the application requests:

```
package com.packt.demo;
import org.springframework.stereotype.Controller;
import org.springframework.web.bind.annotation.RequestMapping;

@Controller
class HomeController {

  @RequestMapping("/")
  String index() {
    return "index";
  }
}
```

The last step is to Bootstrap a servlet configuration. Create a Init class and inherit from SpringBootServletInitializer:

```
package packt.demo;
import org.springframework.boot.builder.SpringApplicationBuilder;
import org.springframework.boot.context.web
  .SpringBootServletInitializer;

public class ServletInitializer extends
  SpringBootServletInitializer {
    @Override
```

```
    protected SpringApplicationBuilder
      configure(SpringApplicationBuilder application) {
    return application.sources(App.class);
    }
  }
```

We can check if the configuration works with Maven using the `mvn clean package` command. The WAR file will be created:

Building war: C:\Projects\demos\spring-boot-thymeleaf\target\spring-boot-thymeleaf-1.0-SNAPSHOT.war

Use Maven to start the application from the WAR file directly using the following command:

java-jar target\spring-boot-thymeleaf-1.0-SNAPSHOT.war

After creating a WAR project, we will run the application in Eclipse. After we have changed the packaging, Eclipse will detect the changes in the project and add a web facet to it. The next step is to configure the Tomcat server and run it. Navigate to **Edit Configurations**, and add the Tomcat server with an exploded WAR artefact. Now you can run the application as any other web application.

Reloading Thymeleaf templates

Since the application is running on a local Tomcat server in Eclipse, we will reload static resources (for example, CSS files) without restarting the server. But, by default, Thymeleaf caches the templates, so in order to update Thymeleaf templates we need to change this behaviour.

- Add the `application.properties` to `src/main/resources` directory with the `spring.thymeleaf.cache=false` property
- Restart the server, and from now on you can reload Thymeleaf templates without restarting the server
- Changing the other configuration defaults

The cache configuration is not the only available configuration we can adjust. Please look at the `ThymeleafAutoConfiguration` class to see what other things you can change. To mention a few: `spring.thymeleaf.mode`, `spring.thymeleaf.encoding`.

Spring security with Thymeleaf

Since we have used Spring security, we will have used custom login forms in JSP in our Spring application. In this section, let's see how we can introduce a Thymeleaf template for securing the Spring based application.

You can use Spring securing dialects like this to display the logged in user information. The attribute sec:authorize renders its content when the attribute expression is evaluated to True. You can use this code in the base file which is displayed after successful authentication:

```
?
<div sec:authorize="hasRole('ROLE_ADMIN')">
  This content is only shown to administrators.
</div>
<div sec:authorize="hasRole('ROLE_USER')">
  This content is only shown to users.
</div>
  The attribute sec:authentication is used to
  print logged user name and roles:
?
  Logged user: <span sec:authentication="name">Bob</span>
  Roles: <span sec:authentication="principal.authorities">
    [ROLE_USER, ROLE_ADMIN]</span>
```

As we know, the following are a few necessary steps that we perform to add Spring security to our Spring application. But, you will observe that we have configured an HTML file which is a Thymeleaf file.

1. Configure the Spring security filter.

2. Configure the applicationContext-springsecurity.xml file as a context parm.

3. Configure the URL that needs to be secured in applicationContext-springsecurity.xml.

4. A sample configuration would look like this:

```
<?
<http auto-config="true">
  <form-login login-page="/login.html"
    authentication-failure-url="/login-error.html" />
  <logout />
  ...
</http>
```

5. Configure the Spring Controller:

```
@Controller
public class MySpringController {

  ...

  // Login form
  @RequestMapping("/login.html")
  public String login() {
```

```
      return "login.html";
    }

    // Login form with error
    @RequestMapping("/login-error.html")
    public String loginError(Model model) {
      model.addAttribute("loginError", true);
      return "login.html";
    }
}
```

6. Let's look at the `Login.html` file, which is Thymeleaf file. This can be
   recognised with XMLNS given in the beginning of the file. Also observe that
   we are handling the error in the JSP file; when login fails it shows an error
   message. We will also create an `error.html` file to handle errors:

```
<!DOCTYPE html>
<html xmlns="http://www.w3.org/1999/xhtml"
  xmlns:th="http://www.thymeleaf.org">
  <head>
  <title>Login page</title>
  </head>
  <body>
  <h1>Login page</h1>
  <p th:if="${loginError}">Wrong user or password</p>
  <form th:action="@{/j_spring_security_check}"
    method="post">
  <label for="j_username">Username</label>:
  <input type="text" id="j_username" name="j_username" />
    <br />
  <label for="j_password">Password</label>:
  <input type="password" id="j_password" name="j_password"
    /> <br />
  <input type="submit" value="Log in" />
  </form>
  </body>
</html>

/*Error.html file*/
?
<!DOCTYPE html>
<html xmlns="http://www.w3.org/1999/xhtml"
  xmlns:th="http://www.thymeleaf.org">
  <head>
  <title>Error page</title>
  </head>
  <body>
  <h1 th:text="${errorCode}">500</h1>
```

```html
<p th:text=""${errorMessage}">java.lang
  .NullPointerException</p>
</body>
</html>
```

This step is all about configuring the error page. The error page can be configured in a `web.xml` file. First, we need to add the `<error-page>` tag to the `web.xml` file. Once we configure the error page, we need to inform the controller class about the error page:

```xml
<error-page>
  <exception-type>java.lang.Throwable</exception-type>
  <location>/error.html</location>
</error-page>
<error-page>
  <error-code>500</error-code>
  <location>/error.html</location>
</error-page>
```

7. Add the request mapping for the `error` page in the controller:

```java
@RequestMapping("/error.html")
public String error(HttpServletRequest request, Model
  model) {
  model.addAttribute("errorCode", request
    .getAttribute("javax.servlet.error.status_code"));
  Throwable throwable = (Throwable) request
    .getAttribute("javax.servlet.error.exception");
  String errorMessage = null;
  if (throwable != null) {
    errorMessage = throwable.getMessage();
  }
  model.addAttribute("errorMessage", errorMessage);
  return "error.html";
  }
}
```

Visit `http://www.thymeleaf.org/doc/tutorials/2.1/usingthymeleaf.html` for more details.

Summary

In this chapter, we have seen how we can integrate the Thymeleaf template engine into a Spring MVC application, and also how to use Spring boot to start a Spring with Thymeleaf application. We have also demonstrated creating custom forms for Spring security using a Spring Thymeleaf template.

In the next chapter, we will look at Spring with web service integration and see what it offers to develop SOAP and REST Web Services.

12
Spring with Web Service Integration

In this chapter, we will see how Spring provides support to the JAX_WS web service and also see how to create a web service in **Spring Web Service (Spring-WS)** framework. We shall also see how the Spring Web Service can be consumed by demonstrating a client application, along with the annotations supported by Spring for Web services.

Spring with JAX-WS

In this section, let's create a simple JAX-WS web service. We shall also see how we can integrate the JAX-WS Web Service with Spring. JAX-WS is the latest version of JAX-RPC, which used remote method invocation protocol to access Web services.

All we need to do here is to expose Spring's service layer as JAX_WS service provider layer. This can be done using the @webservice annotation and involves just a few steps. Let us jot down the steps involved in it.

1. Create a PACKTJAXWS-Spring simple Maven web project or a Dynamic web project in Eclipse.

2. Now, we need to configure JAX-WS servlet in a web.xml file:

```
<?xml version="1.0" encoding="UTF-8"?>
<web-app xmlns:xsi="http://www.w3.org/2001/XMLSchema-
   instance" xmlns="http://java.sun.com/xml/ns/javaee"
   xsi:schemaLocation="http://java.sun.com/xml/ns/javaee
   http://java.sun.com/xml/ns/javaee/web-app_3_0.xsd"
   id="WebApp_ID" version="3.0">
<display-name>JAXWS-Spring</display-name>
<servlet>
   <servlet-name>jaxws-servlet</servlet-name>
   <servlet-class>
```

```
    com.sun.xml.ws.transport.http.servlet.WSSpringServlet
  </servlet-class>
</servlet>
<servlet-mapping>
  <servlet-name>jaxws-servlet</servlet-name>
  <url-pattern>/jaxws-spring</url-pattern>
</servlet-mapping>

<!-- Register Spring Listener -->
<listener>
  <listener-class>org.springframework.web
    .context.ContextLoaderListener</listener-class>
</listener>
</web-app>
```

3. Create a `Context.xml` application file and add the web service information to it. We will be providing the web service name and the service provider class information here.

```
<?xml version="1.0" encoding="UTF-8"?>
<beans xmlns="http://www.springframework.org/schema/beans"
       xmlns:xsi="http://www.w3.org/2001/
         XMLSchema-instance"
       xmlns:ws="http://jax-ws.dev.java.net/spring/core"
       xmlns:wss="http://jax-ws.dev.java.net/
         spring/servlet"
       xsi:schemaLocation="http://www.springframework.org/
         schema/beans
       http://www.springframework.org/schema/
         beans/spring-beans-3.0.xsd
       http://jax-ws.dev.java.net/spring/core
       http://jax-ws.java.net/spring/core.xsd
       http://jax-ws.dev.java.net/spring/servlet
       http://jax-ws.java.net/spring/servlet.xsd">
  <wss:binding url="/jaxws-spring">
  <wss:service>
  <ws:service bean="#packWs"/>
  </wss:service>
  </wss:binding>
  <!-- Web service bean -->
  <bean id="packtWs" class="com.packt.webservicedemo
    .ws.PacktWebService">
  <property name="myPACKTBObject" ref="MyPACKTBObject" />
  </bean>
  <bean id="MyPACKTBObject" class="com.packt.webservicedemo
    .bo.impl.MyPACKTBObjectImpl" />
</beans>
```

4. Next, we need to make all the jars available in a classpath. Since it is a maven project, we only need to update the `pom.xml` file.

```xml
<project xmlns="http://maven.apache.org/POM/4.0.0"
  xmlns:xsi="http://www.w3.org/2001/XMLSchema-instance"
  xsi:schemaLocation="http://maven.apache.org/POM/4.0.0
  http://maven.apache.org/xsd/maven-4.0.0.xsd">
  <modelVersion>4.0.0</modelVersion>
  <groupId>com.javacodegeeks.enterprise.ws</groupId>
  <artifactId>PACKTJAXWS-Spring</artifactId>
  <version>0.0.1-SNAPSHOT</version>
  <dependencies>
    <dependency>
      <groupId>org.springframework</groupId>
        <artifactId>spring-core</artifactId>
        <version>${spring.version}</version>
    </dependency>
    <dependency>
      <groupId>org.springframework</groupId>
      <artifactId>spring-context</artifactId>
      <version>${spring.version}</version>
    </dependency>
    <dependency>
      <groupId>org.springframework</groupId>
      <artifactId>spring-web</artifactId>
      <version>${spring.version}</version>
    </dependency>

    <dependency>
      <groupId>org.jvnet.jax-ws-commons.spring</groupId>
      <artifactId>jaxws-spring</artifactId>
      <version>1.9</version>
    </dependency>
  </dependencies>
  <properties>
    <spring.version>3.2.3.RELEASE</spring.version>
  </properties>
</project>
```

5. We shall now create a web service class with the `@WebService` annotation. We have also defined the kind of binding we might need, such as `SOAPBinding` and `Style`. The `@Webmethod` annotation specifies the method which provides the service.

```java
package com.packt.webservicedemo.ws;
import javax.jws.WebMethod;
import javax.jws.WebService;
import javax.jws.soap.SOAPBinding;
import javax.jws.soap.SOAPBinding.Style;
```

```
import javax.jws.soap.SOAPBinding.Use;
import com.packt.webservicedemo.bo.*;

@WebService(serviceName="PacktWebService")
@SOAPBinding(style = Style.RPC, use = Use.LITERAL)
public class PacktWebService{
  //Dependency Injection (DI) via Spring
  MyPACKTBObject myPACKTBObject;
  @WebMethod(exclude=true)
  public void setMyPACKTBObject(MyPACKTBObject
    myPACKTBObject) {
    this.myPACKTBObject = myPACKTBObject;
  }
  @WebMethod(operationName="printMessage")
  public String printMessage() {
    return myPACKTBObject.printMessage();

  }
}
package com.packt.webservicedemo.bo;
public interface MyPACKTBObject {
  String printMessage();
}
public class MyPACKTBObjectImpl implements MyPACKTBObject {
  @Override
  public String printMessage() {
    return "PACKT SPRING WEBSERVICE JAX_WS";
  }
}
```

6. We should add the Maven JAR files to the build path of our eclipse project.

7. Run the application: `http://localhost:8080/PACKTJAXWS-Spring/jaxws-spring`.

You should be able to see the WSDL URL and on clicking on link, the WSDL file should open up.

Spring Web Services with JAXB marshalling for request

In this section, let's look at developing a simple web service using the Spring Web Service framework. We need JAXB for marshalling and unmarshalling the XML request. The Spring Web Service supports contract first web service. We need to design a XSD/WSDL first and then launch the web service.

We are creating an author web service which will give us a list of authors.

1. **Configuring the web.xml file**: Let us first do a web service configuration in a `web.xml` file. We need to configure the Spring Web Service servlet. The Message Dispatcher servlet needs to be defined and the URL patterns it will handle. The `contextConfigLocation` is specified instead of allowing the default (`/WEB-INF/spring-ws-servlet.xml`) because this location makes the configuration easier to share with the unit test.

```
<?xml version="1.0" encoding="UTF-8"?>
<web-app xmlns:xsi="http://www.w3.org/2001/XMLSchema-
  instance"
  xmlns="http://java.sun.com/xml/ns/javaee"
  xmlns:web="http://java.sun.com/xml/ns/javaee/
    web-app_2_5.xsd"
  xsi:schemaLocation="http://java.sun.com/xml/ns/javaee
  http://java.sun.com/xml/ns/javaee/web-app_2_5.xsd"
  id="WebApp_ID" version="2.5">

  <servlet>
    <servlet-name>spring-ws</servlet-name>
    <servlet-class>org.springframework.ws.transport
      .http.MessageDispatcherServlet</servlet-class>
    <init-param>
      <param-name>contextConfigLocation</param-name>
      <param-value>classpath:/spring-ws-context.xml</param-
        value>
    </init-param>
  </servlet>

  <servlet-mapping>
    <servlet-name>spring-ws</servlet-name>
    <url-pattern>/*</url-pattern>
  </servlet-mapping>

</web-app>
```

2. **Configuring the Spring Context file** (`/src/main/resources/spring-ws-context.xml`): The `EndPoint` class needs to be configured in the `spring-ws-context.xml`. The class is annotated with `@EndPointAnnotation`. The `AuthorEndpoint` is defined as a bean and will automatically be registered with Spring Web Services, since the class is identified as an endpoint by the `@Endpoint` annotation. This configuration uses the `author.xsd`, which is a xml schema descriptor file that was used to generate the JAXB beans to generate the WSDL. The location URI matches the URL pattern specified in the `web.xml`.

The JAXB marshaller/unmarshaller is configured using Spring OXM and also set on the `MarshallingMethodEndpointAdapter` bean.

```xml
<?xml version="1.0" encoding="UTF-8"?>
<beans xmlns="http://www.springframework.org/schema/beans"
    xmlns:xsi="http://www.w3.org/2001/
        XMLSchema-instance"
    xmlns:p="http://www.springframework.org/schema/p"
    xmlns:context="http://www.springframework.org/
        schema/context"
    xsi:schemaLocation="http://www.springframework.org/
        schema/beans
    http://www.springframework.org/schema/beans/
        spring-beans.xsd
    http://www.springframework.org/schema/context
    http://www.springframework.org/schema/context/
        spring-context.xsd">

  <context:component-scan base-package="org.packtws
    .ws.service" />

  <bean id="person" class="org.springframework
    .ws.wsdl.wsdl11
    .DefaultWsdl11Definition"
    p:portTypeName="Author"
    p:locationUri="/authorService/"
    p:requestSuffix="-request"
    p:responseSuffix="-response">
    <property name="schema">
      <bean class="org.springframework.xml
        .xsd.SimpleXsdSchema"
        p:xsd="classpath:/author.xsd" />
      </bean>
    </property>
  </bean>

  <bean class="org.springframework.ws.server.endpoint
    .mapping.PayloadRootAnnotationMethodEndpointMapping">
```

```
    <description>An endpoint mapping strategy that looks
      for @Endpoint and @PayloadRoot
      annotations.</description>
  </bean>

  <bean class="org.springframework.ws.server.endpoint
    .adapter.MarshallingMethodEndpointAdapter">
    <description>Enables the MessageDispatchServlet to
      invoke methods requiring OXM
      marshalling.</description>
    <constructor-arg ref="marshaller"/>
  </bean>

  <bean id="marshaller" class="org.springframework.oxm.jaxb
    .Jaxb2Marshaller"
    p:contextPath="org.packtws.author.schema.beans" />

</beans>
```

3. **Defining the XSD Author.xsd**: A very simple XSD defines an element to indicate an incoming request to get all authors (name element isn't used) and an author response element that contains a list of author elements.

    author.xsd

```
<xsd:schema xmlns="http://www.packtws.org/author/
  schema/beans"
  targetNamespace=" http://www.packtws.org/
    author/schema/beans "
  xmlns:xsd="http://www.w3.org/2001/XMLSchema">

  <xsd:element name="get-authors-request">
  <xsd:complexType>
    <xsd:sequence>
      <xsd:element name="name" type="xsd:string" />
    </xsd:sequence>
  </xsd:complexType>
  </xsd:element>

  <xsd:element name="author-response">
    <xsd:complexType>
      <xsd:sequence>
        <xsd:element name="author" type="author"
          minOccurs="0" maxOccurs="unbounded"/>
      </xsd:sequence>
    </xsd:complexType>
  </xsd:element>
```

```
<xsd:complexType name="author">
<xsd:sequence>
  <xsd:element name="id" type="xsd:int" />
  <xsd:element name="first-name" type="xsd:string" />
  <xsd:element name="last-name" type="xsd:string" />
</xsd:sequence>
</xsd:complexType>

</xsd:schema>
```

4. **Marshalling the AuthorService**: Let us create an Interface `MarshallingAuthorService` for getting authors using the following JAXB generated beans:

   - For the `get-authors-request` element: `GetAuthorsRequst`
   - For the `author-response` element: `AuthorResponse`

   It also has constants for the namespace (matches XSD) and a request constant:

```
public interface MarshallingAuthorService {
    public final static String NAMESPACE = " http://
      www.packtws.org/author/schema/beans ";
    public final static String GET_Authors_REQUEST =
      "get-authors-request";
    public AuthorResponse getAuthors(GetAuthorsRequest
      request);
}
```

5. **Creating an Endpoint class**: Let us create an endpoint class marked with the `@Endpoint` annotation. This class will implement the method of `MarshallingAuthorService`. The `getAuthors` method is indicated to handle a specific namespace and an incoming request element. The endpoint just prepares a static response, but this could very easily have a DAO injected into it and have the information retrieved from a database, which is then mapped into the JAXB beans. The AuthorResponse is created using the JAXB Fluent API which is less verbose than the standard JAXB API.

```
@Endpoint
public class AuthorEndpoint implements
  MarshallingAuthorService {
  /**
  * Gets Author list.
  */
  @PayloadRoot(localPart=GET_AuthorS_REQUEST,
    namespace=NAMESPACE)
  public AuthorResponse getAuthors(GetPersonsRequest
    request) {
```

```
    return new AuthorResponse().withAuthor(
    new Author().withId(1).withFirstName("Anjana")
      .withLastName("Raghavendra"),
    new Author().withId(2).withFirstName("Amrutha")
      .withLastName("Prasad"));
  }


}
```

6. **Adding dependency information**: Also ensure that you add the following dependency in your maven pom.xml file:

```xml
<dependency>
  <groupId>org.springframework.ws</groupId>
  <artifactId>org.springframework.ws</artifactId>
  <version>${spring.ws.version}</version>
</dependency>
<dependency>
  <groupId>org.springframework.ws</groupId>
  <artifactId>org.springframework.ws.java5</artifactId>
  <version>${spring.ws.version}</version>
</dependency>

<dependency>
  <groupId>javax.xml.bind</groupId>
  <artifactId>com.springsource.javax.xml.bind</artifactId>
  <version>2.1.7</version>
</dependency>
<dependency>
  <groupId>com.sun.xml</groupId>
  <artifactId>com.springsource.com.sun.xml
    .bind.jaxb1</artifactId>
  <version>2.1.7</version>
</dependency>
<dependency>
  <groupId>javax.wsdl</groupId>
  <artifactId>com.springsource.javax.wsdl</artifactId>
  <version>1.6.1</version>
</dependency>
<dependency>
  <groupId>javax.xml.soap</groupId>
  <artifactId>com.springsource.javax.xml.soap</artifactId>
  <version>1.3.0</version>
</dependency>
<dependency>
  <groupId>com.sun.xml</groupId>
  <artifactId>com.springsource.com.sun.xml
    .messaging.saaj</artifactId>
```

```
        <version>1.3.0</version>
    </dependency>
    <dependency>
      <groupId>javax.activation</groupId>
      <artifactId>com.springsource.javax
        .activation</artifactId>
      <version>1.1.1</version>
    </dependency>
    <dependency>
      <groupId>javax.xml.stream</groupId>
      <artifactId>com.springsource.javax.xml
        .stream</artifactId>
      <version>1.0.1</version>
    </dependency>
```

7. **Build and deploy the application**: We need to do this on the tomcat to see the WSDL URL. Thus, we have completed all the steps for providing a web service.

Writing a client application for Spring Web Services using JAXB unmarshalling for request

Let us write a simple client application for the author service. The `org.springbyexample.ws.service` package is scanned for beans and will find the `AuthorServiceClient`, and inject the web service template into it. The JAXB marshaller/umarshaller is defined and set on this template.

The import of the `jetty-context.xml` isn't relevant to creating a client, but it creates an embedded Jetty instance that loads the `spring-ws-context.xml` and its services. The client in the unit test is then able to run in isolation.

AuthorServiceClientTest.xml:

```
<?xml version="1.0" encoding="UTF-8"?>
<beans xmlns="http://www.springframework.org/schema/beans"
  xmlns:xsi="http://www.w3.org/2001/XMLSchema-instance"
  xmlns:p="http://www.springframework.org/schema/p"
  xmlns:context="http://www.springframework.org/schema/context"
  xsi:schemaLocation="http://www.springframework.org/schema/beans
  http://www.springframework.org/schema/beans/spring-beans.xsd
  http://www.springframework.org/schema/context
  http://www.springframework.org/schema/
    context/spring-context.xsd">
```

```xml
<import resource="jetty-context.xml"/>

<context:component-scan base-package="org.springbyexample
  .ws.client" />

<context:property-placeholder location="org/springbyexample/
  ws/client/ws.properties"/>

<bean id="authorWsTemplate" class="org.springframework.ws
  .client.core.WebServiceTemplate"
p:defaultUri="http://${ws.host}:${ws.port}/${ws.context.path}/
  authorService/"
p:marshaller-ref="marshaller"
p:unmarshaller-ref="marshaller" />

<bean id="marshaller" class="org.springframework.oxm
  .jaxb.Jaxb2Marshaller"
p:contextPath="org.springbyexample.author.schema.beans" />

</beans>
```

AuthorServiceClient:

At this point, Spring Web Services can handle almost everything. The template just needs to be called and it will return the `AuthorResponse` from the service endpoint. The client can be used like this: `AuthorResponse response = client.getAuthors(new GetAuthorsRequest());`

```java
public class AuthorServiceClient implements
  MarshallingAuthorService {

  @Autowired
  private WebServiceTemplate wsTemplate;

  /**
    * Gets author list.
  */
  public AuthorResponse getAuthors(GetAuthorsRequest request) {
    PersonResponse response =
      (PersonResponse) wsTemplate.marshalSendAndReceive(request);

    return response;

  }
}
```

Summary

In this chapter, we have seen how we can integrate JAX_WS with Spring Web Service. We have also demonstrated how to create Spring Web Services and an endpoint class, as well as how to access the web service by accessing the WSDL URL.

Index

Symbols

A

B

C

S

Sample Batch
application creating, Tasklet
interface used 81-85
application, developing 77-81
configuring, with Quartz Scheduler 92-95
job, intercepting with listeners 106-112
unit testing 112-114
used, for reading CSV file 85-90
used, for reading file 96-101
used, for updating MongoDB
database 96-101
using, with threads to
partition jobs 101-106
with Spring Scheduler 91

Simple Mail Message
used, for sending Spring mail 56-58

Spring
caching, annotations 209
implementing, with MongoDB 11
integration, used for FTP
application 129-132
integration support, to multipart HTTP
Request 141
Map and Reduce job 161
proxy configuration support 140
with JAX-WS 249-252
with MongoDB, application
implementation 6-14

Spring Batch
about 71
architecture 72, 73
dependency 73
enterprise batch, using 73
key components 74-76
processing key goal 72
use cases 71
used, for FTP application 129-132

Spring Bean
Mongo document, mapping 3

Spring Boot
about 189
hot swapping with 193-198
integrating, with Spring Security 198, 199
RestfulWebService used 201-208
URL 189

Spring DataApache Hadoop
used, for Map and Reduce job 166-170

Spring Dynamic Modules
and OSGI 176
integrating, with OSGI 180-188

Spring Expression Language (SpEL) 147

Spring FTP. *See* **File Transfer Protocol (FTP)**

Spring Gradle MVC application 190-193

Spring SpringJMS
Order Management Messaging System,
implementing 31

Spring JmsTemplate
ApacheMq, use case 28, 29

Spring Loaded JAR
URL 194

Spring mail
attachments, sending with 61
handling, process 51, 52
Multipurpose Internet Mail Extension
(MIME) messages, sending 60
preconfigured mail, sending 62, 63
sending, classes used 53, 54
sending, @Configuration
annotation used 54-56
sending, interfaces used 53
sending, MailSender used 56-58
sending, over different thread 66, 67
sending, Simple Mail Message used 56-58
sending, to multiple recipients 59
Spring templates, using with Velocity 63-65
with AOP 68, 69

Spring-MongoDB project
application design 5
setting up 4

Spring MVC
and Thymeleaf 229

Spring namespace
for Hadoop 154

Spring RestTemplate
used, for sending multipart
HTTP request 149, 150

Spring Scheduler
Spring Batch using 91

Spring security
with Thymeleaf 245-248
Spring Boot, integrating with 198, 199

---

[265]

Spring Web Services
  about 249
  client writing for, JAXB unmarshalling for
      request used 258, 259
  with JAXB marshalling, for request 253-258
SSH File Transfer Protocol (SFTP) 115
status codes 138

T

Tasklet interface
  used, for creating sample
      batch application 81-85
Thymeleaf
  and Spring MVC 229
  attributes 227, 228
  dependency 228
  MVC with 230-241
  Spring Boot with 241-245
  Spring security with 245-248
  templates, reloading 245
  URL 248
time-out, handling
  HTTP inbound gateway used 148
  HTTP outbound gateway used 148
Transmission Control Protocol/Internet
      Protocol (TCP/IP) 137

U

URI variables
  mapping as subelement, with HTTP
      outbound gateway 147
  mapping as subelement, with outbound
      channel adapter 147

X

XSD
  for FTP 116, 117
  URL 117

Thank you for buying
Mastering Spring Application Development

About Packt Publishing

Packt, pronounced 'packed', published its first book, *Mastering phpMyAdmin for Effective MySQL Management*, in April 2004, and subsequently continued to specialize in publishing highly focused books on specific technologies and solutions.

Our books and publications share the experiences of your fellow IT professionals in adapting and customizing today's systems, applications, and frameworks. Our solution-based books give you the knowledge and power to customize the software and technologies you're using to get the job done. Packt books are more specific and less general than the IT books you have seen in the past. Our unique business model allows us to bring you more focused information, giving you more of what you need to know, and less of what you don't.

Packt is a modern yet unique publishing company that focuses on producing quality, cutting-edge books for communities of developers, administrators, and newbies alike. For more information, please visit our website at www.packtpub.com.

About Packt Open Source

In 2010, Packt launched two new brands, Packt Open Source and Packt Enterprise, in order to continue its focus on specialization. This book is part of the Packt Open Source brand, home to books published on software built around open source licenses, and offering information to anybody from advanced developers to budding web designers. The Open Source brand also runs Packt's Open Source Royalty Scheme, by which Packt gives a royalty to each open source project about whose software a book is sold.

Writing for Packt

We welcome all inquiries from people who are interested in authoring. Book proposals should be sent to author@packtpub.com. If your book idea is still at an early stage and you would like to discuss it first before writing a formal book proposal, then please contact us; one of our commissioning editors will get in touch with you.

We're not just looking for published authors; if you have strong technical skills but no writing experience, our experienced editors can help you develop a writing career, or simply get some additional reward for your expertise.

Spring MVC Beginner's Guide

ISBN: 978-1-78328-487-0   Paperback: 304 pages

Your ultimate guide to building a complete web application using all the capabilities of Spring MVC

1. Carefully crafted exercises, with detailed explanations for each step, to help you understand the concepts with ease.

2. You will gain a clear understanding of the end to end request/response life cycle, and each logical component's responsibility.

3. Packed with tips and tricks that will demonstrate the industry best practices on developing a Spring-MVC-based application.

Instant Spring Tool Suite

ISBN: 978-1-78216-414-2   Paperback: 76 pages

A practical guide for kick-starting your Spring projects using the Spring Tool Suite IDE

1. Learn something new in an Instant! A short, fast, focused guide delivering immediate results.

2. Learn how to use Spring Tool Suite to jump-start your Spring projects.

3. Develop, test, and deploy your applications, all within the IDE.

4. Simple, step-by-step instructions in an easy-to-follow format.

Spring Security 3.x Cookbook

ISBN: 978-1-78216-752-5   Paperback: 300 pages

Over 60 recipes to help you successfully safeguard your web applications with Spring Security

1. Learn about all the mandatory security measures for modern day applications using Spring Security.

2. Investigate different approaches to application level authentication and authorization.

3. Master how to mount security on applications used by developers and organizations.

Spring Web Services 2 Cookbook

ISBN: 978-1-84951-582-5   Paperback: 322 pages

Over 60 recipes providing comprehensive coverage of practical real-life implementations of Spring-WS

1. Create contract-first Web services.

2. Explore different frameworks of Object/XML mapping.

3. Secure Web Services by Authentication, Encryption/Decryption and Digital Signature.

4. Learn contract-last Web Services using Spring Remoting and Apache CXF.

Please check **www.PacktPub.com** for information on our titles

www.ingramcontent.com/pod-product-compliance
Lightning Source LLC
Chambersburg PA
CBHW060523060326
40690CB00017B/3361